D1495711

the northern heartland kitchen

the northern heartland kitchen

BETH DOOLEY

UNIVERSITY OF MINNESOTA PRESS MINNEAPOLIS LONDON

Published by the University of Minnesota Press
111 Third Avenue South, Suite 290
Minneapolis, MN 55401-2520
http://www.upress.umn.edu

Library of Congress Cataloging-in-Publication Data

Dooley, Beth.
The northern heartland kitchen / Beth Dooley.
p. cm.
Includes bibliographical references and index.
ISBN 978-0-8166-6735-2 (hc : alk. paper)
1. Cooking, American—Midwestern style. I. Title.
TX715.2.M53D6598 2011
641.5977—dc23
       2011023626

Printed in the United States of America on acid-free paper

The University of Minnesota is an equal-opportunity educator and employer.

18 17 16 15 14 13 12 11   10 9 8 7 6 5 4 3 2 1

contents

Introduction: Seasonal Appetites   ix
 Ten Good Reasons to Eat Seasonal and Local   xii
 The Local Kitchen   xiv
Buying a Piece of the Farm:
 Community Supported Agriculture   xv

AUTUMN

Five Fall Dishes in Five Minutes or Less   3
Roast Mushroom, Red Pepper, and Sage Pizza   4
Smoked Trout, Apple, and Fennel Salad
 in Cider Vinaigrette   5
 Lake Superior Smoked Fish   5
Fresh Chestnut Soup   6
 American Chestnuts   7
Wild Rice and Wild Mushroom Soup   8
 Chanterelles   8
Curried Vegetable Soup   9
Asian Chicken Noodle Soup   10
 Simple Chicken Stock   10
Ginger Squash and Apple Soup   11
 University of Minnesota Apples   12
Prosciutto-Wrapped Tilapia with Sage   13
 Farm-Raised Fish   13
Beer-Braised Pork Chops with Pears   14
 Seasonal Beers   14
Venison Medallions with Juniper and Gin   15
Hanger Steak with Fresh Horseradish Sauce   16
Sure Fire Roast Duck   17
 Au Bon Canard, Caledonia, Minnesota   17
Duck Confit   18
Pheasant with Hard Cider, Apples, and Chestnuts   20
Rabbit with Pancetta and Fennel   21
Quick Roast Herb Chicken   22
Thanksgiving Bird—Fast!   23
 Turkey Talk   24

Turkey or Chicken Pot Pie with Cheddar Chive
 Cobbler Crust   25
Harvest Stuffed Squash   26
 Picking Pumpkins   26
Heartland Polenta with Mushroom Ragout   27
 Heartland Polenta   28
Barley Pilaf with Chickpeas and Autumn Vegetables   29
 New Grain Exchange   30
Spicy Savoy Coleslaw   31
Silky Chard   32
No Fail Kale   33
Horseradish and Honey-Glazed Root Vegetables   34
Caramelized Brussels Sprouts   35
Roast Broccoli or Cauliflower with Garlic
 and Hot Pepper   36
Thanksgiving Mashed Potatoes   37
Wild Rice Cranberry Pilaf   38
 Wild Rice   39
Basic Sage Stuffing   40
Savory Cranberry Compote   41
Oven-Dried Pears   42
Scandinavian Brown Beans with a Kick   43
Cranberry Sorbet   44
 Ruby Fields: The Cranberry Harvest   45
Honey Pumpkin Ginger Pie   46
 Honey, Oh Honey   47
Autumn Squash or Pumpkin Bars with
 Cranberry Glaze   48
Oatmeal Chocolate Chip and Dried Cranberry
 Cookies   49
Mom's Fall Fruit Crisp   50
Applesauce and Apple Butter, Savory and Sweet   51
 Upsetting the Apple Cart   52
Rich Applesauce Cake   53
Cranberry Cordial   54
Autumn's Bounty: Harvest Meals   55

WINTER

Five Winter Dishes in Five Minutes or Less   59
Roast Root Salad with Honey Mustard Vinaigrette   60
Potato, Prosciutto, and Rosemary Pizza   61
  Prosciutto Americano   61
Carrot Cashew Bisque   62
  Sweetest Carrots   62
Squash Soup with Thai Spices   63
Caramelized Onion Soup   64
Hungarian Steak and Mushroom Soup   65
  Classic Beef Stock   66
Winter Vegetable Tagine   67
Squash Lasagna with Walnuts and Kale   68
Spicy Bean and Hominy Stew   70
  Heartland Dried Beans and Native
    Harvest Hominy   70
Cornmeal-Dusted Panfish   71
Carnitas   72
  Hello, Goat!   72
Sausage with Apples and Onions   73
Chicken Braised with Mexican Spices   74
  The New Breed   75
Bison Steaks with Blue Cheese Butter   76
  Wild Idea Buffalo   76
  Heartland Blues   77
Oxtails with Stout and Onions   78
  Braising—A Key Technique for Winter   79
Lamb Shanks with Garlic and Rosemary   80
Porketta with Oregano and Fennel   81
Marinated Beef Pot Roast   82
  We Don't Farm with Headlights   82
Carrot and Parsley Salad   83
Parsnip and Chestnut Puree   84
Sweet Potato, Radish, and Walnut Salad   85
  Sweet Spuds in the Heartland   85
Braised Red or Green Cabbage   86
Oven-Blasted Brussels Sprouts   87
Roasted Salsify   88
Braised Root Vegetables in Mustard Sauce   89
Sweet Potatoes with a World of Toppings   90

Simple Potato Gratin   91
  When Are Potatoes in Season?   92
Linzer Cookies   93
  Hazelnuts and Hickories   94
Hazelnut and Dried Cherry Biscotti   95
Cranberry Tartlets in a Sweet Cornmeal Crust   96
Ginger Stout Cake   97
  Sorghum   97
Favorite Carrot Cupcakes   98
Old-Fashioned Bread and Butter Pudding   99
Spiked Chocolate Truffles   100
  White Winter Winery Mead   100
  The Cheese Board   101
Winter's Pleasures: Warm and Cozy Suppers   102

SPRING

Five Spring Dishes in Five Minutes or Less   105
Watercress Salad with a French Twist   106
Pizza with Arugula and Feta   107
Minted Pea Soup   108
  Heartland Peas   108
Spring Spinach and Nettle Soup   109
  Grasp the Nettle   109
Light and Lemony Asparagus Soup   110
  Easiest Vegetable Stock Ever   110
Hot and Sour Vegetable Soup with Tofu   111
Spring Vegetable Curry   112
  Ramps   112
Turkey Cutlets with Spring Vegetables and
    Tangy Pan Sauces   113
Pork Tenderloin with Lemon and Herbs   114
  Pigs at Play   114
Pan-Roasted Lamb Chops with Fresh
    Mint–Cilantro Chutney   115
Crispy Fried Fish   116
  Smelt Run on the North Shore   117
Walleye Meunière   118
  Walleye, Sole of the North   118
Oven-Fried Chicken   119
Potato and Sorrel Gratin   120

Uplands Cheese Pleasant Ridge Reserve
(and Extra Aged Reserve) 121
Showy Spinach Soufflé 122
Vegetable Frittata with Goat Cheese 123
Duck Eggs 123
Spring Greens and Strawberry Salad with
Rhubarb Vinaigrette 124
Wild Watercress 124
New Potato, Fiddlehead Ferns, and Arugula Salad 125
Fiddlehead Ferns 125
Seed Savers Exchange 126
Pan-Roasted Radishes 127
Grilled Asparagus with Chive Vinaigrette 128
Morels and Sunchokes with Toasted Hazelnuts 129
Morel Madness 130
Sunchoke Chips 131
Sunchokes 131
Simple Spring Sauté 132
Cracked Wheat Tabouli with Herbs 133
Chocolate Mousse with Maple Cream 134
Maple Syrup: The Sweet Taste of Spring! 135
Maple Sugar Shortbread 136
Pound Cake with Rhubarb-Strawberry Sauce 137
Once a Year Rhubarb Pie 138
Strawberry Sorbet 139
Rhubarb Lemonade 140
Herbal Elixirs 141
Spring Things: Fresh Fare 142

SUMMER

Five Summer Dishes in Five Minutes or Less 145
Spiced Beet Caviar 146
Panzanella Picnic Salad 147
Tomato, Tomato, and Tomato Tart 148
Good Tomatoes, Worth the Wait 149
Watermelon Gazpacho 150
Sour Cherry Riesling Soup 151
Summer Wines 152
Fresh Tomato Soup with Basil Ice Cream 153
Farmstand Corn Chowder 154

CORN! 155
Fresh Tomato Sauce for Pasta 156
Fourth of July Brats 157
Grilled Tofu with Spirited Marinade 158
Heartland Tofu 158
Classic Tarragon Chicken Salad 159
Whole Grilled Whitefish or Trout with Warm
Tomato Vinaigrette 160
Wisconsin Sturgeon 161
Carp-ing. Can't Beat Them? Eat Them! 161
Planked Whitefish 162
Great Lakes Fishing 162
Tomato, Eggplant, Zucchini, and Potato Bake 163
Beer Can Chicken 164
Dave's BrewFarm 165
Barbecue Ribs with Honey Jalapeño BBQ Sauce 166
Pork Ribs 166
Pesto, Presto Trio 167
Cool Cucumber Yogurt and Mint Salad 169
Fennel Kohlrabi Slaw 170
Melon, Feta, and Arugula Salad 171
Growing Power 171
Zucchini, Summer Squash, and Lemon Salad 172
Great Zukes! 172
Grilled Sweet Corn with Thyme Butter 173
Grilled Cauliflower Steaks 174
Curried Eggplant 175
Considering Eggplant 175
Green Bean, Corn, and Fennel Sauté 176
Stuffed Zucchini Blossoms 177
Gardens of Eagan 178
Slow-Roasted Tomatoes 179
Garlic—a Rose by Any Other Name 179
Fried Green Tomatoes 180
Victory Garden 180
Yogurt and Crème Fraiche 181
Minted Yogurt Cream for Summer Fruit 182
Kiwifruit? 182
Meringue Tart 183
Upside Down Summer Berry Crisp 184
Wild Berry Love 185

Fresh Blueberry Ice Cream   186

   North Shore Blueberries   186

   Organic Milk   187

Melon Ice   188

   Death's Door Spirits   188

Zucchini Spice Cakes   189

Concord Grape Tart   190

Raspberry Cordial   191

Summer's Splendors: Sunshine and Moonlight   192

THE NORTHERN HEARTLAND HEARTH

Many Muffins—One Recipe   194

Muesli   195

Buttermilk Scones, Sweet or Savory   196

   Mary Eckmeier Makes Real Scones   196

Real Cornbread   197

Rich Brown Soda Bread   198

   Daily Bread—Cress Spring Bakery   198

A Daily Loaf   199

   Fresh Flour   200

Whole Wheat Bread   201

   Baking Real Bread with Brett   201

   Forgotten Bread   202

Pizza Dough   203

Simply Granola   204

   Rolled Grains 101   204

Comfort Lodge Buttermilk Pancakes   205

Flaky Butter Crust   206

   Pie Crust Primer   206

Rich Tart Crust   207

Sweet Cornmeal Crust   208

STOCKING THE CUPBOARD:
VINAIGRETTES, DRESSINGS, AND SAUCES

Honey Mustard Vinaigrette   210

   Vinegary   210

The Real Buttermilk Ranch Dressing   211

Apostle Island Dressing   212

Brown Butter Vinaigrette   213

Juniper–Gin Marinade   214

Rosemary-Mint Marinade   215

Honey Jalapeño BBQ Sauce   216

Maple Mustard Basting Sauce   217

Raspberry Vinegar (Fruit Vinegar)   218

   Herb Vinegar   218

Furious Mustard   219

Roasted Tomato Vodka Sauce   220

Sweet Bell Pepper Sauce   221

Compound Butters   222

   Best Butter   222

HEARTLAND PRESERVES
AND CONDIMENTS

Pickle This   226

   Yes We Can   227

   Extending the Seasons   227

Pickled Cherry Peppers   228

Pickled Carrots   229

Dilly Beans   230

Spiced Pickled Beets   231

Pickled Eggs with Horseradish and Beets   232

Roasted Tomato–Chipotle Salsa   233

Fresh Corn Relish   234

Real Ketchup   235

Watermelon Rind Pickles   236

Rhubarb Chutney   237

Green Tomato Marmalade   238

Cranberry Ginger Salsa   239

Apple Jelly, Savory and Sweet   240

Grandmother's Strawberry Jam   241

Backyard Grape Jelly   242

Acknowledgments   243

Sources   244

Index   253

—

seasonal appetites

UNLIKE THOSE WHO LIVE IN WARM TROPICAL CLIMATES, we are governed by the seasons. The weather in this Northern Heartland is dramatic; nature shapes our physical environment as well as our emotional landscape. To live well here is to celebrate the year's changing riches: autumn's crisp air, brilliant colors, and snappy apples; winter's bluster and those simmering, window-glazing stews. How we yearn for spring's greens and pink rhubarb and delight in summer's shimmering gold corn. Come July, those perfect, juice-splitting tomatoes reward our January patience. To eat local means to pay attention to light, temperature, and the land's bounty. When our appetites follow the arc of the sun, we bring balance to our plates.

THRIFT AND BOUNTY

The Northern Heartland Kitchen is a guide to the year's rhythms: autumn, winter, spring, summer. As a geographic term, the Northern Heartland region defies state boundaries. It encompasses Minnesota, Iowa, Wisconsin, the Upper Peninsula of Michigan, and eastern South Dakota and North Dakota. Our climate, topography, ethnic heritage, and native ingredients define our regional character. The challenges and rewards for cooks from International Falls to Sioux Falls are the same. Though our growing season is short, our crops have always been bountiful. These days, local growers and producers are using new technologies and rediscovering heritage practices to enrich our regional selections.

When mindful of local choices, we buy green beans instead of asparagus in September, or toss sweet storage carrots rather than Mexican tomatoes into a February salad. Why buy French butter when the local dairy's tastes of summer's bright pasture? Our artisan cheeses trump the French in international competitions year after year, and our craft brews rival any from Europe. We serve the nation our beef, pork, poultry, game, fish, honey, maple syrup, wild rice, harvest vegetables, and grains. Our local offerings are not limited to niche cottage industries; they needn't be precious or overpriced. Eating local doesn't mean giving up coffee, chocolate, bananas, or spices, but it does imply being aware of where food comes from and how it's produced. When deciding between a lamb chop from New Zealand or Iowa, or between a Washington State Delicious and a Minnesota Haralson, the choice is pretty clear.

We cooks have an opportunity to shape a regional food system based on flavor, health, and sustainability. Shipping, handling, and storage are not high priorities in this paradigm. We've revised the bottom line, valuing flavor, nutrition, the environment, and our local economy above quantity and price. A secure local food system delivers fresh, delicious, nutritious, chemical-free, clean food while protecting our natural resources, provides a fair income for producers, and guarantees access to everyone.

In *Savoring the Seasons of the Northern Heartland*, Lucia Watson and I explored our past to show how the region's cuisine has evolved. Our cooking is farmhouse fare, grounded in the growing cycle, reliant on unprocessed, natural ingredients. These values provide the touchstones to a sustainable future and inform the choices we make today.

REAL LOCAL FOOD

The Northern Heartland Kitchen was born of conversations with growers, urban gardeners, producers, researchers, chefs, and home cooks who like to eat and love to talk about it. Nothing beats knowing the people who grow your food.

SUSTAINABLE GROWERS

Our independent sustainable farmers can hardly keep up with cooks' demands. The Driftless Area in the Upper Mississippi River Valley is home to our nation's early organic farmers. Right after World War II, they employed J. I. Rodale's theories of managing land as a balanced ecosystem, planting diverse crops in rotation without chemicals.

Urban farmers, such as Growing Power, based in Milwaukee, Wisconsin, and community gardeners are creating methods to grow vegetables and raise animals within a city's confines for its urban residents. Such cultivation and composting offer hope to city dwellers with limited access to fresh, healthy, local food at a fair price.

FARMERS' MARKETS

The Dane County Farmers' Market in Madison, Wisconsin, is the nation's largest producer-run market in the nation. It is a splendid forum of the region's heritage meats, artisan cheeses and sausages, and farmstead specialties. Throughout the region, our markets are vibrant with Hmong, Vietnamese, South American, and, most recently, Somali flavors, providing seedbeds for new tastes. This is how cilantro, hot peppers, lemon grass, and bitter melon found their way to our plates.

ENTREPRENEURS

Founded in the 1880s, our region's flour mills, grain companies, dairy co-ops, and meat packers have grown into multinational corporations. The rugged entrepreneurial spirit of those early food companies also thrives in more recently established companies: Organic Valley (LaFarge, Wisconsin), the nation's foremost organic dairy cooperative, which was created by farmers in the shadows of the national farm crisis of the early 1990; La Quercia (Norwalk, Iowa), the first American prosciutto and cured pork producer; Thousand Hills Cattle Company (Cannon Falls,

Minnesota), one of the country's largest free-range beef companies; and Seed Savers Exchange (Decorah, Iowa) have grown into national enterprises.

Start-up businesses are creating ways to extend the seasons through solar greenhouses and by cultivating cold-hardy plants. Because of their efforts, you can find locally grown microgreens, lettuces, tomatoes, safflower oil, and chestnuts in our markets. Soon we'll see kiwi, pawpaw, artichokes, frost-tolerant apples, farro, chickpeas, pecan-hickory nuts, hazelnuts, and nut oils coming in from around our region, not from around the world.

Taking a cue from Old World traditions, small producers are crafting smoked fish and game, processing rough fish (carp and eelpout), and making sheep's milk Roquefort- and Manchego-style cheeses, bison salami, duck sausage, distilled liquors, wine, and vinegar, to name but a few. Don't forget the beer. Microbreweries and home brewers are on the cutting edge of flavor and techniques.

Ojibwe tribes of Native Americans are reclaiming traditions while protecting their natural rights. Hand-harvested wild rice, hominy, jellies and jams made from foraged fruit, and a vigorous fishing industry are providing a healthy income for many Native American tribes.

RELATIONSHIP COMMERCE

Our region hosts the most CSA (community supported agriculture) farms in the nation. In this arrangement, cooks pay for a share of a farmer's harvest in advance of the season and have it delivered once a week. Cooks enjoy heirloom varieties not available in supermarkets. Many CSAs offer grass-fed poultry, meat, flowers, milk, eggs, and cheese through the year. CSA memberships provide the working capital for the season's seeds and equipment and help protect the farmer from the volatile commodity marketplace.

Our burgeoning natural food co-ops were originally founded as neighborhood stores in the 1970s. Today these member-owned enterprises rank among the country's most profitable grocery stores. They have supported start-up organic farmers by providing capital in advance of the growing season in relationships similar to CSAs. Many savvy chefs work with farmers to determine the season's crops, thus securing a market for interesting foods.

RESEARCH: NEW AND HERITAGE FOODS

Think tanks such as the Leopold Institute (Iowa), the Land Institute (Kansas), and the University of Minnesota's Department of Ecology are researching ways to perennialize plants, capture carbon, and offer practical solutions to erosion and diminished fertility. Plant researchers are rediscovering heirloom varieties, hybridizing new cultivars, and promoting woody agriculture's potential for market crops such as chestnuts, hazelnuts, and hickory nuts. NGOs (nongovernmental organizations), like IATP (Institute for Agriculture and Trade Policy), LSP (Land Stewardship Project), SFA (Sustainable Farming Association of Minnesota), and MOSES (Midwest Organic Sustainable Education Service), help fund and foster sustainable solutions to growing, marketing, and policy issues.

TEN GOOD REASONS TO EAT SEASONAL AND LOCAL

1. **Taste** Local food tastes better because it's fresher and has not traveled a thousand miles (or more) to our plates. It was grown or produced for its flavor, not to handle, ship, or store well. This means you will get tomatoes harvested at their peak, not picked green and ripened in a warehouse.

2. **Variety** Farmers' markets and CSA farms offer a range of interesting and delicious heirloom and heritage foods not available in supermarkets.

3. **Health and nutrition** A bag of spinach loses more than half of its health-promoting compounds (folate and carotenoids) after eight days out of the field. It takes bagged California greens twelve days to reach our plates. Grass-fed meat, eggs, and dairy products from pastured animals are richer in antioxidants, higher in good fats (omega-3 and CLA), and do not contain added hormones, antibiotics, or other drugs.

4. **Environment** The concerns are many:
   - Conventional cattle and hogs are raised in CAFOs (confined animal feeding operations), a system that produces the highest output for the lowest cost. The conditions are unsanitary and inhumane. To mitigate disease, they require toxic levels of antibiotics, an issue of grave national and global concern. The manure and runoff from CAFOs are loaded with the drugs fed to these animals as well as the chemicals used to grow their corn and feed. Their holding tanks often leak, polluting the groundwater and wreaking havoc on the environment.
   - Conventional vegetable farmers who grow single crops on large tracts of land rely on fertilizers and pesticides that seep into our groundwater. The continuous tilling and replanting of these crops contribute to erosion. There's no doubt that the sustainable organic system of planting diverse crops in rotation with ground cover is beneficial to water, land, and wildlife.
   - The packaging that preserves produce as it travels great distances creates tremendous waste.

5. **Economy** Every dollar spent on local food returns four dollars to the economy. Economist Ken Meter, president of Crossroads Resource Center, estimates that if rural communities grew food for themselves and for urban markets, there would be no need for the agricultural commodity price supports that suck down trillions of taxpayer dollars every year.

6. **Food safety** The less distance food travels, the less likely it is to become contaminated. Our food system is so highly centralized that when the products of a major processing facility are tainted, millions of people are affected. Local problems are easier to trace. Producers who have a relationship with their customers are more accountable.

7. **Land preservation** Land is expensive and difficult for young farmers to attain, and retiring farmers are often tempted to sell their land to developers for a large return. However, once land is developed, it is all but lost to farming. NGOs like Land Stewardship Project and the Trust for Public Land help retain land and support sustainable farming, but it's also important to support independent farms if we care about the land and the farmers as well as what we eat.

8. **Community** The farm-to-table movement connects farmers, chefs, home cooks, writers, academics, policy makers, and students in a concerted effort to fix our food mess.

9. **Seasonal cooking** The weather and light affect appetite; eating locally keeps us in tune with the natural rhythms of life.

10. **Fair** Promoting a healthy regional food system will help increase the supply of good real food for everyone, including those living in urban and rural food deserts. Access to fresh, clean, fair food is a basic right.

WHAT DO *LOCAL* AND *REGIONAL* REALLY MEAN?

Locavore and *100-mile diet* are catchy terms, but too simplistic. Here are broader, more practical considerations:

1. *Local* should mean from a farm, ranch, or producer locally owned and operated. The management team, as well as many of the workers, should live in the community. (Many small organic farmers in remote rural areas must hire migrant workers to get the harvest in on time, but they do so within the law, treat the workers fairly, provide decent living quarters, and pay a fair wage.)
2. Heirloom foods are tied to the traditions of a landscape or culture with seeds saved over generations.
3. The "food miles" argument needs to be reconsidered. It is not efficient for many farmers to supply restaurants and grocery stores with small amounts of produce when one large biodiesel truck might be able to aggregate and deliver it all at once. The efficient distribution of regional food is yet unresolved.
4. Farm energy and water are key concerns. Small organic farms deserve the kind of financial support currently doled out to large conventional farms through commodity price supports. Organic farms rotate crops and plant cover crops to maintain fertility, cleanse groundwater, and minimize pests without petroleum-based fertilizers and pesticides. They use hoop houses and solar greenhouses to start plants. Their methods improve our environment, yet these farmers do not receive government subsidies or financial incentives for their efforts.
5. Farm inputs are critical. Where does the farm get its hay, compost, and nitrogen? They should come from the region—not California.
6. *Terroir* is the term used in Europe to describe the unique flavors of a place. Our heirloom corn, wheat, wild mushrooms, wild rice, fish, apples, pears, and nuts are regional treasures. They connect us to this place.
7. Direct exchanges with other cultures, localities, and regions that circumvent the middleman are good for everyone's local economy in a global marketplace. Look for the Fair Trade label when purchasing coffee, chocolate, spices, bananas, and other imported foods.

DIY (DO IT YOURSELF)

Hunting, fishing, gardening, raising animals, pickling, brewing—all the home arts remain passionate avocations and social activities. Entries to state fair competitions expand by the year. Faced with economic, political, cultural, and environmental uncertainty, the hands-on work of raising chickens, butchering meat, grinding flour, baking sourdough bread, and brewing vinegar is a mark of self-reliance and instills self-confidence. Plus, it's fun.

Uniting this effort is what was once called "neighboring." When we rap at a friend's screen door to borrow flour, can community-garden tomatoes, and post our recipes online, we share sacred concerns. Each of us puts our money where our mouth is when we join a CSA, plant tomatoes, jump into a "crop mob," and shop at a farmers' market. Cooks, diners, farmers, producers, writers, teachers, and chefs from Duluth to Dubuque, Rapid City to Ann Arbor, are in this together.

COME TO THE TABLE

This book's recipes, notes, advice, and wisdom were gathered in classic Northern Heartland style, over coffee or walking a piece of land. Chefs talked about "nose to tail" cooking; farmers, of heritage breeds raised in pastures; cheese makers, of continuing traditional practices; and butchers, of skillfully cutting meat by hand; while home cooks shared stories and tips. Rich in natural resources, steeped in tradition, our culinary culture is openhanded and generous, grounded in stewardship, guided by love.

Nothing beats knowing the people who grow your food.

A NOTE ABOUT THESE RECIPES

The book is organized by seasons, beginning with autumn, the most bountiful and exciting of the year. The recipes come from a variety of sources and respond to our interest in eating less meat and more plants. Each chapter begins with a selection of five dishes you can have ready in five minutes or less and finishes with suggested menus.

Seasonal, local cooking is spontaneous and simple. It doesn't rely on quirky ingredients or difficult techniques; it means being nimble and flexible. Please consider these recipes as guidelines. Substitute with abandon. Use what you have, and vary the ingredients and flavors according to availability and your own tastes.

Throughout, you will find wisdom for heartland growers, the latest research and discoveries, and insights into how our food comes to the table, plus practical tips, hints, and advice.

The final chapters cover basics to enjoy year-round. Here are recipes for breads and pie crusts, as well as vinaigrettes. Stock your shelves with harvest preserves and jams and jellies so you can open a jar of summer sweetness any dark February morning.

You'll find no recipes calling for apples in May, Italian Parmesan, swordfish, or clams. Whenever possible, I've tried to stick to seasonings and flavors that also come from nearby. Fruit vinegars give the same snap as lemon or orange juice; local beer, wine, and spirits (whiskey, gin, vodka, and apple jack) are specified in lieu of their far-flung relatives; butter or vegetable oils take the place of olive oil; and honey, maple syrup, sorghum, and maple sugar are alternative sweeteners.

This focus on local, seasonal ingredients isn't meant to restrict you or require you to restock your cupboard. Indeed, if you have a favorite olive oil or love lemon juice, do use it as you please. Rather, it is just a way to spark ideas and expand appreciation for the tastes of home.

THE LOCAL KITCHEN

Eating seasonally keeps us flexible and nimble. When we respond to what's coming in from the fields, we're open to inspiration, letting the ingredients guide us into a meal.

Be warned, though, of the dangers in "local overachieving." You don't have to make everything from scratch. Making great cheese or smoked meat requires training and experience. It may seem like a luxury to spend a little more money on these things, but they are worth it.

Misdirected romanticism associated with the local foods movement does us all a disservice. Just seek out ethical, sustainable producers and restaurants, and be grateful for the good they bring to our lives. Why not finish a dinner you've created with a lovely apple pie from the farmers' market and ice cream from a local dairy? No one gets extra points for being wrung out by cooking: it's better to reward top-quality, independent producers for food made with integrity and care.

community supported agriculture

THE BEST WAY TO EAT LOCAL is to grow it yourself. Next best? Join a CSA (community supported agriculture) farm. At their most fundamental, CSAs provide weekly deliveries of organically grown produce to their subscribers through the season (late May to early October) for a fee paid in advance. At their most visionary level, members don't just buy the food; they also engage in the ecological and community activities tied to the farm's production.

Along with the farm-fresh vegetables, cooks delight in the variety of interesting heirloom crops not found in supermarkets, all chosen for flavor, not ship-ability or shelf life. It's a chance to explore unfamiliar flavors and add interest to everyday meals.

Membership arrangements vary greatly. Some CSAs deliver food to neighborhoods for pickup; others arrange for members to come to the farm. Some offer work shares in trade for membership; others expect more than a financial commitment, requiring members to help plant, weed, harvest, and deliver shares. CSA member share the rewards of farming—receiving field-fresh produce the day it is harvested, knowing where the food comes from, enjoying the connection with the farmers, supporting good stewardship of the land—as well as the risks in weather, pests, floods, and droughts.

CSAs make local eating remarkably easy. Choices are confined by what's in the box. This ignites a cook's creativity, spontaneity, and flexibility. There are plenty of CSAs in our area, and the trick is to find one that best suits your needs. Know that they often fill up well before spring. Refer to the CSA directories in your area and team up with neighbors to share the wealth. See a list of directories in Sources (page 244). Here are the kinds of things you should keep in mind while choosing a CSA:

- **Sign-ups** Most farms accept membership sign-ups beginning as early as February, and many fill up quickly. Check the farms' Web sites for application deadlines.

- **Location** Keep in mind the driving distance when you determine your level of involvement.

- **Pick-up site and delivery day** Delivery dates and time vary widely (some CSAs even drop at your door).

- **Length of season and number of deliveries** Most farms begin deliveries in May or June and run through September or October. Some offer winter shares.

- **Types of produce and other foods** Seasonal vegetables, grains, cheese, eggs, meat, flowers, maple syrup, jam, prepared foods, honey—there are a variety of farms with different kinds of shares.

- **Getting involved** Community building is an essential component of CSAs. There are farm events throughout the season, workdays, and time to just drop by.

EATING OUT OF THE BOX

Every week, CSA members are faced with a big box of farm-fresh produce. It's exciting to open and daunting to deal with. It helps to have a strategy: use up the more delicate vegetables now, put away those that will keep a while, and freeze the rest for winter. As you unpack your boxes of produce:

- **Refrigerate greens**—lettuces, kale, cabbage, collards, beet greens, spinach, sorrel—as well as broccoli, cauliflower, kohlrabi, zucchini, summer squash, and roots (beets, carrots, parsnips, radishes) in plastic bags or wrapped in dampened towels in the crisper.

- **Do not refrigerate** tomatoes or eggplant (the cold damages flavor and texture), potatoes, onions, garlic, shallots, and hard winter squash. Keep these in a cool, dark place.

- **Treat herbs like flowers.** Cut off the ends and set them in a vase (or glass) of water, near the cutting board, like an edible bouquet.

- **Corn doesn't keep.** Its sugars start to convert to starch as soon as it's picked. Eat it immediately or freeze it.

Produce from CSAs and farmers' markets is far fresher than anything trucked from over 1,500 miles away, so it will keep a little longer than supermarket food. Use up the delicate foods—tomatoes, peas, lettuces, and summer squash—right away. Save some of the sturdier vegetables—carrots, cabbage, cauliflower, broccoli, radishes, parsnips, potatoes, beets, and onions—for later. To save produce for winter use, you can preserve it (see Heartland Preserves and Condiments), freeze it, or dry it. Here are guidelines for freezing and drying.

Basic Freezing Guidelines

Freeze Directly, without Cooking

- **Corn** Shuck the corn, remove the kernels from the cobs, and transfer the kernels to freezer bags.

- **Tomatoes** Core the tomatoes, cut them into quarters, freeze them on a baking sheet, and then transfer them to plastic bags.

- **Herbs** Lay the leaves out on a baking sheet, freeze them, and then transfer them to a plastic bag. Use freeze-dried herbs in cooked dishes.

Blanch before Freezing

To blanch vegetables, bring a pot of unsalted water to a boil, and then dunk the vegetables in for about 3 to 5 minutes or just until tender, being careful not to overcook them. (You don't want to overcook them because they'll be cooked again after they're thawed.) The rule of thumb is to watch for a change in color: as soon as the vegetables brighten, they're ready. Drain them and immediately place them in a bowl of ice water to halt the cooking. Drain them again, pat them dry, and store them in freezer bags.

These approximate times for blanching vegetables include the time it takes for the water to return to a boil:

- **Carrots** Cut carrots into coins or sticks. Blanch for 3 to 4 minutes.

- **Beans** String, stem, and cut the beans into pieces or leave them whole. Blanch for 3 to 5 minutes.

- **Peas** Shuck shell peas, and string sugar snaps. Blanch for 2 to 3 minutes.

- **Broccoli and cauliflower** Cut into florets. Blanch for 3 to 5 minutes.

- **Brussels sprouts** Halve big sprouts if necessary. Blanch for 3 to 6 minutes.

- **Roots (turnips, rutabaga, parsnips)** Cut into pieces. Blanch for 3 to 6 minutes.

Cook Thoroughly before Freezing

- **Onions** Sauté onions in butter or oil until they are limp, and then freeze them for use in cooked foods.

- **Potatoes** Steam, boil, mash, or roast potatoes.

- **Summer Squash** Sauté or roast.

- **Winter Squash** Roast and then scoop out the interior, or remove the skin and then roast or steam the squash.

- **Eggplant** Roast or sauté.

AUTUMN

roast mushroom, red pepper, and sage pizza

smoked trout, apple, and fennel salad in cider vinaigrette

fresh chestnut soup

wild rice and wild mushroom soup

curried vegetable soup

asian chicken noodle soup

ginger squash and apple soup

prosciutto-wrapped tilapia with sage

beer-braised pork chops with pears

venison medallions with juniper and gin

hanger steak with fresh horseradish sauce

sure fire roast duck

duck confit

pheasant with hard cider, apples, and chestnuts

rabbit with pancetta and fennel

quick roast herb chicken

thanksgiving bird—fast!

turkey or chicken pot pie with cheddar chive cobbler crust

harvest stuffed squash

heartland polenta with mushroom ragout

barley pilaf with chickpeas and autumn vegetables

spicy savoy coleslaw

silky chard

no fail kale

horseradish and honey-glazed root vegetables

caramelized brussels sprouts

roast broccoli or cauliflower with garlic and hot pepper

thanksgiving mashed potatoes

wild rice cranberry pilaf

basic sage stuffing

savory cranberry compote

oven-dried pears

scandinavian brown beans with a kick

cranberry sorbet

honey pumpkin ginger pie

autumn squash or pumpkin bars with cranberry glaze

oatmeal chocolate chip and dried cranberry cookies

mom's fall fruit crisp

applesauce and apple butter, savory and sweet

rich applesauce cake

cranberry cordial

We come and go, but the land is always here.

And the people who love it and understand it

are the people who own it—for a little while.

—WILLA CATHER, *O PIONEERS!*

autumn

SOMETIME AROUND SEPTEMBER, the urgency at the market becomes palpable. It's a mad dash to enjoy the last days of good weather and taste the splendid apples, pears, carrots, beets, kale, cabbages, Brussels sprouts, mushrooms, and more. Our hungers surge as the light fades and the temperatures begin to dip. Farmers consider Thanksgiving the New Year's celebration: the year is complete, the harvest is in. Let the feast begin!

FIVE FALL DISHES IN FIVE MINUTES OR LESS

Autumn Garden Slaw Shred Brussels sprouts, red cabbage, and onion and toss with just enough hazelnut or extra-virgin olive oil to coat. Sprinkle in cider vinegar, salt, and pepper to taste. Let the slaw sit for a few minutes so the flavors marry before serving.

Fresh Apple and Sage Sauce Peel and core an apple or two and finely chop it. Mix in some chopped onions, several minced sage leaves, parsley, a little lemon juice, salt, and pepper to taste. Serve the sauce with grilled or roasted pork or chicken.

Roast Pears Cut pears into quarters and brush all sides liberally with butter. Sprinkle with a little sugar and place them on a baking sheet lined with parchment paper. Roast the pears in a preheated 400-degree oven for about 5 minutes. Serve the pears with a cheese plate, in a salad of dark greens, or alongside roasted meats.

Spiced Roast Carrots Cut some carrots into ½-inch matchsticks. Roll them in melted butter, dust with curry powder or cumin, and roast in a hot (400-degree) oven until just tender, about 5 minutes. Serve the carrots as an appetizer or a side dish.

Grilled Radicchio Slice heads of radicchio in half, brush them with oil, and place them cut-side down on a hot grill until they are just charred, about 5 minutes. Serve drizzled with oil and vinegar.

roast mushroom, red pepper, and sage pizza

This duo shines with the flavors of early fall. Sage perks up the mushrooms' woodsy notes, while the red peppers add a smoky, sweet touch. Pair this with the Ginger Squash and Apple Soup (page 11) for a colorful fall meal. **SERVES 4 TO 6**

1 batch Pizza Dough (page 203)
2 cups thinly sliced mushrooms
2 red bell peppers, seeded and thinly sliced
2 teaspoons chopped fresh sage leaves
2 tablespoons chopped parsley

½ cup mild feta or any cheese of your choice
1 teaspoon chili flakes
Extra-virgin olive oil
Salt and freshly ground black pepper

Preheat the oven to 425 degrees. Line a pizza peel or a baking sheet with parchment paper.

On a lightly floured surface, roll out the dough into a 14-inch circle. Let it rest for 15 to 20 minutes.

Set the dough on the peel or baking sheet; then arrange the mushrooms, peppers, sage, parsley, cheese, and chili flakes on it. Drizzle a little oil over the top and bake until the edges of the pizza are crispy and golden brown, about 15 to 20 minutes. Just before serving, season the pizza with salt and pepper.

smoked trout, apple, and fennel salad
in cider vinaigrette

Smoked trout and crisp apples make a pretty appetizer or a light meal. This recipe works equally well with smoked salmon. It makes a nice start to a festive meal of Sure Fire Roast Duck (page 17) or a fine luncheon salad paired with the Wild Rice and Wild Mushroom Soup (page 8). **SERVES 4**

Salad

2 small smoked trout or 1 smoked whitefish

1 fennel bulb, diced

1 tart, crisp apple, cored and diced

2 cups mixed dark greens

Cider Vinaigrette

2 tablespoons cider vinegar

2 tablespoons apple cider

1 teaspoon Dijon mustard

3 tablespoons hazelnut or vegetable oil

Salt and freshly ground black pepper

Remove the skin from the trout and pick the flesh off the bones. Toss together the fennel and apple and arrange this and the trout on a bed of lettuce.

In a small bowl, whisk together the ingredients for the vinaigrette and season it with salt and pepper to taste. Drizzle the dressing over the composed salad. Pass any additional dressing on the side.

LAKE SUPERIOR SMOKED FISH

Smoked fish is available year-round, even in the winter, as long as it is safe for boats to ply the northern Great Lakes. Business is most brisk in September, when the fattest whitefish and flavorful lake trout are most mature. The weather is fine, and visitors poke along the shores of Lake Superior.

Look for signs for smoked fish outside gas stations and stores on US Highway 2, the main route along the South Shore in Wisconsin and the Upper Peninsula of Michigan, and Highway 61 along Minnesota's North Shore.

Lake Superior smoked fish cannot be compared to lox, gravlax, or cold-smoked Atlantic salmon. Instead, this fish, mostly lake trout and whitefish, is first brined in salt and sometimes brown sugar, then hot-smoked, skin on, over a roaring hardwood fire.

Eat it by laying the fish open and tearing off chunks to serve with Ritz crackers and cold beer. Or, flake it into a salad or mash it with mayonnaise and cream cheese to make a spread. Lake Superior smoked fish is perishable, so buy only what you need and enjoy it within two weeks.

To purchase Lake Superior smoked fish, see Sources.

fresh chestnut soup

This hearty soup showcases the rich, sweet, and earthy flavor of fresh chestnuts with a silky texture that reduces a need for cream. It is delicious as a first course or as a satisfying supper paired with sharp cheddar cheese and hearty bread. A little splash of gin gives it a juniper punch, but white wine works well too. Serve this soup with a salad of Duck Confit (page 18) for a lovely casual supper or as the first course to the Rabbit with Pancetta and Fennel (page 21). **SERVES 4 TO 6**

2 tablespoons unsalted butter

1 large onion, chopped

1 celery rib, chopped, or ½ cup chopped celeriac root

1 carrot, chopped

1 large shallot, chopped

2 sprigs fresh thyme or 1 teaspoon dried

¼ cup gin or dry white wine

4 cups chicken stock (page 10) or vegetable stock (page 110)

1 pound chestnuts, blanched (page 7)

Salt and freshly ground black pepper

Pinch of freshly grated nutmeg

¼ cup chopped fresh parsley, plus additional for garnish

Heavy cream

Toasted croutons

Melt the butter in a heavy soup pot set over medium heat and add the onion, celery, carrot, shallot, and thyme. Cover and cook, stirring occasionally, until the vegetables are very soft, about 8 to 10 minutes. Add the gin and then the stock and the chestnuts. Season with salt and freshly ground black pepper and a little grated nutmeg. Bring the liquid to a boil; then reduce the heat and simmer, partially covered, stirring occasionally, until the vegetables are very tender, about 35 to 40 minutes. Remove the pot from the heat, remove and discard the thyme sprigs (if using), and stir in the parsley.

Puree the soup in batches in a blender and return it to the pot, or use an immersion blender to puree the soup. If you wish for a very smooth soup, pass it through a sieve before returning it to the pot. (Otherwise, it is a nice chunky soup.) To serve, ladle the soup into bowls and garnish each with a swirl of heavy cream, a sprinkling of chopped parsley, and a few toasted croutons.

AMERICAN CHESTNUTS

Until a century ago, millions of majestic chestnut trees, growing taller and straighter than oaks, populated our forests from the Northern Heartland through the East Coast and grew thick along the Appalachians. Come June, their white blossoms made hillsides appear covered with snow. With their shiny canopy of leaves and fine hardwood, they provided shelter and food for wildlife, Native Americans, and settlers. Chestnut trees, often called bread trees, grew nuts that were dried and ground into flour for bread, boiled and mashed, and roasted for snacks. A good source of carbohydrates and protein (equal to beans or maize), highly nutritious chestnuts were dried and stored for winter food. In Virginia, pigs on a diet of chestnuts became the famous Smithfield hams. In the early 1900s, blight caused by a fungus felled nearly all of the American chestnut trees in about 30 years; loggers made quick use of what was left.

Badgersett Research Farm in Canton, Minnesota, is restoring the American chestnut to its former glory. Here, in the southeast corner of the state, Phil Rutter, biologist and ecologist, as well as founder and past president of the American Chestnut Foundation, has been working on breeding hybrid chestnut trees for the past 30 years. The farm sells its breeding stock as well as the nuts.

Tasting this new "old" chestnut is a revelation. Compared with the nuts we find in the stores, which come from Italy and California, the meat is denser, sweeter, and creamier. They are a bit smaller, like mahogany marbles; their soft, pliable shells are easy to score and the meat is free of that bitter dark skin. No more nicked, singed fingers—these nuts are a snap to prepare (see directions below).

Working with his son Brandon and wife, Megan, Rutter sees "woody agriculture" as a viable solution to many of the problems plaguing our farmland while providing a reliable, sustainable source of food, oil, shelter, and fuel. These perennial plants, with their 30-foot root systems, withstand droughts and floods and yield enormous crops year after year. They stem erosion, capture carbon, return nutrients to the soil, and filter water. Yes, they're beautiful too.

Chestnut trees grow quickly, far faster than oaks, absorbing sunlight through the bright green beneath their thin bark and, unlike walnuts, produce crops year after year. Supplies are limited, so when chestnuts appear in the co-ops, it's good to stock up. Chestnuts may also be ordered to ship (see Sources).

COOKING WITH CHESTNUTS

Chestnuts are mildly sweet and earthy tasting, with a fine, silky texture that pairs nicely with assertive flavors and adds body and texture to stuffing, soups, and stews. The American chestnuts have a soft, pliable skin that is easily scored or sliced. Here's how to prepare chestnuts.

Roast Score the flat part of the nut or simply snip the smaller pointy end with a scissors. Roast the chestnuts in a 350-degree oven until the shells begin to curl, about 10 minutes (adjust the time accordingly for Asian or European chestnuts).

Microwave Pierce or score the nuts or cut them in half and cook 10 nuts at a time on high power for about 1 minute.

Open-fire roasting Score the nuts and place them at the edge of the coals. When you see them steaming, about 4 to 6 minutes, remove them from the fire and peel them.

Blanch Slice each nut in half and then blanch them in boiling water for 30 seconds to a minute. Drain the nuts and then, with needle-nose pliers, pinch the back of the nut, gently squeeze, and it will pop out.

Note Store chestnuts in paper bags in the refrigerator until you are ready to use them. Plastic bags trap moisture and can make the nuts too soft. For the best flavor, allow chestnuts to stand at room temperature several days before using them.

wild rice and wild mushroom soup

Although this recipe calls for chanterelle mushrooms, it works nicely with cultivated mushrooms too. Chanterelles are prized by chefs the world over for their texture and flavor. They taste of apricots and pine and complement the smoky notes of wild rice in this soup. This soup makes a satisfying lunch or fine light dinner served with Roast Mushroom, Red Pepper, and Sage Pizza (page 4). **SERVES 6 TO 8**

2 tablespoons unsalted butter
1 large onion, finely chopped
2 shallots, finely chopped
1 pound mixed mushrooms (use as many chanterelles as possible), coarsely chopped
1 tablespoon unbleached all-purpose flour
Generous pinch of freshly grated nutmeg

¼ cup amber beer or red wine
3 cups chicken stock (page 10)
3 cups milk
¼ cup heavy cream
1 cup cooked wild rice (page 39)
Salt and freshly ground black pepper
¼ cup chopped parsley

In a heavy-bottomed pot set over medium heat, melt the butter and sauté the onion, shallots, and mushrooms. Cover and cook until the onions are very soft and the mushrooms have released most of their liquid, about 7 to 10 minutes.

Sprinkle in the flour and nutmeg; then stir and cook over low heat until the flour mixture coats the vegetables like a thick paste, about 1 minute. Whisk in the beer, stock, milk, and cream, and then stir in the wild rice. Simmer for several minutes until the soup thickens to the desired consistency. Season the soup with salt and pepper to taste. Serve garnished with the parsley.

CHANTERELLES

Though morels are best known for their distinct flavor, chanterelles are most prized by chefs worldwide. Chanterelles have a slightly spicy edge and round fruity flavor, reminiscent of apricot and pine. The Italians call them *girolle*, the Germans, *pfifferlinge.*

The best way to eat them is sautéed in a little butter with chopped onion and garlic. Be sure to deglaze the pan with a little wine or sherry. Slather them on toast, pile them on dark bread, or fold them into scrambled eggs.

Chanterelles are tough mushrooms to spot, popping up through the leaf litter after a light rain. It's best to hunt chanterelles in pine forests in the early fall after a light drizzle. To clean fresh chanterelles, just brush them off. If you see insects, dunk the mushrooms in salted water for a few minutes just before cooking them.

For more information on chanterelles and mushroom hunting, see Sources.

curried vegetable soup

This soup, spiced with curry, chock-full of fall vegetables, and sparked with orange juice, makes quick use of backyard chard. The nice thing about red lentils is that they don't have to be soaked in advance. Pair this soup with Rich Brown Soda Bread (page 198) and Spicy Savoy Coleslaw (page 31) for a hearty weekday meal. **SERVES 6 TO 8**

3 tablespoons unsalted butter
1 large onion, diced
4 medium carrots, diced (about 1 cup)
1 small zucchini or summer squash, diced
1 medium potato, diced
Salt and pepper
1 to 2 teaspoons curry powder
1 cup chopped fresh tomatoes
½ cup white wine or water

4½ to 5 cups chicken stock (page 10), vegetable stock (page 110), or water
1 cup red lentils
1 cup chard leaves, thinly sliced
¼ cup fresh orange juice, or to taste
1 teaspoon fresh orange zest
1 cup plain whole-milk yogurt or sour cream
½ cup chopped cilantro

Melt the butter in a wide soup pot set over medium heat. Sauté the onion, carrots, zucchini, and potato until the onion is soft and begins to brown. Sprinkle with salt and pepper and curry powder to taste, cover, and cook until the vegetables are very soft, about 5 minutes.

Add the tomatoes, wine, stock, and lentils. Bring to a boil; then lower the heat and simmer, partially covered, until the lentils are beginning to soften, about 20 minutes. Add the chard and continue cooking until the chard is tender, about 10 minutes. Add the orange juice and zest. Taste the soup and adjust the seasonings. Serve with a dollop of yogurt or sour cream and chopped fresh cilantro.

asian chicken noodle soup

This recipe uses up chicken, turkey, or duck leftover from the Sure Fire Roast Duck (page 17). The stock is seasoned with ginger, star anise, and fish sauce. These flavors, introduced to the Northern Heartland by Vietnamese, Chinese, and Hmong immigrants, enrich our local cuisine. **SERVES 4 TO 6**

4 cups chicken stock (see below)

1 to 1½ inches fresh ginger, peeled and sliced

6 scallions, sliced thinly

2 star anise

1 teaspoon black peppercorns

1 tablespoon fish sauce or soy sauce, or to taste

2 ounces rice noodles

½ cup shredded green cabbage

1 cup cooked chicken, duck, or turkey

¼ cup chopped fresh cilantro or a mix of cilantro and parsley

1 small chili pepper, seeded, deveined, and thinly sliced, or to taste

In a large soup pot, bring the stock to a boil and add the ginger, scallions, anise, and peppercorns. Reduce the heat and simmer for about 30 minutes. Add the fish sauce and set aside.

In a large bowl, pour boiling water over the rice noodles, add the cabbage, and let stand for about 3 to 4 minutes until both are softened. Drain. Add the noodles and cabbage to the stock; then add the chicken, duck, or turkey and heat through. Stir in the chopped fresh herbs and chili and serve right away.

SIMPLE CHICKEN STOCK

This stock takes less than an hour to make and yields a whole cooked chicken to use in a stew or casserole afterward. **MAKES ABOUT 3 QUARTS**

1 whole chicken (an older hen, if possible), rinsed and cut into parts

1 large onion, cut into chunks

2 carrots, cut into chunks

2 celery stalks, with leaves, cut into chunks

2 sprigs fresh thyme or ½ teaspoon dried

Several peppercorns

3 quarts water

Salt to taste

Put all of the ingredients into a large pot. Bring the water to a boil; then reduce the heat so the liquid barely simmers. Partially cover the pot, and cook until the chicken is well done, about 45 minutes to an hour. Remove the chicken and set it aside. Strain off the remaining ingredients, pressing the vegetables to extract as much flavor as possible. Refrigerate the stock and then remove any hardened fat on the surface. Store stock in the refrigerator for about three days, or freeze it for up to three months.

Note You can use a good-quality, low-salt boxed chicken stock in lieu of homemade stock in recipes calling for chicken stock. Doctor it up with sprigs of fresh herbs.

ginger squash and apple soup

Red kuri squash is the prettiest of our local winter squashes. Its hues range from vibrant orange to mustard yellow. Originally from Japan, the red kuri is slightly nutty tasting, not as sweet as our other squash varieties, and is a good choice for this soup. Pair this with the Barley Pilaf with Chickpeas and Autumn Vegetables (page 29) for a casual vegetarian meal. **SERVES 6**

1 medium red kuri, 1 butternut, or 2 small delicata squash (about 2 pounds), cut in half and seeded
Extra-virgin olive oil or hazelnut oil
2 tablespoons unsalted butter
2 large onions, finely chopped
3 cloves garlic, chopped
2 tart apples, peeled, cored, and chopped

1 to 2 tablespoons freshly grated ginger
2 cups vegetable stock (page 110) or chicken stock (page 10)
1 cup fresh apple cider, or to taste
Salt and freshly ground black pepper
Pinch of cayenne pepper
½ cup crème fraiche (page 181) or sour cream
2 tablespoons chopped cilantro, or to taste

Preheat the oven to 350 degrees. Drizzle the cut side of the squash with the oil, turn it cut-side down on a baking sheet, and bake until it's soft, about 45 minutes to 1 hour.

While the squash is baking, melt the butter in a large, heavy soup pot set over medium-low heat; add the onions, garlic, apples, and ginger; and toss to coat. Cover the pan and cook, stirring occasionally, until the vegetables are soft, about 10 minutes. Add the stock and cider, and simmer until the ingredients are very tender, about 10 minutes. Remove the squash from the oven, scoop the meat from the skin, and add it to the pot.

For a smooth soup, puree the mixture using an immersion blender or process it in a blender in batches. For a chunky soup, mash all the ingredients together with a potato masher. Season the soup with salt, pepper, and cayenne, whisk in the crème fraiche, and serve garnished with cilantro.

UNIVERSITY OF MINNESOTA APPLES

Every year, the choice of apples expands, thanks to research conducted by the University of Minnesota College of Food, Agriculture and Natural Resource Sciences. It developed the popular Honeycrisp many years back and recently released the Zestar and SweeTango, both great for eating raw as well as for baking and stewing into sauce.

The SnowSweet apple, with its soft, buttery flesh and rich aromatic overtones, is the new counterpoint to the Honeycrisp. The hard Frostbite apple is perfect for snacking and baking. Here is a partial list of cold-hardy U of M apple varieties.

Early Ripening

Zestar (late August, early September) is distinctly sweet, zesty, and crisp.

SweeTango (early September) is similar to Zestar, crisp and juicy.

Midseason

Honeycrisp (late September) is sweet, juicy, and crisp and stores very well.

SnowSweet (mid-October) is soft fleshed, floral, and slightly tart.

Late Season

Frostbite (mid to late October) is a small cider apple with ultra-sweet flavor and a hard, snappy texture.

All of these new varieties partner beautifully with artisan cheddar and Colby cheeses.

prosciutto-wrapped tilapia with sage

The prosciutto keeps this lean fish moist and adds flavor. Use any fresh herbs available. Serve this with Wild Rice Cranberry Pilaf (page 38) or Scandinavian Brown Beans with a Kick (page 43) and Silky Chard (page 32). **SERVES 4**

4 (8-ounce) pieces tilapia
Salt and freshly ground black pepper
8 slices prosciutto

8 whole fresh sage leaves, plus additional, chopped, for garnish
¼ cup unsalted butter
Chopped parsley

Cut the fillets lengthwise, rinse and pat them dry, then season them with salt and pepper. Wrap each piece of fish with a slice of prosciutto, tucking a sage leaf between the fish and the prosciutto.

Heat half of the butter in a skillet over medium heat and cook two pieces of the fish until cooked through, about 3 to 4 minutes per side. Transfer the fish to a plate and tent it with foil to keep it warm. Cook the remaining fish the same way and serve it immediately, garnished with a little chopped sage and parsley.

FARM-RAISED FISH

Farm trout, catfish, and tilapia are relatively easy to raise with sustainable methods. Unlike salmon, they require no fish or animal components in their feed, and they thrive in enclosed freshwater tanks, ponds, or channels. Farmed salmon present a number of challenges, including pollution, antibiotic contamination, and transfer of diseases and parasites to wild fish.

Star Prairie Trout Farm in Star Prairie, Wisconsin, works hard to raise its trout sustainably. "Exceptionally high water quality is required for fish culture, and it makes sense for the fish farmer to maintain and improve it," explains Nate Wendt, Star Prairie's operations manager. Discharge water from well-run fish farms is cleaner than the waters it runs in to, and sprinkling it on fields is a good way to nourish vegetable crops.

beer-braised pork chops with pears

This method of pan braising is perfect for game and inexpensive cuts of meat. Searing the meat first seals in flavor, and adding beer, wine, or stock keeps it moist while cooking and creates a pan sauce at the same time.

Use a strong beer to add a mysterious bitter edge to the sweet pears and peppery sage. Serve this dish with the Savory Cranberry Compote (page 41) and Horseradish and Honey-Glazed Root Vegetables (page 34). **SERVES 4**

4 boneless pork chops, about 1 inch thick
Salt and freshly ground black pepper
2 tablespoons unsalted butter
2 onions, thinly sliced
2 sage leaves

¼ cup strong-tasting beer (such as Surlyfest, brewed with malted barley and rye) or red wine
½ cup chicken stock (page 10)
1 pear, cored and thinly sliced
Chopped parsley

Trim some but not all of the fat from the chops. Pat the chops dry and sprinkle them with salt and pepper. Melt the butter in a large skillet over medium-high heat; then add the chops to the pan. Brown each side, about 5 minutes total; then set the chops aside on a plate.

Add the onions and sage to the fat in the skillet and cook, stirring, until golden brown, about 5 minutes. Add the beer and stock, and scrape up any browned bits left in the pan. Reduce the heat, cover, and simmer until the onions are very tender, about 15 minutes.

Return the chops, with any juices accumulated on the plate, to the skillet. Scoop some of the onions on top of the pork and add the sliced pears. Cover and cook over medium heat, turning once, until most of the liquid has evaporated and a meat thermometer inserted into the center of a chop reads 145 degrees. Remove the sage leaves and adjust the seasoning as needed. Serve the chops drizzled with the pan juices and topped with the onions and pear slices. Garnish with the chopped parsley.

SEASONAL BEERS

In these storied beer-brewing regions, October is a month of fests. The harvest is in, the pigs are fattened, and the crisp cool air is just right for the slaughter. Plenty of small towns, especially those with an active tourist trade, plan their fests in tune with apple picking, leaf peeping, and Octoberfests.

Surly Brewing, a leader in the area's regional breweries, releases seasonal beers throughout the year. Surly, and a number of other rising artisan breweries, use small-batch methods that once made this region the center of America's brewing industry.

Like many of our young breweries, Surly was started in its owner's garage. When it outgrew that, Surly opened Minnesota's first new brewery west of the Mississippi since 1987. Surly beers are all full-bodied, but Surly is best known for Furious, a crimson-hued hoppy ale. Its seasonal selections include Abrasive Ale, a double IPA, and Hell, brewed for summer sipping. If you're new to this lingo, just take a sip and you'll get it right away. Surly comes in a can with a special lining that protects the brew from damaging light.

venison medallions with juniper and gin

The best venison steaks, cut from the loin, are naturally juicy and tender and best left alone. Here they are panfried and served with a simple sauce seasoned with gin and juniper. Juniper grows wild throughout the Northern Heartland, and its tiny berries, when dried, are as snappy as peppercorns. The berries are the primary seasoning for gin, so here the two work together beautifully. Serve these medallions with Oven-Dried Pears (page 42) and wild rice (page 39). **SERVES 4**

8 venison medallions
Salt and freshly ground black pepper
1 tablespoon vegetable oil
2 tablespoons unsalted butter
¼ cup gin

1 cup chicken stock (page 10)
2 teaspoons juniper berries or black peppercorns
1 tablespoon chopped fresh sage
2 tablespoons chopped fresh parsley,
    plus more for garnish

Season the venison with salt and pepper. Heat the oil and butter together in a large, heavy frying pan set over high heat. Add the medallions and fry until they are browned, about 1 to 2 minutes per side for rare meat or 3 minutes per side for medium. Remove the venison to a plate and cover it.

Add the gin and stock to the pan along with the juniper berries, sage, and parsley, and boil, stirring, until the sauce is reduced to about ½ cup. Season the sauce with salt and pepper to taste. Spoon the sauce over the venison and garnish it with chopped parsley.

hanger steak with fresh horseradish sauce

━━━━━━━━

Hanger steak "hangs" on the last rib of the beef and is similar in texture and flavor to flank steak. This coarse-grained cut can be chewy if overcooked. It is so prized that butchers are known to save it for their families.

Horseradish, a knobby, thick root, grows like a weed across the region. There's a vast difference between the processed sauce in a jar and your own, made fresh. Find horseradish root at farmers' markets and local co-ops, or grow your own. Serve this steak with Silky Chard (page 32) and Scandinavian Brown Beans with a Kick (page 43). **SERVES 4 TO 6**

2 pounds hanger steak (about 1 to 1¼ inches thick)   ½ cup vegetable oil
Salt and freshly ground black pepper

Pat the steak dry on both sides with a paper towel. Season it with salt and pepper. Set a large cast-iron skillet or heavy pan over high heat, add the oil, and heat until smoking, about 5 minutes. Add the steak and sear, turning once, until nicely browned on all sides, about 8 minutes total. Let the steak rest for 5 minutes before slicing. Serve with the horseradish sauce on the side.

Fresh Horseradish Sauce

¼ cup freshly grated horseradish
2 to 3 teaspoons white wine vinegar
Pinch of salt and pepper
Pinch of sugar

1 cup freshly whipped cream, crème fraiche (page 181), sour cream, or plain whole-milk yogurt

Put the horseradish into a bowl with the vinegar, salt, pepper, and sugar. Fold in the whipped cream, crème fraiche, sour cream, or yogurt. This sauce will keep two to three days in the refrigerator.

sure fire roast duck

No longer do you need to know a hunter to get your hands on a good duck. Grocery stores, co-ops, and meat markets are selling good local duck. This recipe will work on any whole duck without much fuss. The trick here is the boiling water—it helps to tighten the skin, keep the meat moist, and prevent the fat from spattering. Serve the duck with Caramelized Brussels Sprouts (page 35) and Wild Rice Cranberry Pilaf (page 38). **SERVES 4**

1 large duck, about 5 to 6 pounds
2 cups boiling water

Coarse salt and freshly ground black pepper

Preheat the oven to 425 degrees. Cut the wing tips from the duck, remove and discard excess fat from the body cavity and neck, and rinse the duck inside and out. Gently prick the top layer of the skin with a sharp fork (being careful not to poke all the way through to the flesh). Set the duck breast-side up on the rack of a roasting pan and pour the boiling water over the duck. Leave the water in the pan, and pour any water that has collected in the duck's cavity into the pan. Pat the duck dry, inside and out, season it inside and out with salt and pepper, and set it breast-side down on the roasting rack.

Roast the duck for 45 minutes, turn it over (using kitchen towels or wooden utensils), and continue roasting until the skin is crisp and brown, about 45 to 50 minutes. Tilt the duck to drain any liquid that has collected in the cavity. Transfer the duck to a carving board and allow it to stand at least 10 minutes before carving.

AU BON CANARD, CALEDONIA, MINNESOTA

In the rolling hills of Southern Minnesota, which are quite like those of the French countryside, Au Bon Canard raises ducks for market. But this farm is known for its foie gras, or duck liver. The delicacy, once limited to the elite, appears on menus nationwide. Au Bon Canard, one of three foie gras producers in the country, limits its sale of this farmstead specialty to local restaurants and shops in and around the Twin Cities.

The ducks, for much of their lives, are free range, and the fattening, or gavage, process is done by hand, duck by duck. The artesian method employed by Christian and Liz Gasset is gentler than others used in the industry. "I don't want to raise too many ducks and grow my business to a large scale," says Gasset, who did not turn a profit for the first four years. "I'm never going to be rich. It doesn't matter. I'm happy with my lifestyle. These ducks are my babies."

duck confit

―――――――

Confit, the oldest way of preserving meat, is becoming very popular. No wonder. It's a cinch to make and yields a silky, flavorful meat that is fabulous served on its own or shredded into a salad, presented on bruschetta, or tossed with pasta. Though this method of cooking meat in its own fat works equally well for pork and goose, duck is the classic choice. Use this luscious meat in a classic Duck Confit Salad (recipe follows). **SERVES 6 (BUT IS REALLY RICH)**

2 large heads garlic, split into cloves and
    peeled, 4 cloves reserved
¼ cup kosher salt
2 teaspoons chopped thyme
1 teaspoon ground black pepper
¼ teaspoon freshly grated nutmeg
¼ teaspoon ground ginger
Pinch of ground cloves

3 shallots, chopped
2 bay leaves, crushed
6 duck legs (about 5 pounds), rinsed
    and patted dry
2 whole cloves
5 cups rendered duck or pork fat
    (directions below)

Using a mortar and pestle, the flat side of a large knife blade, or a food processor fitted with a steel blade, smash all but 4 of the garlic cloves with a little salt to create a paste. Stir in the remaining salt, thyme, pepper, nutmeg, ginger, cloves, shallots, and bay leaves and spread this over the duck legs to thoroughly and evenly coat them. Cover and refrigerate for at least 1 day.

Melt the duck fat in a large, wide pot set over low heat. Add the duck legs and remaining 4 garlic cloves and cook, uncovered, until the fat reaches 190 degrees, about 1 hour. Continue cooking, maintaining the temperature, until the duck is very tender and a wooden toothpick slides easily into the meat, about 2 to 3 hours more.

Remove the duck to a large bowl. Pour the duck fat through a fine-mesh sieve into a large crock, discarding anything that collects at the bottom of the sieve. Pour the strained fat over the legs to cover them completely. Allow to cool to room temperature; then cover and refrigerate for at least 8 hours.

To serve the duck, remove it from the bowl and scrape off the fat. Cook the legs, skin-side down, in a large, heavy skillet over low heat, covered. The skin will crisp up once the duck is heated through.

Rendered Duck Fat

The best thing about rendering your own duck fat is that you end up with delicious cracklings. They're great as snacks sprinkled with a little salt.

Remove the skin and fat from one whole duck, avoiding the neck and tail. Cut it into medium pieces. Put the skin and fat and about ½ cup of water in a heavy pot set over medium-low heat. Bring the water to a simmer and cook until the water evaporates and the skin has released all its fat, about 60 to 75 minutes. Strain the fat through a fine-mesh sieve or a cheesecloth-lined colander. Store the rendered fat in a sealed container in the refrigerator for up to a month or freeze it.

You can also purchase rendered duck or pork fat from gourmet retailers (see Sources).

Duck Confit Salad

This classic salad makes a beautiful appetizer or an elegant lunch. It also partners nicely with Wild Rice and Wild Mushroom Soup (page 8) for a light meal.

Shred the meat and arrange it on a bed of dark greens (such as arugula, watercress, or sorrel) and drizzle with the Honey Mustard Vinaigrette (page 210). Garnish the salad with dried cranberries and toasted walnuts.

pheasant with hard cider, apples, and chestnuts

Pheasant can be tough, but braising it, as called for in this recipe, yields tender, flavorful meat. Serve this pheasant with Roast Broccoli or Cauliflower with Garlic and Hot Pepper (page 36) and barley or roasted potatoes. **SERVES 4 TO 6**

2 pheasants, cut into quarters
½ cup unbleached all-purpose flour seasoned
    with salt and pepper
¼ cup vegetable oil or melted butter
¼ cup hard cider, apple jack, or brandy
6 apples, cored and quartered

2 large onions, cut into wedges
⅔ cup chicken stock (page 10)
1 tablespoon honey
½ pound fresh chestnuts, peeled (page 7),
    or jarred chestnuts
Salt and freshly ground black pepper

Preheat the oven to 350 degrees. Roll the pheasant pieces in the seasoned flour until they are lightly coated. Heat the oil in a large skillet, and then brown the pheasant well on all sides, about 10 to 15 minutes. Add the hard cider and cook for a few minutes, scraping up any of the browned bits from the bottom of the pan.

Put the apples and onions into a baking dish and lay the pheasant on top. Pour the pan juices over the top. Then add the chicken stock and drizzle with the honey. Cover and bake until the pheasant is tender, about 50 minutes. Remove the cover, add the chestnuts, and cook until the chestnuts are browned and heated through, about 10 minutes.

Transfer the pheasant, apples, onions, and chestnuts to a serving platter and cover it to keep the pheasant warm. Transfer the pan juices into a saucepan and set it over medium heat. Simmer until the liquid is reduced by half and has thickened. Season the sauce with salt and pepper and drizzle it over the pheasant before serving.

rabbit with pancetta and fennel

Rabbit's dark meat is light and flavorful, but not gamey. Here it's enhanced by the licorice notes of fennel and sweet dried cherries. Serve this rabbit over Heatland Polenta (page 27) or with Wild Rice Cranberry Pilaf (page 38) for a fine fall meal. **SERVES ABOUT 4**

1 teaspoon coarsely ground black pepper
1 teaspoon fennel seeds, crushed
¼ teaspoon coarse salt
1 clove garlic, crushed or minced
1 teaspoon grated lemon zest
2 teaspoons lemon juice
2 tablespoons olive oil

1 (3-pound) rabbit
2 large fennel bulbs
1 large onion
3 ounces pancetta or very thinly sliced bacon
½ cup chicken stock (page 10)
½ cup dried cherries, plumped in ½ cup warm
   dry white wine or water for about 20 minutes

Preheat the oven to 450 degrees. In a small bowl, mix the pepper, fennel seeds, salt, garlic, lemon zest, and lemon juice with the olive oil. Slather this mixture all over the rabbit and set it aside.

Slice the fennel and onion into ½-inch-thick pieces and lay them in a shallow roasting pan. Lay the pancetta along the back of the rabbit and put one slice on each thigh. Secure the pancetta with several toothpicks or tie it down with cotton kitchen string spaced at 2-inch intervals.

Place the rabbit on the fennel and onion, add the stock with the cherries and their soaking liquid, and roast for 30 minutes. Reduce the heat to 350, baste the rabbit with the pan juices, and continue roasting, basting once or twice more, until the rabbit is tender and an instant-read thermometer inserted into the thigh meat reads 150 degrees, about 20 to 25 minutes. Place the rabbit on a cutting board, tent it with foil, and let it rest for 10 minutes.

Pour the pan juices into a small pot set over medium-high heat and boil until the juices are reduced by about half. Spoon the fennel and onions onto a serving platter, cut the rabbit into pieces and place it on top of the vegetables, spoon the cherries on top of the rabbit, and drizzle with the reduced pan juices.

quick roast herb chicken

This speedy roast cooks in less than half the usual time. This roasting technique requires an ovenproof skillet, another pan or skillet to set on top of the bird, and bricks or a heavy pot to weight it down. The weight helps to keep in moisture while the chicken cooks. Fresh herbs tucked under the skin provide extra flavor. Serve the roast chicken with No Fail Kale (page 33) and Real Cornbread (page 197) or crusty bread for a quick midweek meal. **SERVES 4 TO 6**

1 (3- to 4-pound) chicken, trimmed of excess fat	2 cloves garlic, chopped
1 tablespoon fresh thyme or 1 teaspoon dried	2 tablespoons unsalted butter
2 tablespoons fresh parsley	2 tablespoons olive oil
Salt and freshly ground black pepper	1 teaspoon coarse black pepper

Split the chicken in half and remove the backbone. Put the chicken skin-side down on a cutting board and press the chicken down to flatten it. In a small bowl, mash together the thyme, parsley, salt and pepper, garlic, and butter with the back of a fork. Carefully lifting the skin away from the breast, tuck as much of this mixture as you can under the skin of the chicken, and work it over the flesh. Rub the rest all over the bird.

Preheat the oven to 500 degrees. Set an ovenproof skillet over medium-high heat, add the oil to the pan, and heat it for about 3 minutes (it should sizzle). Put the chicken in the skillet skin-side down. Put the other skillet or pan on top of the chicken and weight it with a couple of bricks or another pot (anything that is heavy and fits will do).

Cook the chicken over medium-high for about 5 to 8 minutes (the skin should be browning). Put the weighted chicken in the oven (be careful, it is heavy) and roast for about 15 minutes. Remove the chicken from the oven and remove the weights. Turn the chicken skin-side up and roast until the skin is crisp and the juices run clear, about 10 more minutes. Remove the chicken from the oven, tent it with foil, and allow it to rest about 5 minutes before serving.

thanksgiving bird—fast!

The popular technique of high-heat roasting has become standard in home and restaurant kitchens. It yields a tender, juicy bird with crisp skin and fabulous gravy. But the high heat can create a mess as the fat from the bird sizzles and pops, setting off the smoke alarm. Here, the turkey starts off in a very hot oven and, after a short time, the heat is turned down so the meat cooks evenly and the oven stays clean. If you're feeding a crowd, you're better off cooking two small turkeys than one great big bird, as the smaller size allows the cook more control.

There are no better partners for turkey than Turkey Gravy (recipe follows), Thanksgiving Mashed Potatoes (page 37), Basic Sage Stuffing (page 40), and Savory Cranberry Compote (page 41). **SERVES 10 OR SO**

1 (10- to 14-pound) turkey, neck and giblets removed and reserved for another use

Salt and freshly ground black pepper
2 cups water

Preheat the oven to 450 degrees and put the rack at the lowest position. Rinse the turkey inside and out, and pat it dry. Season the turkey inside and out with salt and freshly ground pepper. Fold the neck skin under the body and tuck the wings under the body.

Put the turkey breast-side down on a roasting rack in a roasting pan. Add 1 cup of water to the pan. Roast without basting for about 20 minutes, adding water to the pan as necessary to maintain 1 cup. Reduce the heat to 350, carefully flip the bird over (using two wooden spoons or pot holders) so the breast is up, and roast until a meat thermometer inserted into the thigh (without touching the bone) registers about 165 degrees, about 2 to 3 hours depending on the turkey's size. When the turkey is cooked, carefully tilt the turkey so the juices from the cavity run into the roasting pan; then remove the turkey to a platter to rest (the temperature will continue to rise to 180 degrees) while you make the gravy.

Turkey Gravy

Deglaze a metal roasting pan on the stovetop to capture every bit of flavor for your gravy. If you used a glass baking dish for roasting, however, simply transfer the pan juices and drippings to a saucepan.

2 to 3 cups turkey or chicken stock (page 10)
½ cup butter

¾ cup unbleached all-purpose flour
2 teaspoons cider vinegar

Pour the pan juices through a strainer into a measuring cup and skim off and discard the fat. Place the roasting pan across two burners and add 1 cup of the stock. Deglaze the pan by boiling the stock over high heat and scraping up the browned bits. Pour the turkey juices and more stock (you should have 3 to 4 cups of liquid altogether) into the pan, stir, and continue boiling for at least 2 minutes to reduce the liquid.

Melt the butter in a heavy 4-quart pot over moderate heat. Whisk in the flour and cook for about 5 minutes to make a thick roux. Add the stock and juices in a slow, steady stream, whisking constantly to prevent lumps. Bring the gravy to a boil, whisking until it is smooth. Simmer until the gravy is the thickness you desire, between 3 to 5 minutes. Season the gravy with salt, pepper, and vinegar to taste.

TURKEY TALK

Hands down, the flavor of an organic free-range turkey from a local grower is superior to that of a conventionally raised bird treated with growth hormones and antibiotics to prevent diseases spread in tight confinement. Free-range birds have larger thighs from all that exercise, a bonus for dark meat lovers, and their flavor is described as being richer and deeper than that of their conventional counterparts. They tend to cook more quickly too.

Free-range, organic local turkeys are not all that easy to find, even in turkey country. Our grocery stores are flooded with the cheaper, conventionally raised turkeys, making it difficult for small growers to compete. You can find free-range turkeys at farmers' markets, co-ops, and independent meat markets.

In Cannon Falls, Minnesota, John Peterson and his wife, Erica, opened Ferndale Market on his family's turkey farm to bring local turkeys back to turkey country. "We've raised turkeys for seventy years, and yet, until we opened, the turkey in our local grocery store would have been shipped in from the East Coast. It doesn't make sense. Now folks can find local turkeys here."

Several regional farms are also raising heritage turkeys. Brandon Severns, age 15, of Mankato, Minnesota, is a three-time Minnesota State Fair turkey champion who sells his heritage birds to the Wedge Co-op in Minneapolis. "These are closer to wild turkeys," he says. "They are very lean and need a little extra fat to keep them moist while roasting. But they're very flavorful."

Most co-ops, grocery stores, and farmers' markets take orders in advance for organic, free-range, and heritage turkeys (see Sources).

turkey or chicken pot pie
with cheddar chive cobbler crust

This makes quick use of leftover Thanksgiving turkey. It's great with a green salad tossed in Honey Mustard Vinaigrette (page 210). **SERVES 4 TO 6**

Filling

3 tablespoons unsalted butter

1 small onion, chopped

2 cups sliced mushrooms

Salt and freshly ground black pepper

1 ½ cups chicken stock (page 10)

1 tablespoon fresh thyme or 1 teaspoon dried

2 carrots, sliced

1 large potato, peeled and cut into chunks

1 celery rib, sliced

2 boneless chicken thighs, diced, or leftover
     cooked chicken, turkey, or ham

Cobbler Crust

1 recipe Cheddar Chive Scone dough (page 196)

Preheat the oven to 400 degrees. In a Dutch oven or a flame-proof casserole set over medium-high heat, melt the butter and sauté the onion and mushrooms until they release their juices and are soft, about 8 to 10 minutes; then season them with salt and pepper to taste. Add the stock and thyme, and boil until the liquid is reduced by about a third. Add the carrots, potato, celery, and chicken, and reduce to a simmer. Cook until the vegetables are tender and the chicken is cooked through. If you are using leftover cooked chicken, turkey, or ham, add it after the vegetables are cooked.

Drop the dough by spoonfuls on top of the vegetables and chicken in the Dutch oven or casserole, covering most of the surface area as you would a cobbler. Bake for about 35 to 45 minutes or until the crust is golden and the filling is bubbly.

harvest stuffed squash

Use those darling little Cinderella pumpkins, so mild and sweet, for this meatless alternative to Thanksgiving's turkey. The recipe is from Atina Diffley, cofounder of Gardens of Eagan in Farmington, Minnesota. It is a favorite at her table that often doubles as a side dish and as the meatless entrée for vegetarians. Pair this with Fresh Chestnut Soup (page 6) for a hearty vegetarian meal. **SERVES 8**

4 small Cinderella pumpkins or acorn squash,
    halved and seeded

2 tablespoons hazelnut oil or olive oil

1 large onion, chopped

4 cloves garlic, minced

1 fennel bulb, diced

1 red bell pepper, seeded, deveined,
    and chopped

1 large carrot, finely diced

¼ cup chopped hazelnuts

2 cups cooked wild rice (page 39)

½ cup chopped parsley

2 tablespoons rubbed sage

Salt and freshly ground black pepper

Preheat the oven to 375 degrees. Place the squash cut-side down on a baking sheet and bake until it is tender, about 40 minutes.

Meanwhile, heat the oil in a large skillet and sauté the onion, garlic, fennel, red pepper, carrot, and hazelnuts until the onions are translucent, about 5 minutes. Add the wild rice and herbs, and season with salt and pepper to taste. Remove the squash from the oven, turn it over, and place it cut-side up on the baking sheet. Fill the squash with the stuffing. Return the squash to the oven and bake it an additional 30 minutes.

PICKING PUMPKINS

Marvelous looking and easy to carve, field pumpkins make poor eating; they are tough, stringy, and watery. For pies and cakes, look for sugar pumpkins with fine-grained flesh and delicate flavor. These Cinderella pumpkins, bright orange with a lovely, fat, squat shape, make beautiful decorations, containers for soups and stews, and fabulous eating too.

A note about yields:

- A 4-pound pumpkin yields 2 pounds of raw flesh and 6 ounces of seeds.
- To toast pumpkin seeds, rinse them, dry them, toss them with melted butter or oil, and spread them out on a baking sheet. Roast the seeds in a 350-degree oven until they are golden and toasty, about 10 to 12 minutes, shaking the pan occasionally.
- A pumpkin "trims" down to half its original weight when the skin and seeds are removed, though smaller pumpkins tend to be denser and fleshier.
- One pound of cooked pumpkin equals 1 cup of cooked puree.

heartland polenta with mushroom ragout

Polenta is easy to make, and the leftovers are terrific griddled or broiled. Wild, dried, reconstituted mushrooms enhance the flavor of the cultivated button mushrooms in the ragout for a rich-tasting, relatively low-fat dish. Or, you can skip the mushroom ragout and simply finish the polenta with butter and shredded cheese. This makes a marvelous vegetarian meal paired with Caramelized Brussels Sprouts (page 35) or Roast Broccoli or Cauliflower with Garlic and Hot Pepper (page 36). **SERVES 4**

Mushroom Ragout
2 tablespoons butter or vegetable oil
1 pound assorted fresh mushrooms (shiitake,
    button, cremini), trimmed and sliced
Salt and freshly ground black pepper
¼ cup dried wild mushrooms, reconstituted in
    ½ cup boiling water
¼ cup dry white wine, beer, chicken stock
    (page 10), or vegetable stock (page 110)

1 clove garlic, minced
Chopped fresh parsley
2 tablespoons grated Parmesan or Asiago cheese
Polenta
2½ cups water
Salt
1 cup polenta or coarse cornmeal

Heat the butter or oil in a large skillet over medium-high heat. Add the fresh mushrooms, sprinkle them with salt and pepper, and cook, stirring occasionally, until all the juices have been released and the mushrooms are tender, about 10 to 15 minutes. The pan should be relatively dry and the mushrooms beginning to stick.

Add the reconstituted mushrooms with their soaking liquid, the wine, and the garlic. Simmer until the liquid is reduced by half, about 10 to 15 minutes. Stir in the chopped parsley.

Prepare the polenta while the ragout simmers. Put the water and a big pinch of salt into a medium saucepan over medium heat and bring it to a simmer. Add the polenta in a slow, steady stream, whisking all the while to prevent lumps from forming. Reduce the heat to low and simmer, whisking frequently, until thick, about 10 to 15 minutes. The polenta should be the consistency of sour cream. Turn into a warmed serving bowl or individual bowls and top with the mushroom ragout and cheese.

HEARTLAND POLENTA

Mandan Bride is the princess of "flour" corn. With its beautiful, multicolored red, gold, and brown kernels, this heirloom variety, when ground, makes a mean polenta. It's not the golden yellow of southern cornmeal; in fact, it's a pale gray and black-flecked meal, but looks aren't everything.

Freshly ground cornmeal tastes richly of corn, but with a nutty finish. Most commercial cornmeal is made from yellow corn, which has much tougher outer hulls on the kernels. These hulls are removed before grinding, and that robs the cornmeal of nutrients and flavor. Mandan Bride corn ears contain a combination of the flint, or hard, kernels and the softer flour kernels that give the flour substance and flavor.

Mandan Bride was first bred for flavor and nutrients by the Mandan Indian tribes of North Dakota. It is an open-pollinated cultivar, uniquely suited to this area. It is, however, difficult to grow and harvest with big machinery, limiting its commercial appeal. Try getting it through your CSA or at specialty local food stores and co-ops.

barley pilaf with chickpeas and autumn vegetables

Look for hulled barley; loaded with vitamin B, it's the most nutritious form of the grain. Though the cooking time is longer than that for pearl barley that's been polished, it's worth the additional 15- to 30-minute wait. Plus, barley holds nicely in the refrigerator, so don't hesitate to double the amount called for here to save and enjoy through the week.

Pair this with a salad of simple greens tossed in Cider Vinaigrette (page 5) and crusty multi-grain bread. **SERVES 4 TO 6**

1 cup hulled barley, rinsed

3 cups water

2 tablespoons olive oil

1 large onion, diced

4 cloves garlic, smashed

1 stalk celery, leaves included, chopped

1 carrot, chopped

1 (3-inch) sprig fresh rosemary

½ cup dry white wine

½ cup chicken stock (page 10) or vegetable stock (page 110)

1 cup broccoli florets

1 cup diced parsnips

½ cup chopped fresh parsley

2 teaspoons grated orange zest, or to taste

Juice of 1 orange, or to taste

2 cups cooked (or canned and drained) chickpeas

Salt and pepper

¼ cup grated Parmesan cheese

Put the barley and water in a large pot set over high heat, cover, and bring the water to a boil. Reduce the heat and simmer, stirring occasionally and adding a little more water if necessary, until nearly half the grains have split open, about 75 minutes.

While the barley is cooking, heat the oil in a large skillet and cook the onion, garlic, celery, and carrot until the onion is translucent, about 5 minutes. Add the rosemary, wine, stock, broccoli, and parsnips and cook just until the parsnips and broccoli are barely tender. Remove the rosemary sprig.

When the barley is cooked, drain it and return it to the pot, add the broccoli mixture, and toss in the parsley, orange rind, orange juice, and chickpeas. Season the pilaf with salt and pepper to taste. Heat just to warm through and serve sprinkled with the cheese.

Note You can shorten the cooking time for hulled barley by soaking it in enough water to cover for at least 4 hours, or overnight, before cooking. Presoaked barley will cook in about 45 to 50 minutes. If you use pearl barley that has been processed to remove the nutritious hull, reduce the cooking time to 50 minutes.

NEW GRAIN EXCHANGE

No, spelt and farro are not the same. Spelt and farro are ancient strains of modern wheat; both are delicious but quite different. Spelt, a blond grain, can be tough and is best presoaked for a good hour or more before being cooked. It's delicious in soups and casseroles, or ground for flour. Farro, beloved in Tuscany, Italy, resembles light brown barley and cooks in 15 to 20 minutes. It's often used in soups and salads or cooked risotto style and is prized for its delicate wheaten flavor.

According to Abdullah Jaradat, a soil scientist at the University of Minnesota, Morris, planting spelt and farro (sometimes called emmer) in crop rotation may help solve erosion issues as well as provide delicious alternative foods.

Dating to 5000 BC, these ancient grains should have tremendous appeal today. They're loaded with protein and complex carbohydrates and are high in B-complex vitamins as well as mucopolysaccharides, which support the immune system and facilitate blood clotting. Spelt is also slightly lower in gluten than wheat, making its flour accessible to some people suffering from wheat allergies. Because of its tough hull, it is naturally pest resistant.

A few small farms are growing farro and spelt in our region (spelt is easier to come by). Look for it in bulk bins in natural food co-ops.

spicy savoy coleslaw

Savoy cabbage, with its loose, full head of crinkled leaves and mellow flavor, is lighter and crisper than our more familiar tightly wrapped red or green cabbages, though those will work nicely too. Enjoy this with Sure Fire Roast Duck (page 17) or Quick Roast Herb Chicken (page 22). **SERVES 4 TO 6**

2 small or 1 large head savoy cabbage
1 small red onion, thinly sliced
1 jalapeño, seeded, deveined, and thinly sliced
¼ cup chopped fresh cilantro

Juice of 1 lime
⅓ cup extra-virgin olive oil
Pinch of sugar
Salt and freshly ground black pepper

Remove and discard the cabbages' outer leaves. Quarter, core, and then slice the cabbages into thin, ⅛-inch strips. Put the sliced cabbage in a bowl along with the onion, jalapeño, and cilantro. Whisk together the lime juice, oil, and sugar to taste. Toss the cabbage with the dressing. Season the salad with salt and pepper to taste.

silky chard

Chard becomes silky and rich when braised with lots of garlic. This makes a terrific side dish. Toss it with pasta or barley and top it with feta cheese for a light meal. It's a lovely side to Beer-Braised Pork Chops with Pears (page 14); Pheasant with Hard Cider, Apples, and Chestnuts (page 20); or, for a vegetarian meal, Harvest Stuffed Squash (page 26). **SERVES 4**

2 tablespoons olive oil

1 sprig rosemary

3 cloves garlic, minced

1 big bunch Swiss chard leaves, ribs removed

Coarse salt and freshly ground black pepper

¼ cup crumbled feta cheese

Lemon wedges

In a large, heavy, deep pot, heat the oil and rosemary sprig over low. Add the garlic and sauté for about 30 seconds to release its fragrance. Add the chard and sprinkle in some salt and pepper. Toss the chard to coat it in oil and wilt it slightly. Cover and cook, stirring occasionally, until the chard is very tender, about 5 to 10 minutes. Toss in the feta and serve with lemon wedges alongside.

no fail kale

"The cold weather makes kale really sweet. It loses some color from repeated freezing, is no longer crisp, no longer marketable, but it is at its absolute peak for sweetness and tenderness. We can go out and pick it frozen, thaw it out, and cook it. As one of our main cash crops, eating it reminds us to be thankful for another successful farming season," says Atina Diffley of Gardens of Eagan in Farmington, Minnesota. Kale is an excellent source of iron, calcium, vitamin C, folic acid, vitamin K, and carotenoids, providing vitamin A. It's a tasty complement to Hanger Steak with Fresh Horseradish Sauce (page 16). **SERVES 4 TO 6**

1 big bunch organic kale
2 to 6 cloves garlic, minced, to taste
2 tablespoons sesame oil
¼ cup water

Dark sesame oil
Umeboshi (plum) vinegar or rice wine vinegar
Soy sauce

Remove the stems and tough ribs from the kale and coarsely chop the leaves. Heat the sesame oil in a large, deep-sided skillet or saucepan over medium-low heat. Sauté the garlic for about 20 seconds, stirring; then add the kale and toss to coat. Stir in the water and cover the pan. Steam until the kale reaches the desired state of tenderness, about 5 to 10 minutes. Spread the kale on a platter and sprinkle it with dark sesame oil, vinegar, and a little soy sauce to taste.

Crispy Kale

When the CSA box overflows with kale, crisp it. Simply remove the tough stems and ribs from the kale leaves, toss the leaves with a little olive or vegetable oil to coat, and lay them out on a baking sheet, making sure they don't touch each other. Sprinkle with salt. Bake at 250 degrees until the kale is very crisp, about 20 to 25 minutes. Eat crispy kale as you do chips.

horseradish and honey-glazed root vegetables

Sweet, hot, and earthy, these root vegetables are great with the Beer-Braised Pork Chops with Pears (page 14) or Venison Medallions with Juniper and Gin (page 15). **SERVES 6**

1 tablespoon unsalted butter

1 large shallot, sliced

Salt and freshly ground black pepper

2 pounds mixed root vegetables of your choice
(sweet potatoes, parsnips, turnips, carrots,
rutabagas, beets), scrubbed and cut
into ½-inch pieces

¼ cup cider

¼ cup chicken stock (page 10)

2 to 3 tablespoons honey

2 to 3 tablespoons prepared horseradish

Freshly grated nutmeg

Heat the butter in a heavy skillet over moderate heat. Add the shallot and cook, stirring occasionally, until softened, about 2 to 4 minutes. Sprinkle with salt and pepper and then toss in the vegetables, cider, stock, and honey. Cover, bring to boil, then reduce the heat and simmer, stirring occasionally, until the vegetables are tender, about 10 minutes. Remove the cover and continue cooking until the liquid is reduced to a glaze. Stir in the horseradish, fresh nutmeg, and additional salt and pepper to taste.

caramelized brussels sprouts

Sliced thin and then sautéed, Brussels sprouts turn sweet and slightly nutty. Top them with fresh hickory nuts to add crunch. Serve these with Hanger Steak with Fresh Horseradish Sauce (page 16) or Sure Fire Roast Duck (page 17) or Thanksgiving Bird—Fast! (page 23). **SERVES 4**

1 pound Brussels sprouts
2 tablespoons hazelnut oil
4 whole cloves garlic
Water
1 tablespoon fresh lemon juice

¼ cup chopped toasted hickory nuts (see note)
   or pecans
Salt and freshly ground black pepper
Lemon wedges

Prepare the Brussels sprouts by trimming off the dry ends and peeling away any damaged outer leaves. With the stems down, slice them thinly and set aside.

In a large skillet over medium heat, heat the oil and then add the garlic and cook until it is just soft, about 3 minutes. Add the Brussels sprouts, cover, and cook until they are very soft, about 5 minutes. Don't skimp on the time, as extended cooking helps the Brussels sprouts caramelize and take on incredible flavor. If they start to burn or stick to the bottom of the skillet, add a little water, 1 to 2 tablespoons at a time, to deglaze the pan. Continue sautéing until the sprouts start to brown. Toss in the lemon juice along with the hickory nuts. Season to taste with salt and pepper. Serve with lemon wedges passed alongside.

Note Hickory nuts are available in some co-ops and through growers online (see Sources). To toast the hickory nuts, spread them on a baking sheet and bake in a 350-degree oven until they begin to smell nutty and begin to brown. Remove from the oven and proceed with the recipe.

roast broccoli or cauliflower
with garlic and hot pepper

Who knew that roasting broccoli or cauliflower would turn it mellow and nutty? It's a terrific side dish served with a squeeze of lemon or tossed with pasta and cheese for a light meal. Pair it with the Prosciutto-Wrapped Tilapia with Sage (page 13). **SERVES 4 TO 6**

1¼ pounds broccoli or cauliflower florets

3 tablespoons plus ½ tablespoon olive oil

2 garlic cloves, minced

Large pinch of dried crushed red pepper

Lemon juice or cider vinegar

Salt and freshly ground black pepper

Preheat the oven to 450 degrees. Put the broccoli or cauliflower and 3 tablespoons of the oil in a large bowl and toss to coat.

Spread out the vegetables on a rimmed baking sheet, making sure they don't touch. Roast for 15 minutes.

Meanwhile, stir together the remaining ½ tablespoon of oil, garlic, and red pepper in a small bowl. Drizzle the garlic mixture over the vegetables, tossing to coat. Return the vegetables to the oven and roast until the vegetables begin to brown and crisp, about 8 minutes longer. Season to taste with salt and pepper and a sprinkle of lemon juice.

thanksgiving mashed potatoes

You'll want high-starch russet potatoes (aka bakers) for this fluffy mash. Go on and add roasted garlic, mashed root vegetables, chilies, or whatever you please. Still, there is nothing more comforting or delicious than the humble potato elevated to elegance by mashing it with cream.

Always use a potato masher to smash the spuds. Do not whip them or use a food processor; this makes them gluey. Don't make them too smooth—a few lumps are nice. These potatoes are too good to eat only on Thanksgiving. Enjoy them with the Rabbit with Pancetta and Fennel (page 21) or the Venison Medallions with Juniper and Gin (page 15). **SERVES 4 (BUT IS EASILY DOUBLED OR TRIPLED)**

2 pounds russet potatoes, peeled and cut
    into 2-inch pieces
Salt
½ cup whole milk

¼ cup to ½ cup cream, as needed
3 to 4 tablespoons unsalted butter
Salt and freshly ground black pepper

Put the potatoes in a deep pot, cover them with cold water, and add a little salt. Set the pot over high heat, bring the water to a boil, and then reduce the heat and simmer until the potatoes are very tender, about 20 minutes. Drain out all but about an inch of water. Use a potato masher and smash the potatoes, adding in the milk, cream, butter, and salt and pepper to taste. Serve with Turkey Gravy (page 23) or lots of butter.

wild rice cranberry pilaf

Use real wild rice, usually labeled "hand harvested, wood parched." It's available in most grocery stores, natural food co-ops, and farmers' markets. So tasty, it's most delicious cooked simply with a sprig or two of thyme and parsley, a little garlic, and butter. Rinse it well in a colander under cold running water before you begin. Wild rice is the natural partner to game. Serve this with Sure Fire Roast Duck (page 17) or Pheasant with Hard Cider, Apples, and Chestnuts (page 20). **SERVES 4 TO 6**

½ cup wild rice, rinsed under cold water

1¼ cups chicken stock (page 10) or water

1 tablespoon unsalted butter

1 shallot, finely chopped

1 small onion, finely chopped

2 tablespoons chopped fresh parsley

1 (2-inch) sprig fresh rosemary

¼ cup dried cranberries

1 teaspoon grated orange zest

⅓ cup fresh orange juice, or to taste

Salt and freshly ground black pepper

¼ cup chopped toasted walnuts (see note)

In a large saucepan, combine the rice with the chicken stock. Bring the stock to a boil; then reduce the heat and simmer, uncovered, for 20 to 30 minutes. The rice should be tender but not mushy.

While the rice is cooking, melt the butter in a medium skillet over medium heat and sauté the shallot and onion with the parsley and rosemary until the onion is translucent, about 2 to 4 minutes. Stir in the cranberries, orange zest, and orange juice and cook about 2 minutes. Remove the rosemary sprig. Toss the onion mixture into the rice and season with salt and pepper to taste. Fold in the walnuts. Serve hot or at room temperature.

Note To toast walnuts, spread the nuts on a baking sheet and toast them in a preheated 350-degree oven until they begin to smell nutty, about 3 to 5 minutes. Remove and chop.

WILD RICE

Chippewa is a pristine, ancient ricing lake, a pure, spring-fed body of water surrounded entirely by the Chequamegon National Forest. It's the source of the Chippewa River, and the Native people have been ricing here for a long time. This is the domain of the swans, the ducks, the muskrats, the rice worms, the beetles and spiders, the diversity necessary for sustaining life. The productivity, size, and deliciousness of the manoomin (wild rice) from this water is legendary. Chippewa is a lake memories are made of.
—NICK VANDER PUY, WISCONSIN RADIO JOURNALIST AND WRITER WHO RICES ON CHIPPEWA EACH YEAR

True wild rice isn't rice at all but an annual aquatic cereal grass that produces an edible seed. Minnesota is the center of the biodiversity of all wild rice. There are over 60,000 acres of natural wild rice growing throughout the state's northern lakes and rivers in the heart of Ojibwe country. The Ojibwe harvest rice the traditional way. Using sleek canoes that glide through the dense thickets, Native American ricers knock the seeds from the grassy rice heads into the boats. Once on shore, the rice is laid out on tarps to dry and then roasted in galvanized tubs or cast-iron kettles over an open fire to seal the kernels and loosen the husk. Then the rice is thrashed, often by a young, athletic boy or girl who dances on it in the tub, and finally it's winnowed in a birch bark tray to separate the rice from the husks.

Sacred to the Ojibwe, wild rice continues to play a central role in contemporary Native American culture. Communities in Minnesota, Wisconsin, and Michigan honor its place in the region's ecosystem by using the ancient methods that help propagate this important staple.

Biologists are researching wild rice's ability to filter water and its potential for reclaiming endangered wetlands. It's believed that this grass can change nutrient levels in the water and compete with the blue-green algae polluting our lakes and rivers. The plants themselves serve as buffers to winds that stir up lake bottoms. The Great Lakes Indian Fish and Wildlife Commission has been reseeding dozens of ancient rice beds in northern Wisconsin since the early 1990s.

Cultivated paddy rice sold in stores and sometimes mislabeled "wild" is nothing like truly wild rice. This uniformly black, shiny grain is a domesticated hybrid variety cultivated in California, Minnesota, and Canada using fertilizers and herbicides. It is harvested with airboats and processed with metal grinding wheels. It cooks up tough, has little flavor, and sells for less than half the price of real wild rice.

Native Harvest's Wild Rice Campaign seeks to protect the integrity of genuine wild rice from genetic modification and from corporations seeking to patent their breeding methods. Native Harvest's labels and educational materials provide the full story.

Real, hand-harvested wild rice is a pale, variegated brown-black color and never glossy. Though genuine wild rice may seem pricy, it swells to four times its size as it cooks; it was nicknamed pocket money by the early voyageurs, as a little feeds many. Real wild rice cooks in less than 20 minutes, as opposed to the 45 to 50 minutes required for hard paddy rice. Hand-harvested wild rice is nicely chewy, slightly nutty, scented with wood smoke, and tastes of forest and lake.

basic sage stuffing

Many families have a favorite Thanksgiving stuffing recipe passed down through generations, cook to cook. But too often, the quantities aren't noted or something is left out. This recipe gives the amounts needed to build a basic stuffing. Start with it, and then add those important, iconic ingredients that spark memories and honor tradition. **MAKES 8 TO 10 CUPS**

1 pound white bread, cut into ½-inch cubes (about 9 to 10 cups)

¼ cup unsalted butter

1 large onion, peeled and chopped

1 stalk celery, chopped

½ cup minced parsley

1 tablespoon minced fresh sage or 1 teaspoon dried

1 tablespoon minced fresh thyme or 1 teaspoon dried

Pinch of ground cloves

Pinch of ground nutmeg

Salt and freshly ground black pepper

1 or more cups chicken stock (page 10), as needed

Optional ingredients (add any or all to the stuffing)

Handful of chestnuts, blanched or roasted, shelled, and chopped (page 7)

Chopped apple or pear

Cooked and crumbled bacon or sausage

Toasted hickory nuts (page 35) or hazelnuts (page 94)

Dried cranberries or cherries plumped in water, cider, or wine

Preheat the oven to 350 degrees. Spread the bread cubes out on several baking sheets and lightly toast them, about 5 to 7 minutes. Set them aside.

Use some of the butter to heavily grease a casserole or a baking dish. In a medium skillet set over medium heat, melt the remaining butter and sauté the onion and celery until the onion is translucent, about 4 to 5 minutes.

In a large bowl, toss the bread cubes with the parsley, sage, and thyme, and then toss in the sautéed onions and celery. Season with cloves, nutmeg, salt, and pepper to taste. Add enough stock to lightly moisten the bread. Add any or all of the optional ingredients.

Turn the stuffing into the buttered dish and bake until the top is crusty and the stuffing is heated through, about 30 to 40 minutes. If you're roasting a turkey, baste the stuffing with a little of the pan juices.

savory cranberry compote

This makes a wonderful side to Thanksgiving turkey as well as to roast chicken, duck, or pork. It's great on a cheese plate or spread on turkey sandwiches. Make it a day or two ahead and store it in the refrigerator. Serve it warm or at room temperature. It will add spark to a simple meatless dinner of Heartland Polenta with Mushroom Ragout (page 27) or Harvest Stuffed Squash (page 26). **SERVES 4 TO 6**

½ cup dried cranberries
1 cup apple cider
3 cups fresh cranberries, rinsed and sorted
½ cup sugar
3 tablespoons unsalted butter

2 large shallots, thinly sliced
1 large yellow onion, thinly sliced
2 sage leaves
Salt and freshly ground black pepper

In a small saucepan, soak the dried cranberries in ¼ cup of the cider for 30 minutes to plump them. Then add the fresh cranberries and the remaining cider and cook over medium heat until the cranberries pop, about 5 minutes. Add the sugar and stir to dissolve it.

In a large, deep skillet, melt the butter and cook the shallots, onions, and sage over low heat, stirring frequently, until the onions become very soft and begin to brown, about 25 minutes. Add the cranberries with their liquid and cook a few minutes longer, stirring occasionally. Remove the sage leaves, and season with salt and pepper to taste.

oven-dried pears

━━━━━━━━━

The tiny moonglow and honeysweet pears are among the cold-hardy Midwest varieties. Though they are not the prettiest, their flavors are mellow and sweet, and, because they don't ship well, they are often hard to find, except at farmers' markets.

This simple recipe yields a dense, sweet pear that tastes wonderful in a salad with blue cheese or as a delicious garnish for a cheese tray, roast chicken, or pork. They are lovely topped with a scoop of Cranberry Sorbet (page 44). **SERVES 4 TO 6**

4 to 8 pears, depending on size   1 cup sugar
1 tablespoon salt

Slice the pears in half lengthwise and rub each half with a pinch of salt. Line a baking sheet or dish with parchment paper and spread the sugar over the paper so it is about 1/8 inch deep. Set the pear halves cut-side down on the sugar and bake until they are soft and slightly brown, about 45 to 60 minutes. Core and stem the pears after they have cooled.

scandinavian brown beans with a kick

This is a classic Scandinavian dish from Greg Reynolds of Riverbend Farm (Delano, Minnesota). "It's easy," Reynolds notes, "but not very quick." The recipe comes from Greg's grandmother; the kick comes from the serrano chilies he adds. The longer they stew, the hotter the dish will taste. The beans partner nicely with Hanger Steak with Fresh Horseradish Sauce (page 16) or Quick Roast Herb Chicken (page 22). **SERVES 6 TO 8**

1 pound dried Swedish brown beans, cranberry
    beans, or navy beans
¼ pound bacon, chopped
1 onion, peeled and chopped
1 clove garlic, minced
½ cup brown sugar

⅓ cup molasses or sorghum (see page 97)
¼ cup ketchup
1 tablespoon dry mustard
1 teaspoon pepper
1 to 3 whole serrano peppers
Salt

Pick through the dried beans, put them in a pot with enough water to cover them, and soak overnight. Drain and rinse.

Fry the bacon until it is almost crisp; then drain it on a paper towel. Fry the onion in the bacon grease over medium heat until it is brown, about 5 minutes. Add the garlic and sauté another 2 minutes. Add the beans, brown sugar, molasses, ketchup, dry mustard, pepper, serrano peppers, and enough water to cover the beans completely. Bring the water to a boil. Reduce the heat and simmer until the beans are tender, about 15 to 30 minutes, adding water as needed. Taste the sauce as it cooks, and when it is "hot enough," remove the chilies. Season the cooked beans with salt to taste.

cranberry sorbet

Garnet colored and refreshing, this sorbet makes a light finish to an autumn meal. **SERVES 4 TO 6**

4 cups fresh cranberries, picked through
Juice and grated zest of 1 small orange

1 cup sugar

In a medium saucepan set over medium heat, cook the cranberries in just enough water to cover them (about 1 cup) until they pop. Stir in the orange juice, zest, and sugar and continue cooking until the liquid is reduced and the cranberries are quite soft. Turn the mixture into a food processor fitted with a steel blade and puree it. Transfer the puree into an ice-cream machine and freeze it according to the manufacturer's instructions.

Instead of using an ice-cream machine, you can spread the puree in a baking dish and set it in the freezer. After 20 minutes, remove the dish, stir, and return it to the freezer. Stir one more time until the sorbet is frozen. To serve, temper the sorbet at room temperature until it is soft enough to scoop.

RUBY FIELDS: THE CRANBERRY HARVEST

Tiny, bouncy, snapping with tart flavor, cranberries are the last fruit of the harvest, the earth's bonny farewell until spring. Surrounded by a forest of blazing fall leaves, the cranberry marshes are a playground for sandhill cranes, geese, blue herons, and ducks.

Native to North America, cranberries have long been prized for their nutritive value as well as their flavor. A good source of vitamin C and antioxidants, cranberries are considered "superfruit." Their tannins have anticlotting properties and also help fight urinary tract infections. Most of the fresh ruby fruit is harvested in Wisconsin, about two hours southeast of the Twin Cities. You can say that Tomah, Wisconsin, is the fresh cranberry capital of the world. Massachusetts and New Jersey bring in a good haul, but those berries are processed into juice, canned as jellies and relishes, and dried. Wisconsin's fresh berries, plump with holiday promise, are the fairest of them all. Habelman Brothers, a fourth-generation family company headquartered in Tomah, is the largest producer of fresh cranberries in the world.

Harvesting fresh cranberries is tricky. Care is taken not to bruise the fruit or damage the vines. A lot of labor is involved, and the batches are relatively small. Cranberries, close cousins to wild blueberries, grow on low vines with slender wiry stems that sport small, evergreen leaves. At harvest, in late October, they are the color of heather. Pollinated by bees, the berries develop through the summer, turning from white to pale pink to red as they grow. The berries at the bottom of the bush, deprived of sunlight, will remain white, even though they are ripe. Cranberries float, so growers flood the fields and bring the fruit to the surface where a harvester with fork-like paddles tugs them off the vines. They are deposited into gorgeous mounds on flat-bottom boats and then trucked to the nearby plant for winnowing, cleaning, sorting, and bagging.

Besides the more familiar uses in sauce, chutney, and relish, cranberries are terrific added to the roasting pans of pork or chicken—just toss them in with the onions and herbs. Truly fresh cranberries, right off the vines, have a very mild flavor, tart but tasty. Cranberries will keep a good week in the fridge, and they freeze beautifully.

A note about cooking fresh cranberries: one 12-ounce bag yields about 3 generous cups. Do not rinse cranberries until you are ready to use them, but do sort out any that look damaged or soft. They may be stored in the plastic bags they are sold in, either in the refrigerator for about a week or frozen. Once thawed, use the cranberries right away.

honey pumpkin ginger pie

Sweetened with honey and given a kick of ginger, this is a fragrant, comforting pie. Winter squash or sweet potatoes can be used in place of the pumpkin. The pie is great topped with Spirited Whipped Cream (recipe follows). **SERVES 6 TO 8**

1 Flaky Butter Crust (page 206)

1 small (1-pound) pumpkin or 2 cups cooked pumpkin

1/3 cup honey

2 eggs

1/2 cup heavy cream, sour cream, or crème fraiche

1/4 teaspoon salt

1 tablespoon grated fresh ginger

1 teaspoon vanilla

Preheat the oven to 350 degrees. To cook the pumpkin, split it in half horizontally and remove the seeds. Lightly grease the cut sides and lay the pumpkin cut-side down on a baking sheet. Roast the pumpkin until it is very, very tender, about 1 hour. Scrape out the flesh once the pumpkin has cooled. Mash or puree the pumpkin until smooth.

On a lightly floured surface, roll out the dough to a 13-inch round. Transfer it to a 9-inch deep-dish glass pie plate. Trim the overhanging dough to 1/2 inch. Fold the overhang under and crimp the edges. Refrigerate the pie crust for 1 hour.

Preheat the oven to 375 degrees. Line the crust with foil and fill it with pie weights, dried beans, or rice. Bake the crust until the edges begin to brown, about 15 minutes. Remove the foil and beans.

In a medium bowl, whisk together the pumpkin and honey, and then whisk in the eggs one at a time. Whisk in the cream, salt, ginger, and vanilla. Pour the pumpkin mixture into the prebaked crust and bake until the pie is set, about 45 to 55 minutes. The cooking time will depend on how moist the cooked pumpkin is. Set the pie on a rack to cool.

Spirited Whipped Cream
MAKES 2 CUPS

1 cup heavy cream

2 tablespoons sugar, or to taste

1/4 cup whiskey or brandy, or to taste

Whip the cream until it holds soft peaks; then whip in the sugar and whiskey.

HONEY, OH HONEY

Basswood, sweet clover, goldenrod, Dutch clover, thistle, wildflower, buckwheat: the flavor of each single-source honey depends on which flowers the bees feast on. Single-source, raw honey is not exposed to heat or heavily processed or blended, and this raw honey retains vitamins and enzymes that are often removed through processing by large packagers. Raw honey tends to crystallize but never spoils. It will reliquefy when gently heated in a pan of water.

autumn squash or pumpkin bars
with cranberry glaze

These bars are a favorite afternoon treat and work beautifully on a Thanksgiving buffet or a harvest party table. **MAKES 16 BARS**

Bars

½ cup unsalted butter

1½ cups light brown sugar or maple sugar

1 cup squash or pumpkin puree, canned
    or fresh (see page 46)

2 eggs

⅓ cup buttermilk or plain whole-milk yogurt

1¾ cups unbleached all-purpose flour

1 teaspoon salt

1 teaspoon baking soda

1 teaspoon baking powder

1 tablespoon cinnamon

Grated nutmeg

Pinch of cloves

1 cup toasted hickory nuts (page 35) or walnuts
    (page 38), chopped

Glaze

1 cup powdered sugar

¼ cup cranberry juice or apple cider

Preheat the oven to 350 degrees. Lightly butter and flour a 9 × 13-inch baking dish. Tap out any excess flour.

In a large bowl, cream the butter with the sugar until it is fluffy. Beat in the pumpkin, eggs, and buttermilk. In a separate bowl, whisk together the flour, salt, baking soda, baking powder, cinnamon, nutmeg, and cloves. Add the dry ingredients to the pumpkin mixture, blending until the dry ingredients are just moistened. Stir in the nuts.

Spread the batter in the prepared baking dish. Bake until a toothpick inserted in the middle of the cake comes up clean, about 25 to 30 minutes.

To make the glaze, stir together the powdered sugar and the juice. Spread the glaze over the bars while they are still warm.

oatmeal chocolate chip and
dried cranberry cookies

A cookie classic, crisp and flavorful, packed with tart dried cranberries. The recipe is easily doubled for a crowd. **MAKES ABOUT 2 DOZEN COOKIES**

½ cup unsalted butter, softened
1 cup brown sugar
1 egg
2 teaspoons vanilla
1 cup unbleached all-purpose flour
2 teaspoons ground cinnamon

½ teaspoon ground nutmeg
½ teaspoon salt
½ teaspoon baking soda
1 ½ cups rolled oats (not instant)
½ cup dried cranberries or raisins
½ cup semisweet chocolate chips

Preheat the oven to 325 degrees. Lightly grease two baking sheets or line them with parchment paper.

In a large bowl, cream the butter with the sugar until it is light and fluffy, about 2 to 3 minutes; then beat in the egg and vanilla. In a separate bowl, stir together the flour, cinnamon, nutmeg, salt, and baking soda. Stir the dry ingredients into the butter mixture along with the oats, dried cranberries, and chocolate chips and mix well.

Drop the dough by tablespoons about 2 inches apart on the prepared baking sheets. Bake until the cookies are browned but still a little soft in the middle, 20 to 25 minutes. Allow the cookies to cool for a few minutes on the baking sheets before transferring them to a rack.

mom's fall fruit crisp

Pack this crisp with tart, snappy apples—Haralson, Northern Spy, and Greenings—sweet pears, and cranberries. Serve it topped with Spirited Whipped Cream (page 46) or slices of hard Wisconsin cheddar. This crisp is innocent enough to eat for breakfast. **SERVES 6 TO 8**

1 cup brown sugar
1 cup unbleached all-purpose flour
1 cup rolled oats (not instant)
2 teaspoons ground cinnamon
½ teaspoon grated nutmeg
1½ cups unsalted butter

1 pound apples, peeled, cored, and chopped
   (about 2½ cups)
1 pound pears, peeled, cored, and chopped
   (about 2 cups)
¼ pound cranberries (about 1 cup)

Preheat the oven to 350 degrees. In a medium bowl, toss together the brown sugar, flour, oatmeal, cinnamon, and nutmeg. Work in the butter with two knives or your fingertips to make a crumbly dough with pieces about the size of peas.

Turn the fruit into a 2-quart casserole or baking dish and cover it with the brown sugar crumble. Bake until the top is crisp and brown and the fruit is tender and bubbly, about 30 to 35 minutes.

applesauce and apple butter, savory and sweet

This straightforward applesauce is the essence of apples. It is delicious served warm with a splash of cream for dessert or, turned savory with the addition of sage or rosemary, as an accompaniment to roast pork, duck, turkey, or chicken. Savory apple butter also makes a nice garnish to the cheese board.

MAKES ABOUT 3 CUPS APPLESAUCE OR 1 CUP APPLE BUTTER

6 large apples (use a mix of tart, tangy Haralson, Honey Crisp, and Greening), cored, peeled, and cut into chunks (see note)

5 cups fresh apple cider

1 stick cinnamon

About 3 tablespoons sugar or 2 tablespoons chopped fresh sage, rosemary, or thyme

Put the apples, cider, and cinnamon stick into a large pot and bring it to a boil. Reduce the heat and simmer until the apples have begun to soften and break down, about 30 minutes. Continue cooking and stirring until the applesauce begins to thicken, about 15 minutes. Add the sugar for sweet applesauce or the herbs for savory applesauce, taste, and adjust the seasoning if needed. Cook until the applesauce has reached the desired consistency.

To make apple butter, continue cooking and stirring occasionally until the mixture becomes very thick and smooth and is a deep golden brown.

Note You can also cut whole apples into chunks, cook them according to the recipe, and then run them through a food mill to remove the seeds and skin.

UPSETTING THE APPLE CART

Hoch Orchard, an organic apple grower near LaCrescent, Minnesota, grows the newly released and wildly popular SweeTango, developed by the University of Minnesota. The farm is one of the very few to grow these apples organically. SweeTango is tart and sweet and crisp, even better tasting than its parents, Zestar and Honeycrisp.

The University of Minnesota is a pioneer in cultivating and licensing apple varieties. Harry Hoch says that his farm has planted one thousand SweeTango trees, the maximum he is allowed to plant under his license, which controls who grows the trees and how many. "Most of the SweeTango sold in Minnesota grocery stores will have been grown everywhere but in Minnesota," he says. "The local apple stands will be selling the Minnesota-grown SweeTango, but grocery stores will get SweeTango grown in other regions. Only three Minnesota orchards are allowed to grow SweeTango in wholesale volumes." Hoch will have the only certified organic SweeTango available in Minnesota; these will be distributed to local natural food co-ops.

Pepin Heights, the state's largest apple grower, holds a license granted by the University of Minnesota to manage all the wholesale SweeTango apples grown in North America. Many people believe that the marketing program, which requires growers to meet wholesale volume, is a barrier to growing the apple.

"I'm not against the university releasing SweeTango as a managed variety," Hoch says in an open letter on his Web site. "Controlling production and setting quality standards are a great idea and the royalties growers pay help fund the successful research and marketing program. But removing the volume restriction will allow Minnesota apple growers to compete on a level playing field," Hoch says.

For more information about Hoch Orchard apples, see Sources.

rich applesauce cake

This is an old-fashioned snack cake, made with buttermilk to lighten the texture and give it tang. It is great served warm or sliced and toasted for breakfast. **MAKES AN 8 × 4-INCH LOAF CAKE**

Cake

1 ¾ cups cake flour or unbleached all-purpose flour

2 teaspoons baking powder

2 teaspoons ground cinnamon

Pinch of freshly grated nutmeg

½ teaspoon salt

⅓ cup buttermilk

⅓ apple butter or ⅔ cup applesauce (see note)

2 tablespoons unsalted butter, melted

⅓ cup dark brown sugar

¼ cup honey

1 large egg

1 teaspoon vanilla

½ cup dried cranberries, plumped in boiling water and drained

1 small apple, peeled, cored, and finely chopped

½ cup toasted hickory nuts (page 35) or pecans

Glaze

1 cup cider

2 tablespoons brown sugar, or to taste

Preheat the oven to 350 degrees. Grease an 8 × 4-inch loaf pan with butter or vegetable oil. Dust the pan with a little flour and shake out the excess.

In a large bowl, stir together the flour, baking powder, cinnamon, nutmeg, and salt. In a separate bowl, beat together the buttermilk, apple butter, butter, brown sugar, honey, egg, and vanilla.

Gently fold the wet ingredients into the dry ingredients along with the dried cranberries, chopped apple, and nuts. Turn the batter into the prepared pan and bake until a toothpick inserted in the center comes up clean, about 30 to 40 minutes.

To make the glaze, pour the cider into a small saucepan set over high heat and boil until it is reduced by half. Sweeten to taste with the brown sugar.

Pour the hot glaze over the cake as soon as you take it out of the oven. Allow the cake to cool before removing it from the pan.

Note Apple butter will make this a richer-tasting cake. If you don't have apple butter on hand, simply cook ⅔ cup of applesauce in a small pot over medium heat until it is reduced to ⅓ cup.

cranberry cordial

MAKES 1 QUART

1 cup fresh cranberries

1 quart vodka

2 tablespoons sugar

Crush the cranberries and put them in a large jar with the vodka and sugar. Cover the jar and let the vodka infuse for 24 hours. Strain out the cranberries and transfer the cordial to bottles.

HARVEST MEALS

Autumn's colors and flavors are natural partners on these plates. Bright cranberries perk up wild rice; subtly sweet golden squash lightens the darker hues of roasted cauliflower and broccoli. Think of garnishing plates with the recipes' colorful ingredients. Snip a little from the fennel frond to brighten the game and poultry entrées. Add chopped rosy apples and ruby beets to platters of meat and game or roasted vegetables.

HARVEST GAME BUFFET

Salad of Duck Confit in Honey Mustard Vinaigrette
Pheasant with Hard Cider, Apples, and Chestnuts
Rabbit with Pancetta and Fennel
Wild Rice Cranberry Pilaf
Horseradish and Honey-Glazed Root Vegetables
Rich Applesauce Cake
Cranberry Cordial

SPEEDY WEEKNIGHT DINNER

Quick Roast Herb Chicken
No Fail Kale
Real Cornbread
Oatmeal Chocolate Chip
    and Dried Cranberry Cookies

VEGETARIAN COMBO

Ginger Squash and Apple Soup
Heartland Polenta with Mushroom Ragout
Roast Broccoli or Cauliflower with Garlic
    and Hot Pepper
Mom's Fall Fruit Crisp

SOUP FOR SUPPER

Roast Mushroom, Red Pepper, and Sage Pizza
Curried Vegetable Soup
Wild Rice and Wild Mushroom Soup
Spicy Savoy Coleslaw
Autumn Squash or Pumpkin Bars with Cranberry Glaze

THANKSGIVING!

Smoked Trout, Apple, and Fennel Salad
    in Cider Vinaigrette
Thanksgiving Bird—Fast!
Turkey Gravy
Basic Sage Stuffing
Harvest Stuffed Squash
Caramelized Brussels Sprouts
Thanksgiving Mashed Potatoes
Savory Cranberry Compote
Honey Pumpkin Ginger Pie
    with Spirited Whipped Cream
Cranberry Sorbet

roast root salad with honey mustard vinaigrette

potato, prosciutto, and rosemary pizza

carrot cashew bisque

squash soup with thai spices

caramelized onion soup

hungarian steak and mushroom soup

winter vegetable tagine

squash lasagna with walnuts and kale

spicy bean and hominy stew

cornmeal-dusted panfish

carnitas

sausage with apples and onions

chicken braised with mexican spices

bison steaks with blue cheese butter

oxtails with stout and onions

lamb shanks with garlic and rosemary

porketta with oregano and fennel

marinated beef pot roast

carrot and parsley salad

parsnip and chestnut puree

sweet potato, radish, and walnut salad

braised red or green cabbage

oven-blasted brussels sprouts

roasted salsify

braised root vegetables in mustard sauce

sweet potatoes with a world of toppings

simple potato gratin

linzer cookies

hazelnut and dried cherry biscotti

cranberry tartlets in a sweet cornmeal crust

ginger stout cake

favorite carrot cupcakes

old-fashioned bread and butter pudding

spiked chocolate truffles

WINTER

There was so much snow. Would it never end? Snow down
the chimney, snow on the windowsills. Snow as high as the
fences the calves now walked over aimlessly. A little
mountain of snow inside the porch by the crack in the door.
Snow on the roofs. Dirty snow. Clean snow. Snow on top of
snow. Wet snow on the sunny south sides of buildings.
Drifting snow on the north slopes, ravines, plateaus of snow.

    Someone said it was pretty.

    Someone said it brought out the best in people.

    Someone said it would give people time to do what
        they should have done a long time ago.

    Someone said it was good for next year's tulips.

—JIM HEYNEN, *THE ONE-ROOM SCHOOLHOUSE*

winter

AS THE TEMPERATURES PLUNGE and hungers surge, our inspiration is not what's growing but all that we've stored, preserved, and frozen to make the hearty soups, stews, and roasts that will warm us up. Winter is the season for cooks. The choices are fewer but better defined in the soft, clear light: pure white goat cheeses, ruby cranberries, the shocking pink and pale green of the bleeding heart radish. Storage crops such as hard squashes, carrots, parsnips, beets, and potatoes abound.

Creativity and patience plus a few tricks can turn less into more. Roasting concentrates flavors; simmering helps tenderize tasty (but tough) cuts of meat. Hearty whole grains and dried beans become wholesome meals. Bake bread, make yogurt, create holiday treats, let the stew steam the windows and the scent of cinnamon and nutmeg float through the kitchen. It's a great time to eat.

FIVE WINTER DISHES IN FIVE MINUTES OR LESS

Toasted Chèvre Slice chèvre and brush it with hazelnut or walnut oil. Sprinkle it with salt and pepper and chopped parsley and thyme and then roll it in crushed breadcrumbs. Bake the chèvre at 350 degrees until it is soft, about 5 minutes. Serve it with bruschetta or crusty wheat bread.

Spiced Brussels Sprouts Shred 1 pound of Brussels sprouts and cook them in 3 to 4 tablespoons of melted butter with ½ teaspoon each of cumin and coriander, plus freshly ground black pepper, until they are just lightly crisped. Sprinkle on a little cider vinegar or lemon juice. Serve the sprouts as a side dish or on bruschetta.

Smoked Trout or Salmon Spread Remove the skin and flake the salmon or trout into a food processor along with a quarter of a small onion (chopped), several tablespoons of lemon juice, 1 to 2 teaspoons of prepared horseradish sauce, and ½ cup of cream cheese. Process until the spread is light and fluffy. Serve it with crackers or on toasted bread.

Maple Bacon Bites Generously coat strips of bacon with maple sugar, or brown sugar, and lay them on a baking sheet to roast at about 350 degrees until crisp. Cut the bacon into 2-inch pieces. Serve warm or at room temperature.

Speedy Deviled Eggs Split 4 hard-boiled eggs in half. Remove the yolks and mix them with 2 tablespoons of mayonnaise, 1 teaspoon of curry powder, a splash of lemon juice, and salt and pepper to taste. Spoon the yolks back into the egg whites and serve.

roast root salad with honey mustard vinaigrette

Sweet honey and rough mustard perk up sturdy roots in a warm, hearty salad. Serve this salad as an appetizer or pair it with the Potato, Prosciutto, and Rosemary Pizza (page 61) for a simple meal or as a starter to a casual dinner party featuring Oxtails with Stout and Onions (page 78). **SERVES 4 TO 6**

2 pounds mixed root vegetables, such as
    potatoes, golden beets, sweet potatoes,
    turnips, rutabaga, and carrots
3 to 4 tablespoons olive oil or walnut oil

3 tablespoons chopped parsley
1 teaspoon coarse salt
¼ cup Honey Mustard Vinaigrette (page 210)
2 bunches watercress or any dark green

Preheat the oven to 450 degrees.

Cut the vegetables into 1-inch pieces and toss them with enough oil to coat; then toss them with the parsley and salt. Spread the vegetables out on a roasting pan so they do not touch each other. Roast until they are tender and nicely browned, about 25 to 35 minutes, shaking the pan and turning the vegetables so they don't stick.

When the vegetables are cooked, put them into a bowl and toss in just enough dressing to coat the vegetables. Serve over watercress or other greens.

potato, prosciutto, and rosemary pizza

Use Yukon Gold or Yellow Finn potatoes for this pizza, and be generous with the garlic and good olive oil. It's so simple but so warming. The pizza makes a nice dinner served with the Spicy Bean and Hominy Stew (page 70). **SERVES 4**

1 batch Pizza Dough (page 203)
8 ounces fresh mozzarella, thinly sliced
2 pounds potatoes, scrubbed and thinly sliced
2 ounces prosciutto
3 cloves garlic, minced
1 red onion, thinly sliced

½ cup freshly grated Parmesan cheese
2 tablespoons minced rosemary
1 tablespoon minced parsley
Extra-virgin olive oil
Salt and freshly ground black pepper

Preheat the oven to 425 degrees. Line a pizza peel or a baking sheet with parchment paper.

On a lightly floured surface, roll out the dough into a 14-inch circle and let it rest for about 15 to 20 minutes.

Set the dough on the peel or baking sheet, and arrange the mozzarella slices, then the potatoes, and then the prosciutto, garlic, and onion in even layers over the dough. Sprinkle with the Parmesan and then the rosemary and parsley. Drizzle oil over all and bake until the edges of the pizza are golden and crispy, about 15 to 20 minutes. Just before serving, drizzle on a little more oil and season the pizza with salt and freshly ground pepper.

PROSCIUTTO AMERICANO

La Quercia, near Des Moines, Iowa, produces the first and perhaps best prosciutto this side of the Atlantic. Herb and Kathy Eckhouse began making the Italian-style delicacy several years back, using heritage pigs they salt cure and age the traditional Italian way. This silken-textured, nutty-sweet prosciutto is featured on menus in the finest restaurants coast to coast and sold in Whole Foods Markets across the country. La Quercia's product line has expanded to include organic and heirloom prosciutto, lardo, pancetta, speck, coppa, and guanciale. La Quercia has inspired like-minded processors, chefs, and even home cooks to try to create their own cured meats, though doing so requires space, time, money, and a whole lot of faith.

carrot cashew bisque

This rich, warming bisque relies on cashew butter, not cream, for its smooth, velvety texture and flavor. The recipe calls for almond milk, but soy or cow milk works nicely too. Serve this before a dinner of Simple Potato Gratin (page 91) for a lively vegetarian supper or with Bison Steaks with Blue Cheese Butter (page 76) for an elegant meal. **SERVES 4 TO 6**

1 tablespoon vegetable oil

2 medium onions, chopped

2 cloves garlic, smashed

4 large carrots, sliced (about 4 cups)

2 medium potatoes, peeled and cubed

2 cups vegetable stock (page 110) or water

4 cups almond or soy milk

⅓ cup unsalted cashew or almond butter

2 teaspoons freshly grated ginger, or to taste

1 teaspoon freshly grated orange zest, or to taste

Juice of 1 small orange

Salt, pepper, and ground nutmeg

2 tablespoons minced parsley

Toasted unsalted chopped cashews

In a large stockpot, heat the oil over medium heat and sauté the onion and garlic until the onion is translucent, about 3 to 5 minutes. Add the carrots, potatoes, and stock and simmer until the vegetables are very soft, about 5 minutes. Stir in the almond milk. Working in batches, puree the soup in a blender and return it to the pot. Whisk in the cashew butter, ginger, orange zest, and orange juice, plus more almond milk if the soup is too thick. Season with salt, pepper, and a little ground nutmeg to taste. Warm the soup through and serve it garnished with parsley and chopped cashews.

SWEETEST CARROTS

Some of the sweetest carrots don't come to market until February. Though they mature and are harvested in October, they're kept in storage at 33 degrees Fahrenheit with 80 percent humidity, then released three to four months later when their sugars have fully developed. "We plant several different varieties that are meant to be stored. This makes eating locally easy during the winter," says Jack Hedin of Featherstone Farm, located in Rushford, Minnesota.

squash soup with thai spices

The squash for this soup is cooked until just tender, and it isn't pureed. Thai and Vietnamese flavors permeate the Northern Heartland's farmers' markets, and such spices work beautifully with our earthy-sweet winter squash. This makes a lively partner to Cornmeal-Dusted Panfish (page 71). **SERVES 4 TO 6**

1 tablespoon vegetable oil

1 onion, finely chopped

1 celery stalk, finely chopped

2 to 3 tablespoons Thai red curry paste

3 cups chicken stock (page 10) or vegetable stock (page 110)

1 small acorn squash or butternut squash, peeled, seeded, and cut into 1-inch chunks

½ cup coconut milk or heavy cream

1 tablespoon fish sauce or soy sauce, or to taste

2 to 3 tablespoons lime juice

Salt and freshly ground black pepper

Chopped scallions

Chopped cilantro

In a deep, heavy soup pot, warm the oil and cook the onion and celery until they are very soft, about 3 to 4 minutes. Stir in the curry paste and cook for 30 seconds to 1 minute. Stir in the stock and bring it to a boil; then reduce the heat to a simmer and add the squash. Cook until the squash is tender, about 15 to 20 minutes. Whisk in the coconut milk, and season the soup with fish sauce, lime juice, salt, and pepper. Serve the soup garnished with chopped scallions and cilantro.

caramelized onion soup

This recipe is really two in one. The caramelized onions are wonderful on their own as a condiment for meats and poultry, served on bruschetta, or folded into an omelet. The basic recipe calls for cooking the onions a long, long time until they are golden and syrupy. Then the caramelized onions are stewed into a soup and finished with bubbling cheese. The soup is a meal in a bowl when paired with Carrot and Parsley Salad (page 83) and crusty bread. **SERVES 4 TO 6**

Caramelized Onions

4 tablespoons unsalted butter

4 large onions, thinly sliced

1 small sprig fresh rosemary or fresh thyme

Soup

1 cup light ale or beer

5 cups chicken stock (page 10), vegetable stock
  (page 110), or beef stock (page 66)

2 to 3 sprigs fresh parsley

Salt and freshly ground black pepper

4 to 6 slices crusty baguette, toasted

1 cup grated Gruyère cheese

1 cup grated Parmesan cheese

Melt the butter in a large, deep saucepan over medium heat. Add the onions and the rosemary or thyme, spreading the onions out as thinly as possible so they brown evenly and are less likely to steam. Cook the onions, stirring occasionally, until they are very soft and become golden, about 35 to 45 minutes. The darker the onions become, the richer they will taste.

(If you are stopping here, discard the herb sprig and toss the onions with 2 or 3 tablespoons of malt vinegar or balsamic vinegar, a pinch of sugar, and salt and pepper to taste.)

Preheat the oven to 400 degrees. Set the pot with the onions over medium heat and stir in the beer, scraping the bottom of the pan vigorously to release all the browned bits. Stir in the stock and the parsley, and season with salt and freshly ground black pepper to taste. Bring the stock to a boil; then lower the heat and simmer for about 10 minutes. Remove and discard the parsley. (You may prepare the soup up to two days ahead. Cool the soup; then cover and refrigerate it. Reheat before proceeding.)

Place a slice of toasted baguette in each individual ovenproof bowl (or place them all in one large casserole). Ladle the soup into the bowls, distribute the cheese evenly among them, place the bowls on a sturdy baking sheet, and bake until the cheese is melted and bubbly, about 10 minutes.

hungarian steak and mushroom soup

This soup, spiked with sweet paprika, is hearty but not as heavy as stroganoff. The recipe is from Lisa Lindberg, proprietor of the Amboy Cottage Café (Amboy, Minnesota), a place where patrons keep their coffee cups hung on pegs over the endless pot. This hearty dinner in a bowl is sure to have folks sopping up every last bit with a hunk of bread. Serve it with a salad tossed in The Real Buttermilk Ranch Dressing (page 211). **SERVES 4 TO 6**

2 to 3 pieces center-cut bacon, diced

1 pound sirloin steak, cut into small cubes

2 carrots, chopped

1 large onion, chopped

3 cloves garlic

1 teaspoon dried marjoram

2 tablespoons chopped fresh parsley

1 pound mushrooms, plus a few extra, sliced,
    for garnish

2 teaspoons paprika, or to taste

1 quart chicken stock (page 10) or beef stock
    (page 66)

¼ cup whiskey or red wine

Salt and freshly ground black pepper

8 ounces broad flat noodles

1 green bell pepper, cored, seeded, and cut
    into ¼-inch pieces

½ cup sour cream

In a soup pot, cook the bacon over medium heat until crisp, about 5 minutes, and transfer it with a slotted spoon to a paper towel to drain. Remove all but 1 tablespoon of the rendered bacon fat from the pot. Set the pot over medium heat and add the steak, browning the pieces well on all sides. Remove the steak and set it aside. Add one half of the carrots and all of the onion, garlic, marjoram, parsley, mushrooms, and paprika. Cook until the mushrooms release their juices and the onions begin to brown, about 5 minutes.

Return the steak and bacon to the pot along with the stock and whiskey. Season with salt and pepper to taste, bring the liquid to a boil, and then reduce the heat and simmer for about 30 to 45 minutes or until the meat is very tender and the soup is flavorful. Add the noodles, bell pepper, and remaining carrots; then increase the heat and boil until the noodles are tender, about 5 to 8 minutes.

Add a few more sliced fresh mushrooms right before serving. Serve with a dollop of sour cream and a sprinkle of paprika.

CLASSIC BEEF STOCK

Roasting the meat and vegetables first ensures rich, flavorful stock. This freezes nicely. **MAKES 3 QUARTS**

4 pounds beef bones (shank, shin, tail, or short ribs)
2 large onions, peeled and cut into chunks
1 large carrot, cut into chunks
2 sprigs fresh thyme or ½ teaspoon dried
1 bay leaf

1 large bunch fresh parsley
10 peppercorns
1 teaspoon salt
4 quarts water
Salt and freshly ground black pepper

Preheat the oven to 500 degrees. Place the bones, onions, and carrot in a large roasting pan and roast, shaking occasionally, until all are nicely browned, about 45 minutes to 1 hour. Put the roasted bones and vegetables, along with the thyme, bay leaf, parsley, peppercorns, and salt, into a large stockpot. Place the roasting pan across two burners set to medium-high heat, and pour in 1 to 2 cups of the water. Deglaze the pan by simmering and scraping up the browned bits for about 2 minutes. Pour this liquid into the stockpot and add the remaining water. Bring the stock to a boil; then reduce the heat so that the stock is at a very low simmer. Cook until the meat falls from the bones, about 3 hours. Remove the bones, and then strain off and discard the remaining ingredients, extracting as much juice from them as possible. Taste the stock and season it to taste with salt and pepper.

Refrigerate the stock, and then skim any hardened fat from the surface. The stock will keep for 4 days in the refrigerator, or you can freeze it.

Note In lieu of homemade stock, use a good-quality, low-sodium boxed stock.

winter vegetable tagine

This Morocco-inspired one-dish meal is fragrant with cumin, garlic, and chilies. Serve it over couscous drizzled with charmoula, a Moroccan green sauce made with plenty of fresh cilantro and parsley (recipe follows). This tagine is a hearty one-dish vegetarian dinner when paired with a salad tossed with Honey Mustard Vinaigrette (page 210) and also works beautifully in a holiday buffet. **SERVES 4 TO 6**

2 tablespoons olive oil or vegetable oil
1 sweet onion, peeled and chopped
2 shallots, chopped
2 cloves garlic, chopped
½ teaspoon ground cumin
1 teaspoon ground red chili or hot paprika
½ teaspoon ground coriander
1 tablespoon tomato paste

1 cup vegetable stock (page 10)
½ cup vodka or white wine
1 whole jalapeño
Salt and freshly ground black pepper
4 to 5 small new potatoes, scrubbed and cut
   into 2-inch pieces
2 cups cubed winter squash, sweet potatoes, or both
2 cups cooked chickpeas, rinsed

In a large, deep skillet or Dutch oven, heat the oil and sauté the onion, shallots, and garlic with the cumin, ground chili, and coriander until they are fragrant. Stir in the tomato paste and continue cooking until the mixture just begins to brown. Stir in the stock, vodka, and jalapeño and bring the mixture to a boil. Reduce the heat to a simmer, sprinkle with salt and pepper to taste, and then add the potatoes and squash. Cover and cook until the vegetables begin to soften, about 15 to 20 minutes. Toss in the chickpeas and cook until they are warmed through.

Serve on couscous and drizzle with Moroccan Green Sauce.

Moroccan Green Sauce (Charmoula)

Try this sauce on grilled chicken or steak. It's also great as a marinade for fish and terrific tossed with rice. **MAKES ABOUT ¾ CUP**

4 cloves garlic
1 teaspoon salt
¾ cup chopped cilantro
½ cup chopped parsley
2 teaspoons sweet paprika

½ teaspoon ground cumin
⅛ teaspoon cayenne
¼ cup extra-virgin olive oil
Juice of 2 large lemons, or to taste
Ground black pepper

Using a mortar and pestle, pound the garlic with the salt until you have a smooth paste. Add the cilantro and parsley, and pound just long enough to bruise the leaves and release their flavor and fragrance. Stir in the cumin, cayenne, oil, and lemon juice. Season the sauce with pepper to taste.

squash lasagna with walnuts and kale

This recipe may look long, but it comes together in a snap. It is a good way to enjoy leftover baked squash, sweet potatoes, or pumpkin. Use a mix of sharp cheese—Parmesan, aged Gouda, cheddar—to suit your taste. Serve this warming vegetarian dish on the holiday buffet or pair it with the Carrot and Parsley Salad (page 83) for a warming weeknight supper. **SERVES 6 TO 8**

1 large butternut squash (about 3 pounds or less), cut in half and seeded, or about 3 cups cooked

1 head garlic plus 2 cloves garlic, smashed

2 to 3 tablespoons unsalted butter, or more as needed

2 large onions, thinly sliced

Salt and freshly ground black pepper

2 cups milk

1 bay leaf

½ cup chopped parsley

¼ cup chopped fresh thyme or 1 tablespoon dried

2 tablespoons chopped fresh sage or 1 teaspoon dried

½ cup dry white wine

Sprinkling of nutmeg

1 cup lightly toasted walnuts (page 38), coarsely chopped

1 (8-ounce) package no-boil lasagna noodles

1½ cups grated Parmesan, aged Gouda, or cheddar cheese

1 tablespoon vegetable oil

2 bunches kale, rinsed, stems and ribs removed, and chopped

Pinch of crushed red pepper

If you are not using leftover cooked squash, start by roasting a squash. Preheat the oven to 350 degrees. Lightly grease a baking sheet. Place the squash cut-side down on the baking sheet. Cut the top off the head of garlic and roast the garlic alongside the squash until the squash is tender, about 40 to 50 minutes. Set aside to cool.

While the squash and garlic are roasting, melt the butter in a deep skillet set over low heat, add the onions, stir to coat, and season with salt and pepper to taste. Cover and cook the onions, stirring occasionally, until they become caramel colored, about 40 minutes. Set the onions aside.

In a small pot set over medium heat, scald the milk with the bay leaf. Remove the milk from the heat and set it aside.

Remove the squash from its skin, cut it in chunks, and put it in a large bowl. Squeeze the roast garlic cloves from the garlic head, add them to the squash, then toss in the parsley, thyme, sage, and wine, and season to taste with salt, pepper, and nutmeg. Toss in the walnuts.

Lightly grease a 9 × 13-inch baking dish. Lay a base of noodles in the baking dish. Top the noodles with a layer of squash, a layer of onions, and some of the cheese. Then add another layer of noodles. Drizzle some of the scalded milk over the noodles. Repeat the layers, drizzling with the milk as you go. Pour any remaining milk over the dish and top with the remaining cheese. Cover the pan loosely with aluminum foil and bake for about 30 minutes. Remove the foil and, if the dish looks dry, drizzle a little more milk or wine over the dish and continue baking, uncovered, until the lasagna is bubbly and golden, another 20 minutes or so.

To prepare the kale, heat the oil in a skillet; then add the smashed garlic cloves and the kale. Season with salt and pepper and toss to coat the leaves. Cover and cook until the leaves are tender, about 10 minutes. Season the kale with the crushed red pepper. Arrange the sautéed kale on top of the lasagna and serve.

spicy bean and hominy stew

This stew makes a filling vegetarian meal when served over creamy polenta (see page 27) or on cooked barley with a side of Real Cornbread (page 197). **SERVES 4 TO 6**

1 cup mixed dried beans, soaked overnight

1 cup hominy, soaked overnight

1 tablespoon vegetable oil

1 onion, peeled and chopped

2 cloves garlic, chopped

1 carrot, chopped

1 stalk celery, chopped

1 to 2 teaspoons chili powder

1 cup canned tomatoes with their juices

½ cup amber ale

1 to 2 tablespoons cider vinegar or lime juice

Salt and freshly ground black pepper

½ cup finely chopped fresh cilantro

½ cup sour cream

Drain the beans and the hominy, put each in its own pan, and add enough cold water to cover by 1 inch. Bring both pots to a boil; then reduce the heat, cover, and simmer until the beans and the hominy are tender. Depending on age and size of the beans and the hominy, they may require different cooking times, between 20 and 45 minutes. Drain each and set aside.

In a large soup pot, heat the oil and sauté the onion, garlic, carrot, and celery until the onion is wilted, about 5 minutes. Stir in the chili powder, tomatoes and their juices, and then the ale. Add the beans and hominy. Bring to a boil, reduce the heat, and simmer until the liquid is reduced and thickened. Season to taste with vinegar, salt, and pepper. Serve the stew topped with chopped cilantro and sour cream.

HEARTLAND DRIED BEANS AND NATIVE HARVEST HOMINY

If you think hominy and black-eyed peas are Southern fare, try Native Harvest's hominy from the White Earth Land Recovery Project (Callaway, Minnesota) and any of the many different dried beans sold in area farmers' markets and co-ops.

Hominy is dried corn kernels that have been treated to remove the germs and hulls. Cook it as you would dried beans. To speed the process, soak the hominy overnight in enough water to cover it. Drain the hominy and put it in a pot along with enough water to cover the kernels. Bring the water to a boil, cover the pot, reduce the heat, and simmer until the hominy is tender, about 40 minutes to an hour, adding more water to the pot if the hominy becomes dry. Once cooked, hominy will keep up to a week in the refrigerator or may be frozen. With its slightly sweet corn flavor, hominy is great is soups and stews.

Area farmers have been growing a range of beans to dry. The most interesting are scarlet runner beans, cowpeas, lima and fava beans, Swedish brown beans, and Jacob's cattle beans. All are delicious fresh or dried and provide more balanced protein when partnered with hominy. Recently, the University of Minnesota, Morris, introduced chickpeas (garbanzo beans) to farmers to plant as a third crop in rotation with soybeans and corn. They make good eating and are very nutritious. We will see them in local markets before long.

cornmeal-dusted panfish

Panfish is just about any freshwater fish of legal size that will fit in a frying pan. Hoping to catch perch, walleye, northern pike, crappies, and catfish, winter anglers auger holes in frozen Northern Heartland lakes on the darkest and coldest days of the year. The fish emerge especially firm and sweet.

Aquaculture is making sustainably raised panfish available to those less inclined to wait for dinner at the end of a line in subzero temperatures. Find farmed catfish, tilapia, and perch in co-ops and fish markets.

In this recipe, buttermilk adds a nice tang to the crunchy nut and cornmeal crust. Serve the fish topped with a heap of Sweet Potato, Radish, and Walnut Salad (page 85). **SERVES 4**

1½ pounds catfish, tilapia, crappie, or any white, light fish

1½ cups unbleached all-purpose flour

2 teaspoons salt

1 teaspoon freshly ground pepper

2 large eggs

1 cup buttermilk

1¾ cups fresh breadcrumbs (see note)

½ cup cornmeal

½ cup hickory nuts (page 35) or pecans, toasted and finely chopped

¼ cup chopped fresh parsley

¼ cup canola oil

Preheat the oven to 375 degrees. Rinse and pat the fillets dry and lay them out on a plate.

In a shallow bowl, combine the flour, salt, and pepper. In a second shallow bowl, whisk together the eggs and buttermilk.

In a third shallow bowl, toss together the bread crumbs, cornmeal, nuts, parsley, and some additional salt and pepper. Line up the three shallow bowls with the egg mixture in the middle.

Line a baking sheet or tray with parchment paper. Dredge each fillet in the seasoned flour, then the egg mixture, and then the breadcrumb mixture, pressing the crumbs and nuts into the fillets.

Heat the oil in a large skillet over medium-high heat. When the oil is rippling slightly and a light smoke appears over the surface of the pan, it's ready. Carefully set the breaded fillets into the pan, being careful not to crowd them, and brown them quickly on each side for 2 minutes, turning once.

Remove the fillets and place them on a baking sheet; put them in the oven and cook until the fish feels firm when pushed with a finger, about 5 minutes.

Note To make fresh breadcrumbs, whiz 2 slices of fresh bread in a food processor fitted with a steel blade or a blender until fine.

carnitas

Crispy cubes of roasted savory meat, carnitas is a staple of the Mexicans and Guatemalans who have settled in this region. It's terrific tossed with pasta or folded into a tortilla. Serve carnitas over creamy polenta (see page 27) or mashed sweet potatoes or with Real Cornbread (page 197) and a side of Braised Red or Green Cabbage (page 86). **SERVES 4 TO 6**

2 pounds pork, lamb, or goat,
    diced into ½-inch cubes
¼ cup vegetable oil
4 cloves garlic, minced

1 jalapeño, minced
1 onion, halved and thinly sliced
1 tablespoon ancho chili powder
Salt and freshly ground black pepper

Preheat the oven to 450 degrees. In a mixing bowl, toss the meat with the oil, garlic, jalapeño, onion, and ancho chili powder. Season the meat with salt and pepper. Spread the meat on a baking sheet and roast, stirring once or twice, until it is nicely browned and crisp, about 15 to 20 minutes.

HELLO, GOAT!

Goat meat (chevon), the most widely consumed meat in the world, is a staple in Mexican, Indian, Greek, Southern Italian, and North African cuisines. The meat is lower in fat than chicken but higher in protein than beef. Goat meat varies greatly depending on the breed.

As immigrants make the Northern Heartland their home, it's no wonder we are seeing more goat in our markets. The increased popularity of raising these animals may also have to do with the goat's easy nature, a plus for the new crop of farmers. "I find my does to be wise and tender mothers; my bucks stately and kind. Kids are indeed, of course, quite silly," Pamela Betts, a breeder in Lohman, Missouri, notes. "No creature expresses the pure joy of being young and alive quite so well as a young goat."

Note Because goat is so lean, it can dry out and toughen quickly if cooked at too high a heat for too long. The two basic rules are (1) cook goat slowly at a low temperature, and (2) cook goat with moisture. The most tender cuts of meat are the legs, shoulder, loin roast, and breast. Less tender cuts include shanks, riblets, and stew.

sausage with apples and onions

Make this dish with pork or turkey sausage (the turkey is a bit lighter). Be sure to serve it with plenty of crusty bread to sop up the juices. It's great with a side of baked sweet potatoes (page 90) or Simple Potato Gratin (page 91). **SERVES 6 TO 8**

1 pound sweet Italian sausage
3 tablespoons unsalted butter
Approximately ½ to 1 cup water
4 medium onions

4 tart apples (Haralson or Cortland), peeled, cored, and cut into 1-inch chunks
¼ to ½ cup apple cider

Cut the sausage into 3- to 4-inch lengths and place them in a large skillet or sauté pan with enough water to come about ⅓ inch up the sides of the sausage. Place over medium heat and cook, stirring occasionally, until the water has evaporated, about 15 to 20 minutes.

Add 1 tablespoon of the butter and continue cooking until the sausage is lightly browned, about 8 to 10 minutes. Transfer the sausage to a platter and cover it to keep it warm.

Add the remaining butter to the skillet and place it over medium heat. Add the onions and cook, stirring, until slightly wilted, about 4 minutes. Add the apples to the onions and sauté until both the apples and the onions are lightly browned, about 3 minutes. Pour enough cider into the pan to cover the bottom. Stir to release any of the browned bits sticking to the bottom, and then reduce the liquid to create a thick glaze. Spoon the apples and onions over the sausage and serve with warm crusty bread.

Note To make this a day ahead, prepare the recipe and allow it to cool. Transfer the mixture to a baking dish, cover it with aluminum foil, and store it in the refrigerator. Before serving, allow the mixture to come to room temperature and place, covered, in a low (325-degree) oven until it's warmed through, about 20 minutes. Peek occasionally and, if it's drying out, splash on a little more cider.

chicken braised with mexican spices

This braise creates a tender chicken for a simple weeknight supper. Serve it over steamed rice, boiled potatoes, or with Simple Potato Gratin (page 91) and Carrot and Parsley Salad (page 83). **SERVES 4**

3 tablespoons unbleached all-purpose flour
    seasoned with salt and pepper
1 (3-pound) chicken, cut into 8 pieces and skinned
2 tablespoons unsalted butter
½ cup beer
½ cup chicken stock (page 10)
1 cup canned tomatoes with their juices

1 teaspoon ancho chili powder, or to taste
2 tablespoons chopped fresh parsley
1 to 2 tablespoons fresh lime juice
Sour cream or crème fraiche
Chopped cilantro
Lime wedges

Spread the seasoned flour on a dinner plate and roll the chicken pieces in the flour to coat them evenly. Tap off the excess flour.

In a large, heavy skillet, melt the butter over medium-high heat and sauté the chicken in batches until it is golden, about 3 minutes on each side. Transfer the chicken to a platter.

Reduce the heat under the pan, stir in the beer and stock, scraping up any browned bits from the bottom of the pan, and simmer for a minute or two. Stir in the tomatoes, breaking them up into pieces, then the chili powder, parsley, and lime juice. Return the legs and thighs to the pan, bring the sauce to a simmer, cover, and cook for about 7 minutes. Return the breast meat to the pan, cover, and cook until all the chicken parts are tender, about 15 more minutes. Remove the chicken and continue cooking until the liquid is reduced to a thick sauce. Serve the chicken with its sauce over rice or with steamed potatoes or baked sweet potatoes garnished with sour cream, cilantro, and lime wedges.

THE NEW BREED

Regi Haslett-Marroquin, founder of Hillside Farmers Cooperative in Northfield, Minnesota, learned to raise poultry on his family's land in Guatemala. The founder of Peace Coffee, a Fair Trade coffee importer and roaster, he is currently working with the local Latino community, the city of Northfield, and regional businesses to create a co-op poultry business. His plan is to build clusters of small chicken operations using simple, modular barns scaled for a single family on a quarter acre of land. The barns can be assembled quickly in the field and are easy to move if the family relocates.

"When there are 80 barns in working order, the co-op will have the capacity to raise and sell chickens for mass market," he says. But these chickens are different from the birds of large-scale, conventional farms. They are heritage breeds that feast on grasses and kitchen scraps. Because they live in the open with plenty of room to strut, they do not require the antibiotics administered to commercially raised birds kept in unclean, crowded conditions. These grass-fed birds are slaughtered when they are a little older, so their meat is more mature and flavorful—denser, richer, and more chickeny than corn-feed birds.

Eventually, when the co-op of poultry farmers has reached capacity, Haslett-Marroquin plans to build a processing facility capable of supplying local supermarkets with local free-range chickens. "There is nothing I am doing today that I did not learn by working on farms in Guatemala," Haslett-Marroquin says. "Latino immigrants bring to farming a strong work ethic, practical knowledge, and experience. We need more immigrant farmers."

bison steaks with blue cheese butter

Bison, lacking fat, rely on their wooly coats to stay warm through the winter. The meat is very red, even when cooked to medium rare, so a thermometer is key to checking doneness. This simple presentation is terrific for entertaining. Pair this dish with Oven-Blasted Brussels Sprouts (page 87) and Parsnip and Chestnut Puree (page 84) for a lively winter meal. **SERVES 4**

4 bison tenderloin steaks (about 2 pounds total)
Salt and freshly ground black pepper
2 tablespoons butter, oil, or both

4 tablespoons Blue Cheese Butter (page 223)
Chopped parsley

Preheat the oven to 450 degrees. Pat the steaks dry and season them with salt and pepper. Heat the butter in a heavy skillet over high heat. Add the steaks and sear them, turning once, until they are browned, about 4 minutes per side. Transfer the steaks to a baking sheet and roast the steaks in the oven until a meat thermometer inserted 2 inches into one of the steaks reaches 130 degrees, about 5 minutes. Transfer the steaks to a platter and top each with a dollop of the blue cheese butter. Allow the steaks to stand about 5 minutes before serving.

WILD IDEA BUFFALO

I live in a land suspended between the laws of nature and the laws of economics. The North American grasslands are too fragile to be treated like a factory. Their degradation has harmed the public welfare in ways we have not yet imagined. Their restoration is vital. So, while I could make more money by rejoining the cattle/grain/meat-packer cycle, I choose to do what seems clearly right. I raise and process buffalo with honor and respect for the animals and the land. As a result, this ranch produces the condensed essence of the Northern Great Plains in the form of pure buffalo meat, and I take pride in that.
—DAN O'BRIEN, BUFFALO FOR THE BROKEN HEART

HEARTLAND BLUES

Real Roquefort cheese, the king of cheeses, is one of the oldest in the world and traditionally made from sheep's milk. French law protects the moniker, so Heartland cheesemakers usually refer to their Roquefort-style creations as blue cheeses. Shepherd's Way Farms, in Nerstrand, Minnesota, makes its mighty Big Woods Blue the traditional way, with sheep's milk, and ages it for at least three months in temperature-controlled rooms. Sheep's milk cheese from LoveTree Farmstead Cheese replicates the robust barniness of Roquefort by introducing special molds to the milk. Maytag Dairy Farms and many others create Roquefort-style cheese from cow's milk, taking the process one step further from its origins. All are quite different; all are very good. But the sheep's milk versions are the most complex and closest to those of France.

Note These Heartland blues are great on steak and make a fine, creamy finish with a lovely bitter edge to hearty stews. Try blue cheese as a garnish on the oxtail stew (page 78) and the lamb shanks (page 80).

oxtails with stout and onions

Savvy, independent butchers are serving the increasing demand for flavorful, less expensive cuts of meat and the desire to use the entire animal. Clancey's Meats and Fish, located in the Linden Hills neighborhood of Minneapolis, cuts meat to order and carries a wide range of grass-fed and sustainably raised fare.

One of the most flavorful yet cheapest cuts, oxtails make great stew. Provide extra napkins or towels, because this is finger food. Dish up this stew with heaps of Parsnip and Chestnut Puree (page 84) alongside. **SERVES 6**

6 pounds oxtails, cut into 1 ½-inch lengths

4 cups dark stout

1 onion, sliced

2 ribs celery, sliced

2 carrots, sliced

1 teaspoon juniper berries

1 teaspoon whole black peppercorns

¼ cup chopped parsley

2 tablespoons chopped fresh thyme or
    2 teaspoons fresh

3 teaspoons salt

Freshly grated black pepper

2 tablespoons flour

2 tablespoons unsalted butter

¼ cup tomato paste

2 cups chicken stock (page 10) or beef stock
    (page 66)

Chopped parsley

Trim the oxtails of excess fat and place them in a large bowl with the stout, onion, celery, carrots, juniper berries, peppercorns, parsley, and thyme. Cover the bowl and let the oxtails marinate at room temperature about 15 minutes, or refrigerate them, covered, overnight.

Preheat the oven to 375 degrees. Drain the oxtails, reserving the liquid and vegetables in separate bowls. Season the oxtails with salt and pepper, and dust them with the flour. Heat the butter in a large Dutch oven over medium heat, and brown the oxtails on all sides, about 10 to 15 minutes, working in batches if necessary. Remove the oxtails from the pan; then add the vegetables and brown them, stirring, for about 10 minutes. Remove the vegetables and set them aside.

Return the oxtails to the pan along with the marinade, and stir in the tomato paste and stock. Cover and bake until the meat is very tender, about 3 hours. Add the vegetables to the pot and continue cooking until they are tender, another 20 minutes.

To skim off the fat, put an edge of the pot on the stove over high heat and, using a spoon or a bulb baster, remove the fat as it collects in the cooler side of the pot. Adjust the seasoning, and serve the stew garnished with chopped parsley.

BRAISING—A KEY TECHNIQUE FOR WINTER

Braising turns large hunks of meat tender and silky and yields a rich, luscious sauce. It's a great way to make tougher cuts of meat, which are often older and have more muscle and sinew, more flavorful. Every braise begins by searing the meat to seal in juices and then adding some liquid, but not enough to cover the meat. This creates steam heat that draws out the meat's juices to create a rich sauce. Toward the end of the cooking time, the cover is removed so the meat browns. Stewing is like braising, but the meat and vegetables are cut into pieces.

lamb shanks with garlic and rosemary

These succulent shanks take time, but not your time. Use a slow cooker or just put them in a very low oven. Either way, you will get a silky, unctuous result that you would never get cooking the shanks high and fast. Serve these over barley, wild rice, white beans, or hominy with plenty of crusty bread to soak up the juices and a simple green salad tossed in Honey Mustard Vinaigrette (page 210). **SERVES 4**

4 lamb shanks
Salt and freshly ground black pepper
2 tablespoons unsalted butter or vegetable oil
3 carrots, coarsely chopped
1 celery rib, leaves included, chopped
1 onion, chopped

6 cloves garlic, smashed
1 cup dark stout
2 cups chicken stock (page 10)
2 bay leaves
3 sprigs fresh rosemary or 1 teaspoon dried
Malt vinegar

Preheat the oven to 300 degrees. Remove most of the fat from the shanks, and season them with salt and pepper. Heat the oil or butter in a heavy skillet over medium-high, and sear the lamb until it is very well browned on all sides, about 10 minutes. Remove the shanks and set them aside. Add the carrots, celery, onion, and garlic and stir to coat them with the oil. Cover the pan and let the vegetables sweat until they release their juices and begin to brown, about 5 to 7 minutes. Add the stout, stock, bay leaves, and rosemary and bring the stock to a boil, scraping up any of the browned bits stuck to the bottom of the pot. Turn off the heat, add the shanks, cover the pot, and cook in the oven until the lamb is very tender, about 2½ to 3 hours or more.

When the lamb is so tender it falls from the bone, remove the bay leaves and rosemary. Taste and season with additional salt and pepper and malt vinegar. Place the lamb shanks in a warmed deep dish. To serve, spoon them over barley, wild rice, white beans, or hominy.

porketta with oregano and fennel

On the Iron Range of Minnesota, the hearty flavors of southern Italy are big. Take porketta, for example. Fennel spiked and oregano fragrant, it figures in church suppers and town potlucks. Made with a butt roast or a shoulder roast, it needs a long time in a low oven, but requires little more than patience from the cook. It's great, rib-sticking party food; pile any leftovers on crusty rolls for a two-fisted sandwich. Serve this roast with Braised Root Vegetables in Mustard Sauce (page 89) or Sweet Potato, Radish, and Walnut Salad (page 85). **SERVES 6 TO 8**

6 cloves garlic

1 tablespoon coarse salt

2 tablespoons fresh oregano or 2 teaspoons dried

3 tablespoons fennel seed, crushed

1 tablespoon freshly ground black pepper

2 tablespoons apple cider vinegar

1 picnic shoulder or butt roast (about 5 pounds)

3 slices bacon, cut into pieces

1 large onion, thinly sliced

2 fennel bulbs, thinly sliced

½ cup beer

½ cup chicken stock (page 10)

In a food processor fitted with a steel blade or in a mortar and pestle, smash together the garlic, salt, oregano, fennel, and pepper. Then add the apple cider vinegar to make a paste.

With a paring knife, cut deep tunnels into the exposed fleshy ends of the roast and stuff the herb mixture into them. Spread any leftover herb mix over the roast. Wrap the roast tightly in aluminum foil and refrigerate it for one or two days.

Preheat the oven to 325. In a large, deep Dutch oven or a flameproof roasting pan, cook the bacon until it is crisp. Remove the bacon, leaving the grease in the pan. Sauté the roast in the bacon fat until it is browned on all sides, about 10 minutes. Lift out the roast, add the onions and fennel to the pan, and cook until they are wilted, about 5 minutes. Set the roast on top of the onions and fennel, and add the beer and the stock. Cover the pan and place it in the oven.

Roast until the pork reaches 160 degrees on a meat thermometer, about 2½ to 3½ hours. Remove the roast to a platter and let it stand for about 20 minutes before carving. Serve the pork topped with the onions, fennel, and pan juices.

marinated beef pot roast

This one-pot supper relies on balsamic vinegar to boost flavor and keep the meat tender. It's an updated version of German sauerbraten and is delicious served with Braised Red or Green Cabbage (page 86), Thanksgiving Mashed Potatoes (page 37), and crusty bread. Marinate the roast ahead of time, if possible. (Otherwise, allow the meat to sit in the marinade at room temperature while you are readying the rest of the meal.) **SERVES 4 TO 6**

2 to 3 pounds beef or buffalo chuck, rump,
    or shoulder roast, with fat on one side
3 cloves garlic, slivered
1 cup balsamic vinegar
2 tablespoons chopped fresh rosemary

3 medium onions, sliced
Salt and freshly ground black pepper
1 (14½-ounce) can tomatoes, chopped,
    with their juices

Poke the meat all over with a thin-bladed knife, making slits about ½ to 1 inch deep, and insert the garlic slivers into the holes. In a large ceramic dish or bowl, or in a zippered plastic bag, combine the vinegar and rosemary. Add the meat and turn to coat completely. Cover the bowl and refrigerate the roast overnight.

Preheat the oven to 350 degrees. Spread the sliced onions in a large casserole or a small roasting pan. Nestle the meat into the onions and pour in the marinade. Season the meat with salt and pepper. Add the tomatoes with their juices. Cover the pan tightly with a lid or aluminum foil. Cook until the beef is easily pierced with a fork and its juices run clear, about 3 to 3½ hours.

Remove the roast from the oven and allow it to rest in the pan for 5 to 10 minutes before carving. Serve the sliced meat with the tomatoes, onions, and pan juices.

WE DON'T FARM WITH HEADLIGHTS

"We don't farm with headlights," says Audrey Arner of Moonstone Farm, in Montevideo, Minnesota. "Many farmers have to work well into the night to get their crop in," she says, explaining the real difference between the conventional mono-crop system where farmers plant a single crop (such as corn) and the organic system in which farmers plant different crops in rotation. Harvesting one crop all at once requires big, expensive equipment, and there is a small window of time for the harvest. Conventional corn and soybean farmers work well into the night to get everything out of the fields on time.

"We are working from a different knowledge base," Arner explains. "We realized we had to either purchase updated equipment and go into debt to keep up or change how we farmed." Arner and her husband, Richard Handeen, turned to raising beef cattle and diversified their crops, committing to organic methods. "We are not making the same kind of money we might, but our expenses are far less. And we lead a sane life."

Arner and Handeen manage an ecosystem comprising an orchard, a vineyard, vegetables, and nut trees that filters water from the neighbors before it reaches the Chippewa River. "You can't have a stable farm without plant diversity," she adds.

carrot and parsley salad

Best known for adding zest, color, and style to dishes, parsley makes a bold, refreshing contribution to salads. This perky combo pairs parsley's strong, clean taste with carrot's sweet, earthy nature. This salad is tart with raspberry vinegar and dried cranberries, and the vibrant crunch keeps you digging in for more. (That's okay, because the salad is so light that you might burn calories just munching away.)

Be sure to use organic carrots. They taste better and you won't have to peel them. (Peeling removes the layer of skin that contains many essential nutrients.) These make a great side dish to a meal of Caramelized Onion Soup (page 64) or Lamb Shanks with Garlic and Rosemary (page 80). **SERVES 4 TO 6**

7 to 8 organic carrots, grated (3½ cups)
1 large bunch parsley, finely chopped
    (about 2 cups)
⅓ cup dried cranberries
1 large clove garlic

2 tablespoons raspberry vinegar (or any
    fruit vinegar)
2 to 3 tablespoons vegetable oil
½ teaspoon salt
1 tablespoon smashed fennel seeds

In a medium bowl, toss together the carrots, parsley, and dried cranberries.

Force the garlic through a garlic press and put it in a small bowl. Whisk in the vinegar, oil, salt, and fennel seeds. Toss the dressing with the carrot mixture.

Cover the bowl and store the salad in the refrigerator for a few hours, or overnight, so the flavors blend.

Variation Substitute 2 bleeding heart or other large, mild radishes (about ¼ cup, shredded) for 2 of the carrots.

parsnip and chestnut puree

This puree will convert doubters to the pleasures of parsnips. It's an old-fashioned dish, just right in this season. It's best to steam or microwave the parsnips (rather than boiling them) so they don't become waterlogged. Serve these alongside Bison Steaks with Blue Cheese Butter (page 76) or Oxtails with Stout and Onions (page 78). **SERVES 4 TO 6**

About 1 ½ pounds parsnips, cut into chunks
1 cup blanched or roasted and peeled chestnuts
    (page 7)
Salt and freshly ground black pepper
2 tablespoons unsalted butter

Pinch of nutmeg
2 tablespoons chopped parsley, plus additional
    for garnish
¼ cup cream or milk, as needed

Place the parsnips and the chestnuts in a steamer above 1 or 2 inches of water, and set the pan over medium heat. Cover, bring the water to a simmer, and cook until the parsnips are easily pierced. Alternately, cook the parsnips in the microwave: put the parsnips and chestnuts in a shallow bowl with ¼ cup of water, cover, and microwave on high for 6 minutes, stopping to shake the container every 2 minutes, until the parsnips are easily pierced. Drain the parsnips and chestnuts.

Transfer the cooked parsnips and chestnuts into a food processor fitted with a steel blade, and add the salt and pepper, butter, nutmeg, and parsley. Process, adding the cream as needed. Reheat if necessary before serving and garnish with more parsley.

sweet potato, radish, and walnut salad

This salad tastes better the day after it's made. If you can't wait, allow it to stand at least an hour or two at room temperature before serving so the potatoes absorb the sweet, rough marinade. Bleeding heart radishes add a lovely crunch. This salad makes a nice side to the Cornmeal-Dusted Panfish (page 71). **SERVES 6 TO 8**

3 medium sweet potatoes (about 1½ to 2 pounds)
½ cup walnut oil
2 large cloves garlic, minced
¼ cup white wine or raspberry vinegar, or to taste
1 tablespoon dry mustard
1 tablespoon honey

Salt and freshly ground black pepper
½ cup diced bleeding heart radishes or any
    other mild radish
¼ cup toasted walnuts (page 38)
¼ cup dried cranberries

Peel the sweet potatoes, cut them in half and then into thin slices, and steam them over boiling water until just fork tender, not mushy, about 5 to 7 minutes. Set them aside while making the marinade.

In a large bowl, whisk together the oil, garlic, vinegar, mustard, and honey until well blended. Add the hot sweet potatoes to the marinade and toss gently; then season with salt and freshly ground black pepper to taste. Allow the salad to stand on the counter for at least one hour before serving, or tightly cover the bowl and refrigerate it overnight. When ready to serve, toss in the radishes, walnuts, and dried cranberries.

SWEET SPUDS IN THE HEARTLAND

Let's get this straight. A sweet potato is not a yam. Yams grow in the tropics; sweet potatoes, though identified with the south, grow quite well in the Northern Heartland. With names like Jersey, Centennial, garnet, and jewel, sweet potatoes are sweeter, more delicate and nuanced, than any yam or starchy tuber can ever be. Their colors range from soft gold to rich maroon, and they can taste of chestnuts, honey, or molasses. Highly nutritious and relatively low in calories, the sweet potato's mild flavor works well in hot, tart, or salty dishes. Don't let the cloying marshmallow-topped casserole image dissuade you; sweet potatoes can dance to Latin, Indian, Asian, and Middle Eastern beats.

Extremely high in antioxidants, sweet potatoes are loaded with vitamins A and C. They contain nutrients that help eliminate free radicals that can lead to heart disease, colon cancer, and atherosclerosis. They're considered anti-inflammatory and have been shown to help reduce the severity of conditions related to asthma and arthritis.

Sweet potatoes are grouped into two different categories depending on their cooked texture: some are firm, dry and mealy, and less sweet; the others become soft and moist. Color is no indication of sweetness. The pale golden Jersey is sweeter than the brick-colored garnet.

Our local sweets are so right for this time of year. Their warming hues and mellow nature blend nicely with roasts and in stews. They are delicious simply baked in their jackets, split, and served with just a little butter and salt, and they perk up with a splash of vinegar.

braised red or green cabbage

When braised, seared in a little butter or oil, and then cooked over low heat with aromatic liquid, cabbage turns tender and a bit spicy. Here is a simple method that will work for both red and green cabbage. Simply vary the liquid to suit each. **SERVES 4 TO 6**

1 tablespoon vegetable oil

1 small onion, thinly sliced

1 small head red or green cabbage, thinly sliced

For Red Cabbage

¼ cup cider

2 apples, peeled, cored, and chopped

1 tablespoon apple cider vinegar

1 tablespoon brown sugar

Salt and freshly ground black pepper

For Green Cabbage

¼ cup sweet white wine (such as Riesling) or
  2 tablespoons fresh lemon or orange juice
  plus 2 tablespoons water

1 teaspoon caraway seed

Salt and freshly ground black pepper

In a large, deep skillet, heat the oil and toss in the onions and cabbage. Cover and cook until the cabbage is just tender, about 5 minutes.

If you are making red cabbage, add the cider, apples, apple cider vinegar, and brown sugar; toss; and cook about 5 more minutes, until the apples are tender. Season the cabbage with salt and black pepper to taste.

For green cabbage, simply stir in the wine and caraway seeds, and season with salt and freshly ground black pepper to taste. No additional cooking is required.

oven-blasted brussels sprouts

Blasting these pretty mini-cabbages in a hot oven caramelizes their edges, calling forth their sweetness. Finishing them with a splash of vinegar adds snap. Serve the Brussels sprouts warm or at room temperature. They make a nice starter course or a fine side dish to Sausage with Apples and Onions (page 73) or Lamb Shanks with Garlic and Rosemary (page 80). **SERVES 4 TO 6**

1 pound Brussels sprouts, halved, or quartered
   if very large

2 shallots, coarsely chopped

1 to 2 tablespoons olive oil or vegetable oil

Coarse salt

Cracked pepper

1 to 2 tablespoons aged malt, balsamic,
   or sherry vinegar

Preheat the oven to 450 degrees. Toss the Brussels sprouts and shallots with just enough oil to generously coat them and sprinkle on a little salt. Spread them out on a baking sheet in one layer so that they don't touch. Roast, shaking the pan once or twice, until the sprouts are brown on the edges and very tender, about 25 minutes. Remove, turn into a serving dish, and sprinkle with the pepper and drizzle with vinegar to taste. Serve warm or at room temperature.

roasted salsify

This old-fashioned root vegetable, sometimes called goat's beard, looks like a gnarled white carrot. It's especially nutritious and has an unusual nutty, parsley taste. Roasted, it's a terrific companion to Marinated Beef Pot Roast (page 82). **SERVES 4**

1 pound salsify, scrubbed and cut into 2-inch pieces
2 tablespoons hazelnut or olive oil
Salt and freshly ground black pepper

¼ cup chopped fresh parsley
Squeeze of lemon or splash of vinegar

Preheat the oven to 375 degrees. Toss the salsify with the oil and spread it out on a baking sheet. Roast, turning occasionally, until the salsify is tender and brown, about 30 to 35 minutes. Turn into a serving bowl and toss with the parsley. Season with lemon juice or vinegar to taste and serve right away.

braised root vegetables in mustard sauce

You can use any combination of root vegetables you like, but this is a great recipe for turnips and rutabagas. Both turn earthy and sweet as braising softens their bitter, cabbage-like edge. Serve these with Bison Steaks with Blue Cheese Butter (page 76) or Marinated Beef Pot Roast (page 82). **SERVES 4 TO 6**

2 tablespoons butter
1½ pounds mixed root vegetables (turnips,
    rutabagas, carrots), peeled as needed and
    cut into 1-inch pieces
Salt and freshly ground black pepper

1 tablespoon maple syrup or honey
1 cup chicken stock (page 10)
2 tablespoons coarse Dijon mustard
Chopped fresh parsley

In a large saucepan, melt the butter over medium heat to film the pan and then add the vegetables, spreading them out in one layer. Sprinkle with salt and pepper and cook, stirring, until the vegetables begin to soften and brown, about 10 minutes.

Add the maple syrup and just enough stock to cover the vegetables. Bring the stock to a boil, reduce the heat, and simmer until the vegetables are tender and the liquid has reduced to a shiny glaze, about 20 to 30 minutes. Stir in the mustard. Serve garnished with the fresh parsley.

sweet potatoes with a world of toppings

───────

Scrub the sweet potatoes and poke several holes in them to allow steam to escape. Bake in a preheated 400-degree oven for about 40 to 50 minutes, or until tender when poked with a thin, sharp knife. Slit the sweet potatoes, press in at both ends to open them, and top with one of the following. **ONE 8-OUNCE POTATO PER SERVING**

Mexican Add a dusting of chili powder, lime juice, sour cream, and chopped cilantro.

Asian Drizzle on dark toasted sesame oil, soy sauce, and toasted sesame seeds.

Yankee Add a drizzle of maple syrup, butter, and toasted chopped walnuts.

Italian Drizzle on extra-virgin olive oil and balsamic vinegar, and add chopped parsley.

Northwoods Roast equal numbers of apples and sweet potatoes. When they are cooked, turn the apples into a food processor and puree them with a little cream or plain yogurt, honey, cinnamon, ginger, nutmeg, grated orange rind, and salt and pepper to taste.

simple potato gratin

This dish makes use of the fluffy, high-starch potatoes available this time of year, although buttery Yukon Gold and Yellow Finn potatoes work nicely too. Although gratins are most often made with cream, this recipe is lightened by poaching the potatoes in stock and wine before baking them with a little cheese. Serve the gratin with roasts or pair it with a hearty vegetable dish for a meal. It also goes well with Sausage with Apples and Onions (page 73), Lamb Shanks with Garlic and Rosemary (page 80), or Oxtails with Stout and Onions (page 78). **SERVES 4 TO 6**

1 tablespoon unsalted butter
1½ to 2 cups chicken stock (page 10) or
    vegetable stock (page 110)
1 cup dry white wine
2 bay leaves
1 clove garlic, smashed

Salt and freshly ground black pepper
Pinch of nutmeg
2 pounds (about 6 to 8 medium) baking
    potatoes, peeled
2 ounces grated aged hard cheese such as
    cheddar, Parmesan, or Gouda

Preheat the oven to 350 degrees. Grease a 1½-quart gratin dish with a little of the butter.

Combine the stock, wine, bay leaves, garlic, and a little salt, pepper, and nutmeg in a medium saucepan set over high heat. Bring the stock to a boil, and cook until the liquid is reduced to 2 cups, about 10 to 15 minutes.

Slice the potatoes very thin, about ⅛ inch thick. Add the potatoes to the stock, and simmer until the mixture begins to thicken and the potatoes are just tender but not fully cooked, about 10 to 15 minutes. Remove the bay leaves and turn the potatoes and liquid into the gratin dish. Dot the potatoes with the remaining butter.

Cover and bake the gratin until the potatoes become very tender and the liquid is reduced, about 40 minutes. Remove the cover, sprinkle on the shredded cheese, and continue baking until the gratin is set and the top is crusty and golden, about 20 to 25 more minutes.

WHEN ARE POTATOES IN SEASON?

Potatoes fall into two general categories—high starch and low starch.

High-starch potatoes (such as russets) are drier, mealier, and more floury when cooked. They tend to fall apart, so are better for baking, mashing, and frying.

Low-starch potatoes (boiling or red) are wetter and waxier. They hold their shape when cooked and are best suited to potato salads and gratins.

The happy medium, Yukon Gold and Yellow Finn, are medium starch, great for both mashing and salads.

New potatoes are not a separate group but rather the new crop of any potato. Generally, they are lower in starch than mature potatoes and do not keep well. New potatoes are harvested as early as April or May in most climates, while mature potatoes are harvested through the middle of October, before the ground freezes. After that, the plant tops are cut and the potatoes are left in the ground until they are harvested. By this time, they have stopped growing but continue to age, albeit not as rapidly as they would in a warehouse or on the shelf. November potatoes therefore taste different from those harvested in summer.

To tell a high-starch from a low-starch potato, cut the raw potato with a sharp knife. If there is a lot of milky liquid on the blade and it feels like the potato is grabbing the knife, it's a high-starch potato.

Store all potatoes in a cool spot away from light (both artificial and sunlight) that may cause them to turn green and give them a bitter taste.

linzer cookies

The dark, toasty flavor of hazelnuts shines in this delicate cookie. Delicious as is or sandwiched with jam, they are terrific for the holiday cookie platter. **MAKES 24 SANDWICHES OR 48 COOKIES**

1 cup unsalted butter
⅔ cup sugar
1 tablespoon fresh orange zest
1 egg
2 teaspoons vanilla extract
2 cups unbleached all-purpose flour

1 teaspoon cinnamon
½ teaspoon freshly grated nutmeg
½ teaspoon salt
1½ cups toasted hazelnuts (page 94),
    finely chopped
½ cup raspberry preserves for filling cookies

Preheat the oven to 325 degrees. Line a baking sheet with parchment paper or lightly grease it.

In a large bowl, cream the butter, sugar, and orange zest. Add the egg and beat it in; then cream in the vanilla.

In a separate bowl, stir together the flour, cinnamon, nutmeg, and salt. Turn the dry ingredients into the butter mixture and stir to make a stiff dough. Add the hazelnuts and stir just until they are mixed in.

Divide the dough into two pieces and flatten each piece into a disk. Wrap each disk in plastic and refrigerate them for at least 30 minutes (or overnight).

On a lightly floured surface, roll out each disk until the dough is about ⅛ inch thick. Cut out the cookie shapes (if you are making sandwiches, cut a small hole in the center of the top shape). Gather the scrap dough and roll it out again to cut more cookies.

Place the cookies on the baking sheet and bake for about 14 to 16 minutes, or until the edges have browned slightly. Cool the cookies before filling them with the preserves.

HAZELNUTS AND HICKORIES

Badgersett Research Farm in Canton, Minnesota, breeds hazelnut trees and is currently working on a hickory-pecan hybrid whose pale nuts are buttery and lush. Hazelnuts are delicious in baked goods, salads, and snacks. Fresh off the tree, their taste is reminiscent of fresh coconut, a flavor that deepens as they cure. Badgersett's hazelnuts are smaller than those we find in the stores and, once cracked, their covering, or pellicle, is paler and less bitter. It doesn't interfere with the nut's flavor but can be removed quickly (see below).

Hazelnut oil is golden, fragrant, and wonderful in vinaigrettes and baked goods. Because its smoke point is higher than that of olive oil, it works nicely in stir-fries and sautés. The future of local hazelnuts relies on a processor capable of shelling and packaging fresh nuts and pressing them for oil.

Cracking Local Hazelnuts

Hazelnuts can be tough to crack. Look for the "seam" on the shell, place a nutcracker or pliers at opposite ends, and then squeeze so the shell splits along the seam. To remove the nut's thin, papery covering, place the shelled nuts on a baking sheet and roast them in a 350-degree oven for about 3 to 5 minutes. Put the warm nuts in a dishtowel and rub them until the skins flake off. For more information on local hazelnuts, see Sources.

hazelnut and dried cherry biscotti

This twice-baked biscuit is hard and porous, perfect for dunking into Alexis Bailly's orange-infused Ratafia or Saint Croix Vineyards' Raspberry Infusion or even Surly's Coffee Bender. These cookies store beautifully and make terrific holiday gifts. **MAKES ABOUT 24 BISCOTTI**

1 ¾ cups unbleached all-purpose flour

¼ teaspoon salt

1 teaspoon baking powder

1 cup light brown sugar

2 eggs, beaten

1 cup toasted and chopped hazelnuts

¼ cup dried cherries, plumped in ½ cup
    apple cider

Preheat the oven to 350 degrees. Line a baking sheet with parchment paper or lightly grease it.

Stir together the flour, salt, baking powder, and brown sugar. Mix in the eggs, and then fold in the nuts and the cherries, along with any remaining cider. The dough will be sticky, so flour your hands before shaping it into 3 to 4 logs, each about 6 inches long and 1 to 2 inches wide. Space them out on the baking sheet and bake until firm, about 25 minutes. Remove the baking sheet from the oven, and reduce the temperature to 275 degrees.

Allow the biscotti to cool for about 15 minutes; then slice them diagonally into ¾-inch slices and lay the slices on the baking sheet. Return the biscotti to the oven and bake for about 10 minutes. Flip the biscotti and continue baking for an additional 10 minutes, or until they are golden.

cranberry tartlets in a sweet cornmeal crust

Tart cranberries peek through a golden lattice crust in these bright tartlets. Serve them with Spirited Whipped Cream (page 46) or vanilla ice cream. **MAKES 6 TARTLETS OR ONE 9-INCH TART OR PIE**

1 recipe Sweet Cornmeal Crust (page 208)
2 cups cranberries, rinsed and picked over
1½ cups sugar

¼ cup crystallized ginger
2 pears, peeled, cored, and diced

Prepare the dough and divide it into two balls. Divide 1 of those balls into 6 pieces and return the other to the refrigerator. On a floured surface with a floured rolling pin, or between two sheets of parchment paper or plastic wrap, flatten each piece of dough and roll it out to fit a 4- or 5-inch tartlet pan (you will need 6 tartlet pans). Fit each rolled-out crust into a pan, pressing it against the sides, and trim the tops even. Roll out the remaining dough into an ⅛-inch-thick rectangle. Cover and chill the prepared crusts while you prepare the filling.

In a food processor fitted with a steel blade, process 1 cup of the cranberries with the sugar and ginger until the berries are coarsely chopped. Turn the chopped cranberries into a bowl, and stir in the remaining cranberries and the pears.

Preheat the oven to 375 degrees. Place the tartlets on a baking sheet and distribute the filling among the crusts. With a sharp knife, cut the remaining dough into strips about ½ inch wide for tartlets or an inch wide for a 9-inch tart. Lay half of the strips over the filling so they are parallel and evenly spaced. Lay the remaining strips over the top, running in the other direction. Press the ends of the strips into the crust at the sides and trim off the excess dough. Bake until the crust is golden and the filling is bubbly, about 25 to 30 minutes (about 10 minutes more for a large pie or tart). If you are using tart pans with removable bottoms, liquid may leak through, but don't be alarmed.

ginger stout cake

The stout gives this moist cake a lovely bitter edge, perfect with ginger. It's one of those sweets that work beautifully with coffee at midday and later on with a beer and sharp cheese. The cake will stay moist for several days and freezes nicely. The slices toast well. This recipe calls for sorghum, but molasses or dark buckwheat honey is good too. **1 10-INCH BUNDT CAKE**

2½ cups unbleached all-purpose flour
1 tablespoon ground ginger
2 teaspoons baking powder
½ teaspoon baking soda
½ teaspoon salt
1 cup unsalted butter, at room temperature

1¼ cups packed light brown sugar
2 large eggs plus 1 egg yolk
1 cup sorghum, molasses, or dark
   buckwheat honey
½ cup stout or mead (page 100)
Powdered sugar for dusting

Preheat the oven to 350 degrees. Grease and flour a 12-cup Bundt pan.

In a large mixing bowl, combine the flour, ginger, baking powder, baking soda, and salt. Set the bowl aside.

Using an electric mixer, cream the butter and brown sugar in a large bowl until fluffy, about 3 minutes, scraping down the sides of the bowl as needed. Add the eggs and egg yolk and beat for 30 seconds. Add the sorghum and slowly blend.

With the mixer on low speed, blend the flour mixture into the butter mixture until just mixed, about 30 seconds. Do not overmix.

Scrape the batter into the prepared pan, and place it in the center of the oven. Check on the cake frequently. If the top starts to brown too quickly, cover it with aluminum foil. Bake until the top springs back when touched and a cake tester inserted into the center comes out clean, about 50 to 60 minutes.

Use a toothpick to make several holes about halfway through the cake. Drizzle the stout onto the cake, making sure that it is distributed evenly. Let the cake cool in the pan on a rack for 10 minutes, and then invert the cake onto the rack to finish cooling. Dust the cake with sieved powdered sugar. Serve warm or at room temperature.

SORGHUM

From a distance, sorghum, with its wide blade-shaped leaves arching out in a whorl around a thick stalk, looks a lot like corn. However, it doesn't have ears. Sweet sorghum is grown for the syrup made by cooking juice from the plants' stalks. It resembles molasses in taste but is a little lighter. In the Midwest, small farmers grow and process it for themselves and their neighbors. These days, the Sandhill Farm community in Rutledge, Missouri, produces about 800 gallons of sorghum syrup per year and distributes it to stores across the region. Look for it in local natural foods co-ops and small independent grocery stores.

favorite carrot cupcakes

These lovely spicy-sweet cupcakes are topped with traditional cream cheese frosting. Grate the carrots on a box grater because the bright orange slivers give these mini-cakes color and texture. **MAKES 12 CUPCAKES**

Cupcakes
⅔ cup unbleached all-purpose flour
½ cup light brown sugar
1 teaspoon baking soda
½ teaspoon baking powder
1 teaspoon cinnamon
½ teaspoon grated nutmeg
¼ teaspoon ground cloves
½ teaspoon salt
⅓ cup walnut, hazelnut, or vegetable oil
    (or a combination)
2 eggs

3 medium carrots, grated (about 1 cup)
1 cup toasted walnuts (see page 38), chopped
1 apple, peeled, cored, and diced
Cream Cheese Frosting
1 (8-ounce) package cream cheese,
    at room temperature
6 tablespoons unsalted butter,
    at room temperature
1 teaspoon vanilla extract
Pinch of salt
2 cups confectioners sugar
Milk or cream as needed

Preheat the oven to 350 degrees. Line a cupcake pan with paper liners.

In a medium bowl, stir together the flour, brown sugar, baking soda, baking powder, cinnamon, nutmeg, cloves, and salt.

In a small bowl, whisk together the oil and the eggs. Stir this into the dry ingredients. Stir in the carrots, walnuts, and apple.

Turn the batter into the prepared cupcake tins and bake until a toothpick inserted into the center comes up clean, about 18 to 22 minutes. Remove the cupcakes from the tin, and let them cool completely on a wire rack.

To make the frosting, beat the cream cheese with the butter until fluffy, and then beat in the vanilla and salt. Beat in the sugar, adding a little milk or cream if it seems too dry, until the frosting reaches a thick consistency that's easy to spread.

When the cupcakes have thoroughly cooled, spread a generous amount of frosting on each one.

old-fashioned bread and butter pudding

The scent of sizzling maple syrup that finishes this pudding will draw everyone into the kitchen. It's especially good baked in a cast-iron skillet, which creates a lovely firm golden crust. Serve with Spirited Whipped Cream (page 46). **SERVES 4 TO 6**

Unsalted butter for greasing the pan
¼ cup dried cranberries or dried blueberries
¼ cup dried cherries
4 eggs
¼ cup sugar
2 cups milk, or a little more as needed
½ cup heavy cream
1 teaspoon vanilla

1 teaspoon cinnamon
Pinch of nutmeg
Pinch of salt
12 slices good-quality bread or a mixture of
    bread and muffins, cut into 1½- to
    2-inch pieces
¼ cup chopped hickory nuts, walnuts, or hazelnuts
¼ cup maple syrup

Preheat the oven to 350 degrees. Generously butter a casserole, a 9 × 9-inch baking dish, or a cast-iron skillet.

Put the dried fruit in a bowl, cover it with hot water, and allow it to steep for at least 10 minutes.

In a large bowl, whisk together the eggs and sugar; then whisk in the milk, cream, vanilla, cinnamon, nutmeg, and salt. Toss in the bread cubes. Drain the fruit; then gently mix it in. Turn the mixture into the prepared dish; then sprinkle the nuts on top. Bake until the pudding is puffy and a knife inserted in the center comes up clean, about 40 to 45 minutes. If the top browns too quickly, cover it loosely with a piece of buttered foil. Remove the pudding from the oven and pour the maple syrup over the top right away. Serve immediately.

Note It is best if the bread is a little stale. If it's very moist, spread the pieces on a baking sheet and toast them in a 350-degree oven until they begin to firm up, about 3 to 5 minutes.

spiked chocolate truffles

There's a reason Valentine's Day falls in February: chocolate is the sweet to lift spirits on a glum afternoon. These truffles make a simple dessert or a lovely gift. Use Alexis Bailly's orange-infused Ratafia in this recipe, and then enjoy a glass with the truffles. **MAKES ABOUT 24**

8 ounces semisweet or bittersweet chocolate

2 tablespoons unsalted butter

¾ cup heavy cream, at room temperature

¼ cup mead, fortified wine, or whiskey

¼ cup unsweetened cocoa

In a small saucepan over low heat, melt the chocolate with the butter, stirring continually to blend. Very gradually add the cream, stirring after each addition, until the mixture is smooth. Remove the pan from the heat and stir in the mead. Turn the chocolate mixture into a low bowl and refrigerate until it is cool and stiff, about an hour.

Sift some cocoa powder onto a plate. Line another plate with waxed paper. Use two spoons or your hand to make small balls, about 2 inches in diameter, out of the chocolate mixture, and roll them in the cocoa powder. Place the truffles on the waxed paper and serve them immediately, or place them in an airtight container and refrigerate for up to a day or two.

WHITE WINTER WINERY MEAD

An ancient drink brewed from honey and yeast, mead can be dry or sweet, robust or refreshing. It is also known as honey wine. The White Winter Winery in Iron River, Wisconsin, makes traditional meads. Its Black Harbor Dessert Mead is brewed from black currants grown on the Bayfield peninsula on the shores of Lake Superior. It's a rich and spicy elixir, one of the many traditional varieties employing local grains, fruit, and honey. This mead is especially good with dessert cheese or sprinkled over fresh or dried fruit. See Sources.

THE CHEESE BOARD

Cheese makes an elegant end to any meal. Our region's artisan cheesemakers are drawing on traditional German, Italian, and Welsh methods using milk from free-range cows, sheep, and goats.

Alemar Cheese Company (Mankato, Minnesota) creates a triple-cream Camembert-style cheese using single-source milk from Cedar Summit Farm, just up the road. The Bent River cheese ages beautifully from the inside out. "Milk is to cheese what grapes are to wine," says Keith Adams, Alemar cheesemaker. "Quality milk means everything."

Mary Falk, of LoveTree Farmstead Cheese in the Trade Lakes region of Wisconsin, raises a special breed of dairy sheep that thrive in the harsh climate. Dairy sheep, unlike cows, are not under pressure to perform and produce great quantities of milk. Cheesemaker Jodi Ohlsen Read of Shepherd's Way Farms (Nerstrand, Minnesota) makes cheeses on the farmstead that reflect the land they come from. Cheesemakers and brothers Brian and Kevin Donnay of Stickney Hill Dairy (Kimball, Minnesota) make award-winning chèvre from the milk of their own goats.

The vast and growing selection of great local cheese can be overwhelming. Here's some basic advice for assembling a cheese board.

- Don't offer more than three kinds of cheese, and make each different—young and creamy, hard and aged, mild yet firm. Think of contrasting flavors and textures.
- Serve cheese at room temperature.
- Remember that cheese is as wonderful an ending as it is a start to any meal.
- Soft and fresh cheeses such as chèvre, mascarpone, ricotta, and feta are delicious with honey and soft fruit.
- Soft-ripened cheeses (Camembert- and Brie-style cheeses) may be baked until bubbly and lightly browned.
- Blue-veined blue and Gorgonzola cheeses are crumbly, strong tasting, and salty. Pair these with fruit and nuts.
- Semi-soft cheeses range from buttery to earthy. Think of Havarti, fontina, and Muenster to serve with roasted vegetables or poached fruit and sugared nuts.
- Mexican cheeses, such as asadero and queso fresco, bring mild balance to spicy dishes and salsas.
- Semi-hard cheeses have a wide range of flavor profiles. Cheddar with crisp apples and sweet pie is classic. Smooth, buttery Gouda and Edam are lovely with spiced nuts and peppers.
- Hard cheeses, such as Asiago, Parmesan, and Romano, are terrific with grilled vegetables and cured meats, but they are also wonderful at the end of the meal with dried fruit and nuts.

WARM AND COZY SUPPERS

Homey stews and warming soups are sparked with vibrant salads of bleeding heart radishes, brilliant carrots, or the sharp-sweet magenta of braised red cabbage. The subtle cozy flavors of a crusty onion soup, for example, get a lift from lively carrot salad.

SIMPLE FIRESIDE DINNER
Potato, Prosciutto, and Rosemary Pizza
Caramelized Onion Soup
Carrot and Parsley Salad
Ginger Stout Cake

CASUAL VEGETARIAN SUPPER
Winter Vegetable Tagine
Spicy Bean and Hominy Stew
Braised Green Cabbage
Favorite Carrot Cupcakes

HOLIDAY BUFFET
Sweet Potato, Radish, and Walnut Salad
Squash Lasagna with Walnuts and Kale
Porketta with Oregano and Fennel
Parsnip and Chestnut Puree
Braised Red Cabbage
Linzer Cookies
Cranberry Tartlets in a Sweet Cornmeal Crust
Spiked Chocolate Truffles
Selection of Heartland Cheeses

APRÈS-SKI DINNER
Roast Root Salad with Honey Mustard Vinaigrette
Lamb Shanks with Garlic and Rosemary
Simple Potato Gratin
Hazelnut and Dried Cherry Biscotti

WINTRY WEEKNIGHT SUPPER
Carrot Cashew Bisque
Sausage with Apples and Onions
Roasted Salsify
Buttermilk Scones, Sweet or Savory
Old-Fashioned Bread and Butter Pudding

watercress salad with a french twist

pizza with arugula and feta

minted pea soup

spring spinach and nettle soup

light and lemony asparagus soup

hot and sour vegetable soup with tofu

spring vegetable curry

turkey cutlets with spring vegetables and tangy pan sauces

pork tenderloin with lemon and herbs

pan-roasted lamb chops with fresh mint–cilantro chutney

crispy fried fish

walleye meunière

oven-fried chicken

potato and sorrel gratin

showy spinach soufflé

vegetable frittata with goat cheese

spring greens and strawberry salad with rhubarb vinaigrette

new potato, fiddlehead ferns, and arugula salad

pan-roasted radishes

grilled asparagus with chive vinaigrette

morels and sunchokes with toasted hazelnuts

sunchoke chips

simple spring sauté

cracked wheat tabouli with herbs

chocolate mousse with maple cream

maple sugar shortbread

pound cake with rhubarb-strawberry sauce

once a year rhubarb pie

strawberry sorbet

rhubarb lemonade

herbal elixirs

SPRING

One Swallow does not make a summer, but one skein of geese, cleaving the murk of March thaw, is the spring.

—ALDO LEOPOLD, *A SAND COUNTY ALMANAC*

spring

SUDDENLY, IT'S SPRING. The earth softens and we come to our senses. Damp forests of morels, sizzling trout from ice-crusted streams, tangy delicate chèvre, the palette of flavors and colors is sunny and light. Just as we trade out wool for cotton, roasting and simmering give way to quick, light techniques such as sautés and stir-fries. Think peppery watercress, lemony sorrel, spicy radishes, and bold herbs to wake sleepy taste buds from wintery comforts.

FIVE SPRING DISHES IN FIVE MINUTES OR LESS

Spring Sauté Heat 2 tablespoons of olive oil, butter, or a mixture of both in a large skillet and sauté 1 handful of chopped garlic greens plus 2 cups of spring vegetables (snap peas, radishes, turnips, spinach, asparagus) cut into ½–inch pieces. Cook until the vegetables are just wilted, about 2 to 4 minutes. Sprinkle with fruit vinegar or lemon juice, salt, and pepper. Serve as a side dish or toss with pasta or cheese.

Warm Spinach Salad Film a sauté pan with hazelnut, walnut, or olive oil and sauté chopped shallots for a minute or two; then toss in several handfuls of spinach and heat another minute until the spinach is wilted. Add a splash of raspberry or strawberry vinegar and serve topped with crumbled feta and toasted hazelnuts or walnuts.

Radish Sandwiches Slice radishes very, very thin. Spread a generous layer of sweet butter on dark pumpernickel bread, top it with the radishes, and sprinkle on some coarse sea salt.

Honeyed Chèvre Mix ½ cup of fresh chèvre with 1 to 2 tablespoons of light honey, to taste. Shape the cheese into a log and serve it with gingersnap cookies or crackers.

Roast Sunchokes with Herbs Rinse and slice sunchokes into ½-inch slices. Toss them with oil, sprinkle on some herbs de Provence and coarse salt, and roast in a hot (425-degree) oven until they're tender and the cut side is browned, about 5 minutes. Serve as a side dish or on bruschetta.

watercress salad with a french twist

This classic French bacon-and-egg salad makes a terrific appetizer, light lunch, or brunch dish paired with lots of crusty bread and some good cheese. The fun is in poking the yolk and making a joyful mess of it all.

Though frisée is the classic green for this salad, try tossing in watercress, sorrel, and dandelion greens too. Some recipes call for lardoons (a fancy name for thick-cut bacon), but thinner rashers cooked crisp work well too. Be sure to use eggs from free-range chickens. **SERVES 4**

4 slices bacon	4 to 6 cups mixed greens
1 teaspoon Dijon mustard	1 bunch watercress, stemmed
1 medium shallot, finely chopped	1 small red onion, chopped
2 to 3 tablespoons apple cider vinegar	1 teaspoon fresh thyme
4 eggs	Salt and freshly ground black pepper

Cook the bacon in a skillet over low heat, turning it occasionally, until crisp. Set the bacon on paper towels to drain. Reserve the bacon fat.

In a small bowl, whisk together the mustard, shallot, and vinegar to taste. Then whisk in 2 to 3 tablespoons of the bacon fat.

Bring about 2 quarts of water to a boil in a saucepan; then lower the heat to a steady simmer. Lightly grease or butter four ramekins. Break one egg into each ramekin and set them in the simmering water. Partially cover the pan and cook just until the yolks are set, about 3 to 4 minutes.

Toss the greens with the red onion and most of the dressing. Arrange the dressed greens on four separate plates and crumble the bacon over top. Using a spoon, carefully slide one egg onto each salad. Spoon the remaining dressing over the eggs, and garnish them with the fresh thyme, salt, and freshly ground black pepper.

pizza with arugula and feta

Arugula, also called roquette and rocket, is mild in the spring but turns peppery as the season moves on; combine it with assertive dandelion greens for additional snap. Here, wispy arugula leaves wilt a little as they season the pizza, sizzling from the oven. Pair this pizza with Light and Lemony Asparagus Soup (page 110) for a bright spring dinner. **SERVES 4**

1 batch Pizza Dough (page 203)
3 tablespoons extra-virgin olive oil
2 cloves garlic, smashed
⅛ teaspoon crushed red pepper
1 teaspoon chopped fresh oregano or
    ½ teaspoon dried

1 bunch spring onions, white parts only,
    finely chopped
4 to 6 ounces feta, crumbled
1 large handful baby arugula or
    dandelion greens

Preheat the oven to 425 degrees. Line a pizza peel or baking sheet with parchment paper.

In a small dish, whisk together the olive oil, garlic, crushed red pepper, and oregano and set it aside.

On a lightly floured board, roll out the pizza dough into a 14-inch circle and let it rest for about 15 minutes.

Set the dough on the peel or baking sheet, arrange the chopped onions and the crumbled feta over the dough, drizzle a little oil over all, and bake until the edges of the pizza are golden and crispy, about 15 to 20 minutes. Just before serving, pile on the arugula and dandelion greens. Season the pizza with salt and pepper and a little more oil.

minted pea soup

In this soup, sugar snaps and English peas are whirled into a lush puree. Fresh garden mint adds a light, bright note. This soup makes an easy and elegant beginning to a dinner of Pan-Roasted Lamb Chops with Fresh Mint–Cilantro Chutney (page 115). **SERVES 4 TO 6**

1 tablespoon unsalted butter

1 small yellow onion, chopped

3 cups vegetable stock (page 110) or chicken stock (page 10)

1 small baking potato, peeled and sliced

1 sprig fresh thyme

Pinch of freshly grated nutmeg

1 pound sugar snap peas, chopped

1 pound English peas, shelled, or 1 cup frozen and thawed

2 tablespoons fresh flat-leaf (Italian) parsley

2 tablespoons lemon juice, or to taste

½ cup cream

Salt and freshly ground black pepper

2 tablespoons chopped fresh mint, or to taste, plus more for garnish

Melt the butter in a heavy soup pot over medium heat. Add the onion and sauté until the onion is translucent, about 5 minutes. Add the stock, potato, thyme, and nutmeg and bring the stock to a boil. Reduce the heat to medium-low, partially cover the pot, and simmer until the potato slices are very tender, about 10 minutes.

Add the sugar snap peas and simmer until they are tender, about 10 to 15 minutes. Add the English peas and simmer until they are cooked, about 3 to 5 minutes. Stir in the parsley.

Use an immersion blender to puree the soup or puree it in a blender in batches. Pour the soup through a sieve placed over a bowl resting in a bowl of ice. Stir the soup slowly until it has cooled to room temperature (this sets the green color). Stir in the lemon juice, cream, salt, and pepper, and then remove the soup from the ice bath.

If serving the soup warm, return it to the pot over low heat and warm it through (do not let it boil). If serving it cold, cover the bowl and refrigerate until the soup is well chilled.

Just before serving, stir in the chopped mint, taste the soup, and adjust the seasonings as needed. Ladle the soup into bowls or cups and garnish each with more chopped mint.

HEARTLAND PEAS

The sugar snap, darling of pea lovers, is a cross of the snow pea (called *mange tout*, which is French for "eat it all") and the English shell pea and is sweeter and more succulent than its forebearers. At the farmers' markets in Minneapolis and St. Paul, Hmong farmers sell sugar snaps on the vine by the case.

To prepare pea shoots, remove the pea pods and steep the vines a few minutes in simmering water to make a luscious stock, rich with sweet pea flavor. Use it as you would any stock; it's great in sauces and stir-fries, and in the Minted Pea Soup.

spring spinach and nettle soup

Loaded with nutrients, delicious and light, this vibrant soup is a sure spring tonic. If you don't have nettles (or don't want to use them), double the amount of spinach for an equally vibrant soup. It makes a healthy partner to a meatless supper when paired with the Potato and Sorrel Gratin (page 120). **SERVES 6**

2 tablespoons unsalted butter
1 cup finely diced onion
1 small potato, peeled and thinly sliced
2 sprigs fresh tarragon
6 cups vegetable stock (page 110), chicken stock
    (page 10), or water
6 cups spinach, thinly sliced

6 to 8 ounces (about 1 cup loosely packed)
    nettle leaves (see below)
Pinch of nutmeg
Salt and freshly ground black pepper
½ cup crème fraiche or plain
    whole-milk strained yogurt

Melt the butter in a soup pot set over medium-high heat, and sauté the onion until it is translucent, about 5 minutes. Add the potato, tarragon, and stock. Bring the stock to a boil; then reduce the heat and simmer until the potato is very soft, about 15 minutes. Stir in the spinach and the nettles, and simmer until the spinach turns bright green, about 2 to 3 minutes. Remove and discard the tarragon.

Working in small batches, puree the soup in a blender (or use an immersion blender); then return it to the pot. Season the soup with nutmeg, salt, and freshly ground black pepper. Stir in the crème fraiche.

GRASP THE NETTLE

"Our grandmothers would laugh if they knew what chefs were paying for nettles, pesky weeds that sting like mad. They grow like crazy along the borders of our fields," says Atina Diffley, cofounder of Gardens of Eagan, Minnesota's largest organic farm. Nutritious, loaded with anti-inflammatory properties, and a remedy for spring allergies, nettles are surprisingly good, tasting a bit like artichokes and asparagus.

To harvest nettles:
* Wear gloves and use tongs or a fork. Don't touch them with your bare hands.
* Harvest only the top four inches of the plant.
* Remove the thick stems from the nettle tops before blanching the tops in boiling water for about 2 minutes. Remove and discard the stems.
* Once blanched, nettle leaves can be quickly sautéed in a little butter or oil, then served on pasta or a pizza.

light and lemony asparagus soup

Ramps and asparagus, both members of the lily family, make natural partners in this lively soup. Serve this as a lively first course to the Pork Tenderloin with Lemon and Herbs (page 114). **SERVES 4 TO 6**

2 tablespoons unsalted butter

2 ramps or 1 leek, white and pale green parts only, rinsed and finely chopped

2 large shallots, chopped

Salt and freshly ground black pepper

2 pounds asparagus, trimmed and cut into 1-inch pieces, with the tips set aside

4 to 5 cups chicken stock (page 10) or vegetable stock (see below)

2 tablespoons fresh lemon juice, or to taste

Melt the butter in a large, heavy pot set over medium-low heat, and add the ramps and shallots, a little salt, and pepper. Cook, stirring, until the ramps are soft, about 3 minutes. Add the asparagus tips and the stock and bring the stock to a boil; then reduce the heat and simmer until the asparagus tips are tender, about 2 or 3 minutes. Remove the asparagus tips with a slotted spoon and set them aside. Add the asparagus stalks and continue simmering the soup until the asparagus stalks are very tender, about 7 or 8 minutes longer. Working in batches, puree the soup in a blender (or use an immersion blender) and return it to the pot. Add a little water if the soup is too thick. Stir in lemon juice to taste. Gently reheat the soup and serve it garnished with the asparagus tips.

EASIEST VEGETABLE STOCK EVER

You can double the recipe to have extra to freeze, but it comes together so quickly, why bother? **MAKES ABOUT 1 QUART**

2 large carrots, cut into big chunks

1 small onion, cut into chunks

1 celery stalk, cut into chunks

3 cloves garlic

20 sprigs parsley

Salt and freshly ground black pepper to taste

Put all of the ingredients into a large pot with about 4 to 5 cups of water. Bring the water to a boil; then reduce the heat and simmer until the vegetables are very tender (the longer the simmer time, the more flavorful the stock). Strain out and discard the vegetables; then adjust the seasonings. The stock will keep in the refrigerator about 3 days, or you can freeze it for up to 3 months.

Note In lieu of homemade stock, use a good-quality, low-sodium boxed stock.

hot and sour vegetable soup with tofu

The Hmong, who immigrated to the Midwest from Laos in the 1970s, brought with them seeds to grow searing peppers and cooling cilantro and a taste for spicy, tangy vegetable dishes like this soup. They grew these foods for themselves, then for the farmers' markets, expanding the region's flavors. This is a one-dish supper when partnered with Rich Brown Soda Bread (page 198) and Spring Greens and Strawberry Salad with Rhubarb Vinaigrette (page 124). **SERVES 4 TO 6**

6 cups chicken stock (page 10) or vegetable stock (page 110)

1 inch fresh ginger, peeled and cut into 5 slices

1 teaspoon whole black peppercorns

6 scallions, trimmed, white and light green parts only, chopped

1 cup sliced mushrooms

6 shiitake mushrooms, stemmed and sliced

1 medium sunchoke, scrubbed and cut into matchsticks

1 cup sliced sugar snap peas

2 cups fresh spinach, thinly sliced

1 (12-ounce) package silken tofu, cut into ½-inch cubes or strips

1 tablespoon rice wine, mild cider, or fruit vinegar, or to taste

2 teaspoons dark sesame oil, or to taste

2 teaspoons soy sauce, or to taste

¼ cup chopped fresh cilantro

Put the stock, ginger, peppercorns, scallions, mushrooms, sunchoke, and sugar snap peas into a big, heavy pot set over medium-high heat and bring the stock to a simmer. Cook until the vegetables are just tender, about 5 minutes. Add the spinach and tofu and cook to heat through, about 1 to 2 minutes. Season with the vinegar, sesame oil, and soy sauce and stir in the cilantro.

spring vegetable curry

This spicy, sweet stew steeped in rich coconut milk is a nice meal for transitioning into spring from late, rainy winter. Garnish it with dried cherries and dried cranberries. Serve the curry over mashed sweet potatoes, barley, or noodles, or partner it with Cracked Wheat Tabouli with Herbs (page 133). **SERVES 4**

2 tablespoons unsalted butter or vegetable oil

3 tablespoons good-quality curry powder

1 yellow onion, diced

3 ramps or 1 large leek, white part only, slit vertically and rinsed, then sliced into 1-inch pieces

1 cup diced carrots

1 cup diced potatoes

1 cup shelled peas, fresh or frozen

2 cups fresh spinach

4 cups cooked, or canned and rinsed, chickpeas

1 cup coconut milk

Juice of ½ lime, or to taste

Salt and freshly ground black pepper

½ cup chopped fresh cilantro

½ cup dried cherries, dried cranberries, or both

Heat the butter in a wok or a large skillet set over medium-high heat; then add the curry powder, onion, and ramps and stir-fry for about 1 minute. Add the carrots and potatoes, tossing to coat them; then cover the pan and steam until the vegetables release their juices and soften a little, about 1 or 2 minutes. If they begin to burn or stick, add a little water.

Stir in the peas, spinach, chickpeas, and coconut milk and cook, uncovered, until the vegetables are tender, about 2 to 3 minutes. Season the curry with lime juice, salt, and pepper to taste. Serve garnished with the chopped fresh cilantro and the dried fruit.

RAMPS

Ramps sprout through the damp forest floor as soon as the snow is but a thin crust. Often called wild leeks, these relatives of the lily are so fragrant that after a spring rain, you'll sniff them before they become apparent, right under your boots.

Ramps look like small tulips or big lily of the valley. Native Americans used them as a lifesaving source of vitamin C after a long winter and to cure coughs, colds, and bee stings. The Menominee called ramps skunk plant. Because ramps grew abundantly along the shores of Lake Michigan, they named their settlement *Shikako*, or "skunk place." This name evolved into Chicago.

If you find ramps, pick only what you will use and always leave a few plants in each patch so that you'll have more next year.

turkey cutlets with spring vegetables and tangy pan sauces

Turkey cutlets make weekday dinners quick and easy. Here, they're tossed in with lots of spring vegetables for a dinner that is ready in less than 10 minutes. This method of cooking thin pieces of meat and vegetables in a pan on the stove is simple and quick, just right for spring's delicate flavors. Vary the meat and the vegetables to suit what you have on hand. This makes a quick dinner served with the New Potato, Fiddlehead Ferns, and Arugula Salad (page 125). **SERVES 4 TO 6**

2 tablespoons unsalted butter

1½ to 2 pounds turkey cutlets, cut into
    2 × 4-inch strips

5 heads green garlic or scallions, white and
    light green part only, chopped

½ cup sliced mushrooms

2 morel mushrooms (optional)

Salt and freshly ground black pepper

½ cup chicken stock (page 10)

½ cup white wine

1 cup fresh peas

¼ cup chopped fresh chives

2 tablespoons chopped fresh parsley

Heat the butter over medium-high heat and sauté the turkey, green garlic, and mushrooms, tossing until the turkey is browned on all sides, about 2 to 4 minutes. Season the sauté with salt and pepper, add the stock and the wine, and cook for a minute or two, scrapping up any of the browned bits stuck to the bottom of the pan. Toss in the peas and cook through. Finish the dish with the chives and parsley and serve it immediately.

pork tenderloin with lemon and herbs

This is a simple dish bright with lemon and fresh spring herbs. Serve it over noodles or with new potatoes and the Simple Spring Sauté (page 132). **SERVES 4 TO 6**

1 whole pork tenderloin (1¼ to 1½ pounds)
¼ cup flour seasoned with salt and pepper
2 tablespoons unsalted butter
½ cup dry white wine
½ cup chicken stock (page 10)
2 teaspoons fresh thyme
2 teaspoons chopped chives

Juice of 1 lemon, or to taste
1 teaspoon grated lemon zest
2 tablespoons heavy cream, sour cream,
    or crème fraiche (optional)
2 tablespoons chopped parsley
Lemon wedges

Cut the pork into thin slices, about ½ inch thick, and lightly pound them between parchment paper or plastic wrap until they are not quite flat. Dip each slice of pork into the seasoned flour, shaking off the excess.

Melt the butter in a large skillet and sauté the pork until it is browned and cooked through, about 30 seconds to 1 minute per side. Remove the pork from the pan, set it on a warm plate, and tent the plate with the aluminum foil to keep the meat warm.

Deglaze the pan by pouring the wine into it and scrape up any browned bits with a fork or a spatula. Bring the wine to a boil over high heat and reduce the wine to a syrupy consistency, about 2 to 3 minutes. Add the stock, thyme, and chives and reduce the sauce again until it is thick, about 5 to 8 minutes. Season the sauce with the lemon juice and lemon zest. Stir in the cream, if using, and cook until the sauce has reached the desired consistency. Serve the sauce over the pork, garnished with the chopped parsley, with the lemon wedges on the side.

PIGS AT PLAY

"Heritage breeds like Chester Whites and Durocs are smaller and heartier than other breeds, so they can withstand our weather, and because they can stay outside in the fresh air, they don't need antibiotics," says Tom Nuessmeier, who with his brother, Tim, produces Pig in the Patch pork on a farm in Le Sueur, outside the Twin Cities. "The Berkshire is noted for high-quality, flavorful meat, with more fat and a whole lot of flavor."

"The quality of life—being outside, having room to run and play—is really important for quality meat," says Lynn Anderson of Anderson Farms in Arkansaw, Wisconsin. "It's also important that when it's time for slaughter, they are not traumatized, but handled gently and respectfully."

Tim Fischer, of Fischer Family Farms Pork in Waseca, Minnesota, supplies the Twin Cities' best restaurants. He advises not to overcook the meat. "When raised in clean conditions, not on a factory farm, pork meat does not carry diseases old cookbooks warn against. It's cooked and safe at 165 degrees. Anything close to the formerly recommended 180 dries it out."

pan-roasted lamb chops with fresh mint–cilantro chutney

Simple yet seasoned with brilliant flavors, these chops are a snap. Double the recipe for a party—just be sure to cook the lamb in batches so as not to crowd the pan. It's lovely with Pan-Roasted Radishes (page 127) and Cracked Wheat Tabouli with Herbs (page 133). **SERVES 4**

1 teaspoon ground cumin
1 teaspoon ground cardamom
1 teaspoon salt
1 teaspoon freshly ground pepper

8 (¾-inch thick) lamb rib chops (about 2 pounds), trimmed
2 tablespoons olive oil or vegetable oil
8 cloves garlic, smashed
2 lemons, cut into wedges

In a small bowl, stir together the cumin, cardamom, salt, and pepper. Rub both sides of each chop with the mixture. For extra flavor, season the chops up to a night ahead; then cover and refrigerate them.

Put 1 tablespoon of the oil in a heavy skillet over medium heat and add 4 cloves of the garlic. Cook the garlic just until it begins to turn golden. Remove and discard the garlic.

Increase the heat to medium-high, add 4 of the chops, and cook, turning once, about 6 to 8 minutes for medium rare. Transfer the lamb to a platter and cover it with foil to keep the meat warm. Repeat this process with the remaining chops, adding the rest of the oil to the pan and browning the garlic before adding the chops to the pan. Let the chops stand a few minutes before serving with the lemon wedges and Fresh Mint–Cilantro Chutney.

Fresh Mint–Cilantro Chutney
MAKES ABOUT ½ TO ⅓ CUP

1 cup cilantro leaves
1 cup mint leaves
2 to 4 small green Thai chilies, stemmed and seeded

2 to 3 tablespoons apple cider or white wine vinegar
Pinch of sugar
Salt and freshly ground black pepper

By hand, or in a food processor, chop the cilantro and mint with the chilies; then turn it into a bowl and stir in vinegar, sugar, salt, and pepper to taste.

crispy fried fish

Who needs calamari? Smelt, perch, and sunnies from our cold, clear lakes and streams fry up tender, sweet, and crisp.

Tiny fish such as smelt, crappies, and sunnies can be fried whole, after being cleaned and dressed. Don't worry about the bones; like bones in anchovies and sardines, these are barely noticeable. Walleye, catfish, and other larger fish should be boned and cut into strips. Serve them classic supper club style—in paper cones with a little apple cider vinegar or tartar sauce for dipping. Sunchoke Chips (page 131) make a perfect partner. **SERVES 4 TO 6**

2 eggs

2 cups milk

1 ½ cups fine cracker crumbs (use your favorite cracker)

1 ½ cups unbleached all-purpose flour

1 tablespoon minced fresh thyme

1 teaspoon salt

1 teaspoon finely ground pepper

About 1 ½ to 2 pounds fresh fish; cleaned if smelt, perch, or sunnies; skinned, boned, and cut into 2- to 3-inch strips if larger fish

3 to 4 cups peanut or canola oil for frying

Whisk together the eggs and milk in a low, flat bowl. In a separate bowl, stir together the cracker crumbs, flour, thyme, salt, and pepper. Working in batches, dip the fish into the egg mixture, let the excess drip off, then dredge it in the flour mixture. Coat the fish with the egg and flour mixture a second time, then transfer it to a tray lined with waxed paper.

In a deep, heavy skillet set over high heat, heat 1 inch of the oil to 350 degrees. Fry the fish in batches, being careful not to overcrowd the pan. Cook the fish, turning, until golden, about 2 to 3 minutes per batch. Return the oil to 350 degrees between batches. Drain the fish on paper towels and season it with salt and pepper.

SMELT RUN ON THE NORTH SHORE

I remember smelting as a 12-year-old. It was dark; I could smell the cold water rushing by and smell the fish as they piled up in the bucket. I could feel the icy water and the warmth of the spring air. The excitement was palpable as the nets dipped into these rivers and pulled up, in one swipe, dozens of squirmy fish.
—ANDREW SLADE, WRITER, DULUTH

Back in the 1960s and through the '70s, for a few days in the spring, the waters of Lake Superior on the North Shore literally came alive with fish and revelers. Whoever dumped smelt into the Great Lakes back in the 1910s couldn't have known that a spring ritual might be born. As the lamprey eel and commercial fishermen reduced the numbers of lake trout, the smelt had few predators and their population soared. When smelt numbers peaked, thousands could haul home buckets of fish.

Though smelting remains popular, it's no longer the carnival it once was. Smelt numbers have declined as the lake trout population has increased and Pacific salmon have become more established. Lake Superior is being restored to a more natural state, the DNR reports.

Smelt, silver-colored fish about 6 to 9 inches long, run through Lake Superior and Lake Michigan come mid-April, heading from the lakes to streams. They're light sensitive, so they tend to run in shallow water at night, hence the storied moonlit parties.

walleye meunière

Light, delicate, and slightly sweet, fresh walleye is the sole of Midwestern lakes. The French term
meunière refers to anything dusted with flour, and no doubt the technique for lightly panfrying walleye
and finishing it with brown butter trickled through the Great Lakes region via French Canada. A little
vinegar or lemon juice sparks things up.

Start off with the Minted Pea Soup (page 108) and pair the walleye with the Grilled Asparagus with
Chive Vinaigrette (page 128) and steamed new potatoes for an elegant spring meal. **SERVES 4**

1 cup unbleached all-purpose flour

2 (6-ounce) walleye fillets

Coarse salt

4 tablespoons unsalted butter

1 tablespoon chopped fresh flat-leaf parsley

1 fresh lemon, quartered, or a splash of vinegar

Spread the flour on a plate. Pat the fish dry and season it with salt. Dredge the fish in flour, shake off
the excess, and transfer it to another plate.

Heat 3 tablespoons of the butter in a 12-inch nonstick skillet over moderately high heat until it is
golden brown and fragrant. Add the parsley, shaking the skillet to distribute it, and then add the fish.
Reduce the heat to moderate and cook until the undersides are golden, about 2 minutes.

Flip the fish and cook it until it is golden and cooked through, about 2 more minutes. Be careful not to
overcook. Serve with the lemon wedges or a drizzle of vinegar.

WALLEYE, SOLE OF THE NORTH

The nation's only hook-and-line commercial walleye fishery, Red Lake Fisheries in Redby, Minnesota,
is providing a livelihood for the residents of Red Lake Indian Reservation and Redby while protecting
Upper Red Lake and Lower Red Lake. The walleye population has been growing thanks to efforts
to limit the use of commercial nets in order to prevent overfishing. Hook and line, a trickier but more
traditional fishing method, insures that fewer but larger fish are caught.

Fishing is legendary on this lake, the namesake of the Red Lake Band of Chippewa Indians. The
lake provided a ready supply of food through the year generations ago. Now it does again. Fresh
and frozen fillets can be shipped directly from Red Lake Fisheries, and they are a far better catch than
anything that comes out of Canada or environs farther away (see Sources).

oven-fried chicken

This simple preparation brings dinner to the table quickly and easily, without the fat and mess associated with classic fried chicken. It's terrific on a busy school night. The Simple Spring Sauté (page 132) is the perfect side. **SERVES 4 TO 6**

2 cups panko (Japanese bread crumbs)
Salt and freshly ground black pepper
Poultry seasoning
½ cup unsalted butter, melted

1 (3½ to 4 pound) chicken, rinsed, patted dry, and cut into serving-sized pieces (breasts cut in half)

Preheat the oven to 450 degrees. Lightly season the panko with salt, pepper, and poultry seasoning and put it on a flat plate or a pie plate. Coat each piece of chicken with a little butter and press into the crumb mixture, coating it evenly on all sides; then set it in a shallow baking dish or on a baking sheet, skin-side up.

Bake the chicken until it is well browned and cooked through, about 35 to 40 minutes. Transfer the chicken to a rack and let it stand, uncovered, for about 5 minutes to crisp.

potato and sorrel gratin

There's something old-fashioned and substantial about lemony sorrel, that slender green that resembles spinach but is longer leaved and lighter green. Terrific tossed in with spring greens and baby spinach, sorrel also imparts its subtle flavor to poached and baked fish. It has an affinity for potatoes. Be warned, though, that sorrel's pretty green goes army gray when cooked, so add a few chopped herbs (parsley or basil) to perk things up.

Make this easy gratin with buttery Yukon Gold or Yellow Finn potatoes and vary the cheese to taste. It makes a simple dinner served with the Spring Greens and Strawberry Salad with Rhubarb Vinaigrette (page 124) for a meatless spring meal. **SERVES 6 TO 8**

3 tablespoons butter, melted
25 to 30 sorrel leaves
3 pounds Yukon Gold or Yellow Finn potatoes
Salt and freshly ground black pepper
Grated nutmeg
½ cup chopped fresh parsley

1 cup milk (or half-and-half for a rich gratin)
1 cup chicken stock (page 10) or vegetable stock (page 110)
½ cup grated Pleasant Ridge Reserve (page 121) or aged Gouda cheese

Preheat the oven to 375 degrees. Butter a large gratin dish or casserole with a tablespoon of the melted butter.

Wash, stem, and coarsely chop the sorrel. Peel and thinly slice the potatoes. Layer half the potatoes in the gratin dish. Season the potatoes with salt, pepper, and nutmeg, add a layer of the chopped sorrel and parsley over the potatoes, and then layer on the remaining potatoes. Season with more salt, pepper, and nutmeg, and add enough milk and stock to almost cover the potatoes. Drizzle the surface with the remaining butter and sprinkle on the grated cheese. Bake about 1 hour or until the surface is nicely browned and the liquid is nearly absorbed. Serve garnished with more chopped fresh parsley.

UPLANDS CHEESE PLEASANT RIDGE RESERVE (AND EXTRA AGED RESERVE)

The partnership between the Gingrich and Patenaude families in Uplands Cheese Company, located in Dodgeville, Wisconsin, is flavored with great success. Mike Gingrich understood immediately that the key to good cheese is good pastures and seasonality. Having identified French Gruyère as the style best suited to his herd and the land, he makes cheese only when the pastures are in excellent condition and only through the grazing season. "We make the cheese right on the farm, starting within minutes after the last cow has been milked. This eliminates the possibility of the milk developing any off flavors. We pay meticulous attention to the traditional cultures and enzymes to be sure the cheese develops deep, complex flavor profiles."

Pleasant Ridge Reserve raw milk cheese is aged between two and five years, or longer, in rooms that replicate the temperature and humidity of France's limestone caves. The ten-pound wheels need continuous TLC, and are washed and turned daily.

Mike notes, "In this age of industrialized food production, we offer a hand-crafted cheese using ancient methods to create flavor and quality that have been compromised in the drive for mass production and labor efficiency."

showy spinach soufflé

Here's a showy dish. The transformation from flat cake batter to golden puff is magical and far easier than it looks. The real trick is in using very fresh eggs, and spring is a great time to get them from the farmers' market. As soon as it's ready, get the soufflé to the table before it deflates (along with your pride).

The local spinach just coming into market is a perfect foil to the eggs and cheese, adding color and a fresh grassy flavor. You can bake it in several individual dishes or one large dish. Make it quick. Spring's tender baby spinach is as ephemeral as this lovely, light soufflé. Pair it with Morels and Sunchokes with Toasted Hazelnuts (page 129). **SERVES 4 TO 6**

1 pound baby spinach, stems removed
½ cup chopped yellow onion
1 tablespoon water
5 tablespoons unsalted butter
4 tablespoons grated sharp cheddar cheese

¼ cup unbleached all-purpose flour
1½ cups milk
6 eggs, separated
Salt and freshly ground black pepper
Pinch of cayenne pepper

In a saucepan, combine the spinach, onion, and water. Cover the pan, place it over medium-low heat, and cook until the spinach is bright green, about 3 to 4 minutes. Drain the spinach, pressing out any liquid. Chop the spinach and set it aside.

Preheat the oven to 400 degrees. Butter a 2-quart soufflé dish or four 2-cup individual soufflé dishes. Sprinkle the insides of the dish with about 1 tablespoon of the cheese, tilting the dish to coat the bottom and sides evenly.

In a saucepan over medium heat, melt the remaining butter. When it foams, add the flour and reduce the heat to medium-low. Cook, stirring, until the mixture darkens a bit, about 3 minutes. Whisk in the milk a little at a time, whisking vigorously after each addition to prevent lumps. When all of the milk has been added, cook over low heat, still whisking, until the mixture is thick, about 1 to 2 minutes longer. Remove the pan from the heat.

In a small bowl, beat together the egg yolks, salt, black pepper, cayenne pepper, and remaining 3 tablespoons of cheese. Stir the egg mixture into the milk. Add the cooked, drained spinach and onions and stir to combine.

In a small bowl, beat the egg whites with a pinch of salt until they hold stiff peaks. Stir a couple of spoonfuls of the beaten egg whites into the spinach mixture to lighten it. Gently fold in the remaining whites. Transfer the batter to the prepared dish (or dishes).

Bake until the soufflé has risen and is browned on top, about 30 to 40 minutes or 15 to 18 minutes for individual soufflés. Use a knife to check the interior—it should be a little moist. If it looks wet, bake for another 5 minutes. Serve the soufflé immediately.

vegetable frittata with goat cheese

Frittata is just a fancy name for an oven omelet or a crustless quiche. Frittatas are easy to make—no tricky timing—and can be varied with whatever you might have on hand. Once you get the proportions down, add a range of spring vegetables, such as spinach and young greens, and your favorite cheese. The best thing about frittatas is that they can be served warm or at room temperature and can be prepared ahead. This one makes a simple supper or brunch dish. Or cut it into small wedges to serve as a snack or an appetizer. It is terrific with the Minted Pea Soup (page 108). **SERVES 4 TO 6**

2 tablespoons unsalted butter
1 small shallot, peeled and chopped
1 bunch spring onions, thinly sliced
½ pound sugar snap peas
½ pound asparagus, cut into 1-inch pieces
1 cup chopped spinach

1 dozen eggs
¼ cup chopped Italian parsley
3 tablespoons chopped fresh thyme
Salt and freshly ground black pepper
1 cup crumbled goat cheese, or shredded
    mild cheddar or Colby

Preheat the oven to 400 degrees.

Melt the butter in a large oven-proof skillet set over medium heat, and lightly sauté the shallot, onions, snap peas, asparagus, and spinach until the spinach is limp, about 1 minute; then cover the pan and continue cooking until the asparagus is just tender, another minute or so.

In a large bowl, beat the eggs, and then beat in the parsley and thyme and a little salt and pepper. Pour the eggs over the vegetables in the skillet and cook over medium-low heat until the bottom of the frittata is firm, about 10 minutes. Sprinkle the cheese on top and transfer the skillet to the oven. Bake the frittata, checking it every 5 minutes or so, until the top is no longer runny and the cheese is melted and bubbly, about 10 to 20 minutes.

DUCK EGGS

"Duck eggs are so creamy and delicious that I decided I needed my own supply," says Khaiti Kahleck of LTD Farm, located in Clayton, Wisconsin. Kahleck sells duck eggs at her farm and through her CSA. No doubt they're pricy, but they are about twice the size of chicken eggs. Duck eggs can be used interchangeably with chicken eggs: use one duck egg for every two chicken eggs called for. They taste terrific in the frittata recipe.

spring greens and strawberry salad
with rhubarb vinaigrette

Rhubarb and strawberries usually pair up in dessert, but here they are tossed in a salad. The dressing relies on rhubarb's tangy nature to take on vinegar's bite. This vibrant salad makes a nice starter to an elegant dinner of Pan-Roasted Lamb Chops with Fresh Mint–Cilantro Chutney (page 115) or a fine companion to the Showy Spinach Soufflé (page 122) for a meal. **SERVES 4 TO 6**

Vinaigrette

½ cup rhubarb, peeled and finely diced

½ cup water

¼ cup sugar, or to taste

1 shallot, diced

¼ cup fruit wine or apple cider vinegar

½ cup vegetable oil

Salt and freshly ground black pepper

Salad

¼ pound baby spinach, stemmed, rinsed, and
   dried (about 3 cups)

¼ pound baby greens or mesclun mix, rinsed
   and dried (about 3 cups)

¼ cup toasted and chopped hickory nuts,
   hazelnuts, pecans, or walnuts (page 38)

1 cup sliced fresh strawberries

Put the rhubarb and water into a small saucepan, bring the water to a simmer, and cook the rhubarb until it is tender but not soggy, about 5 minutes. Add just enough sugar to sweeten the rhubarb. Turn the rhubarb into a small bowl and allow it to cool to lukewarm. Whisk in the shallots, vinegar, and oil. Season the vinaigrette with salt and pepper to taste.

Put the greens into a large bowl and toss them with just enough rhubarb vinaigrette to coat. Top the salad with the nuts and sliced strawberries and serve it immediately.

WILD WATERCRESS

Watercress is the easiest of plants to forage. It looks exactly like the watercress you buy in the store—a tangled dark-green mat—but costs far less, perhaps only a bit of sunburn. There are no dangerous watercress look-alikes. Find watercress growing along the edges of a clean, swiftly moving stream, and snip the part of the plant that is above the water. Be sure, of course, that it is coming from unpolluted waters and soak it in clean water before eating it. Watercress is loaded with vitamin A and is a pretty good source of calcium, iron, and trace minerals as well.

If you are interested in foraging greens and other wild things, seek out Teresa Marrone's works, especially her book *Abundantly Wild: Collecting and Cooking Wild Edibles in the Upper Midwest* (see Sources). Your backyard will never look the same again. Marrone's books will guide you to foraging food in the tamest of places—corporate campuses, suburban office parks, urban playing fields. Ramps, morels, watercress, purslane, lamb's quarters, stinging nettles, and fiddleheads are all, literally, out our back doors. With her keen eye and wit, Marrone shows us how to find a free lunch.

new potato, fiddlehead ferns, and arugula salad

Use the tiny, tender new potatoes that are harvested early in the year (page 92). They range in size from as small as marbles to as big as golf balls, and they don't need to be peeled. Their flavors range, depending on the variety, from slightly sweet and nutty to tangy and celery-like. Often named for their shape and color, new potatoes put a whole new spin on classic potato recipes. Russian fingerlings (stubby, oblong yellow potatoes), Reddale (marble-sized red potatoes with pure white flesh), huckleberry (pink fleshed), French fingerling, and Nosebag (yellow flesh with rose skin) are delicious choices for this salad. It's a nice partner to the Pork Tenderloin with Lemon and Herbs (page 114) or the Walleye Meunière (page 118). **SERVES 4 TO 6**

1 pound tiny new potatoes, scrubbed and cut in half if bigger than an inch across
2 cups cleaned and trimmed fiddlehead ferns
1 tablespoon apple cider vinegar
3 tablespoons hazelnut oil or extra-virgin olive oil
1 teaspoon Dijon mustard
¼ cup chopped dill pickle
½ cup chopped parsley
1 hard-boiled egg, peeled and chopped

Put the potatoes and the ferns in a large pot and add just enough water to cover. Set the pot over high heat, bring the water to a boil, and cook until the potatoes are tender and the ferns are bright green yet still crisp, about 8 minutes. Drain the potatoes and ferns, rinse them under cold running water, and turn them into a serving bowl.

In a small bowl, whisk together the vinegar, oil, and mustard, and then stir in the pickle and parsley. Season the dressing to taste; then pour it over the potatoes and toss in the egg. Serve the salad garnished with more fresh parsley.

FIDDLEHEAD FERNS

Fiddleheads, the tiny, violin-shaped heads of the ostrich fern, are sometimes called poor man's asparagus, but that's a stretch. Among the first real green things to poke through the crusty snow-covered woods, fiddleheads must be harvested and enjoyed ASAP. Once the heads unfurl, they're bitter and tough. Their flavor is quite mossy, like the scent of the woods after a cold rain.

The first step in preparing fiddleheads is to trim the dark ends from the stems and then soak them for a few minutes in a big bowl of cold water. Swirl them around, rubbing off the thin flakes of chaff, which are tough and bitter tasting. Strain the fiddleheads in a colander, turn them onto a towel, and pat them dry, rubbing off any remaining chaff. Once cleaned, fiddleheads can be simply sautéed in olive oil or butter in a hot skillet for 3 to 4 minutes, covered, then about 3 to 4 minutes uncovered, or until tender yet crisp, and you're good to go. Some books recommend blanching fiddleheads before sautéing them, but that step is unnecessary.

SEED SAVERS EXCHANGE

The fertile soil waits, full of possibility, full of seed for a gentle rain. Those first brave blades of grass that struggle through the crust create better conditions for the next blades, for the delicate wildflower, for the seedling oaks and so on, until the earth is once again clothed in a green mantle.
—VIRGINIA GOEKE, FARMER, VIROQUA, WISCONSIN

Home gardeners may be the front line in the effort to protect our food's diversity. The most valued plants are those raised from heritage seeds, planted and collected through generations.

Heritage Farm, near Decorah, Iowa, is home to Seed Savers Exchange and its seed bank of over 25,000 endangered vegetable varieties, mostly from Europe, the Middle East, Asia, and around the world. It was founded by Diane Ott Whealy and Kent Whealy when Diane's grandfather gave them the seeds of two garden plants descended from seeds his parents had brought from Bavaria when they immigrated to Iowa in the mid-1800s. Since Seed Savers Exchange was founded in 1975, its members have distributed over 1 million samples of rare garden seeds, which are widely used by seed companies, small farmers supplying local and regional markets, chefs, home gardeners, and cooks.

Once you've planted heritage seeds and harvested a good crop, save the seeds from your favorite vegetables to plant the next year. See Sources for more information.

pan-roasted radishes

These radishes are a complete surprise. With a simple dance in the pan, radishes turn pale pink and their peppery flavors remain intact. A fabulous side dish, they're great on bruschetta, sprinkled with grated Parmesan. Enjoy them with the Oven-Fried Chicken (page 119) or the Crispy Fried Fish (page 116). **SERVES 2 TO 4**

2 tablespoons unsalted butter
1 bunch small spring radishes
4 garlic cloves, smashed

Salt and freshly ground black pepper
Parmesan or aged sharp cheese

Melt the butter in a sauté pan set over medium heat, and sauté the radishes and the garlic until the radish skins becomes slightly translucent and the radishes become tender but remain slightly crisp. Season with salt and pepper to taste. Serve the radishes garnished with the grated cheese, hot or at room temperature.

grilled asparagus with chive vinaigrette

Choose thick asparagus for grilling. The stalks will remain succulent and not overcook in the high heat. In the vinaigrette, use the fresh chives that pop up around the same time as asparagus. Serve the asparagus with Walleye Meunière (page 118) or Pork Tenderloin with Lemon and Herbs (page 114). **SERVES 4**

Asparagus

2 pounds thick asparagus, woody ends trimmed

Extra-virgin olive oil

Coarse salt

Vinaigrette

2 tablespoons raspberry vinegar or lemon juice

1 tablespoon chopped fresh chives, plus additional for garnish

1 small clove garlic, minced

½ teaspoon sugar

Salt and freshly ground black pepper

⅓ cup extra-virgin olive oil

Prepare a charcoal grill or preheat a gas grill to medium. Toss the asparagus with enough oil to coat it and sprinkle it with a little salt. Put the asparagus on the grill and cook, rolling it frequently to avoid burning, until it is brown and tender yet still slightly crisp, about 5 to 7 minutes depending on the thickness of the asparagus.

To make the vinaigrette, whisk together the vinegar, chives, garlic, sugar, and salt and pepper. Whisk in the oil in a slow, steady stream. Toss the asparagus with enough vinaigrette to coat. Garnish the asparagus with snipped chives.

morels and sunchokes with toasted hazelnuts

Sunchokes, or Jerusalem artichokes, appear around the same time as morels. If you don't have enough morels for this recipe, simply increase the amount of cultivated mushrooms. Serve this dish with the Vegetable Frittata with Goat Cheese (page 123) for an elegant brunch. **SERVES 4 TO 6**

2 tablespoons unsalted butter or hazelnut oil

1 large shallot, chopped

½ pound cremini or portabella mushrooms, stemmed, rinsed, and cut into 1-inch pieces

⅓ cup morel mushrooms, cut in half horizontally if large

¼ cup dry white wine or 2 tablespoons lemon juice

⅓ pound sunchokes, peeled and sliced into 1-inch matchsticks

Salt and freshly ground black pepper

½ cup hazelnuts, toasted and chopped (page 94)

In a large skillet, melt the butter or heat the oil over medium heat. Add the shallot and mushrooms and sauté, stirring often, for a few minutes. Cover the skillet and cook to release the mushrooms' juices, about 5 minutes. Remove the lid and cook until the juices dry; then add the wine and the sunchokes. Continue cooking, uncovered, until the sunchokes become tender, about 5 minutes. Serve topped with the nuts.

MOREL MADNESS

Look for morels when lilacs are the size of a mouse's ear, when dandelions are in full yellow bloom, when cottonwood trees begin to green, when apple trees blossom, when snakes come out of hibernation, when turtles cross the road. Look near dead elms in the deep woods or ash trees or old apple trees in abandoned orchards. They poke up through dead leaves and detritus. Seek them on a damp morning. They are light and cone shaped and honeycombed.

Morels are the result of symbiotic disruption. A suffering or dying tree stimulates the morel fungus inside the root system, causing it to withdraw. The hardened nodules, or sclerotia, form below the ground and, with enough water and light in the spring, swell to form morels. When you discover morels in the woods, here's what you do.

Cut the morels off at ground level. This protects the mycelium, allowing more morels to grow. Put them in a clean container but do not use plastic bags, as these trap moisture and heat that encourage decomposition; use paper sacks or baskets. Once home, store the mushrooms in a paper bag in the refrigerator; do not wash them until you are ready to use them.

To prepare morels, cut the mushrooms in half and then soak them in salted water for about 20 minutes to clean them and remove any insects that may hide within. Pluck the morels from the water by hand, and drain them on dish towels for at least 20 minutes.

Morels are best sautéed in butter or oil. Cook morels completely; never eat them raw. An active enzyme in morels can cause stomach pain but is made harmless when they are cooked.

Note that false morels are nasty, dangerous fungi. They are similar to morels, but their heads are misshapen, their stems are not hollow, they're solid or fibrous. False morels range in color from brown to deep rust or red. Do not eat them. When in doubt, pitch them out.

Dehydrating is the best way to preserve morels. Follow the directions for washing; then let them air-dry on dish towels. Put the morels in a dehydrator or on a cookie sheet in an oven set to the lowest heat; remove the mushrooms when they are dry and crisp. Once they are dehydrated, store them in a cool, dry place. To use the dried mushrooms, rehydrate them in hot water for at least 30 minutes before cooking; add the soaking liquid to the dish you're preparing, as it makes a very flavorful stock. If you're not heading into the woods, you'll find morels at farmers' markets and co-ops.

sunchoke chips

Crunchy and satisfying, these chips are a hit as an appetizer or served alongside grilled burgers or Crispy Fried Fish (page 116). **SERVES 4 (RECIPE IS EASILY DOUBLED)**

1 pound sunchokes, scrubbed but not peeled
Vegetable oil for frying

Coarse salt and cracked pepper

Fill a large bowl with ice water. Slice the sunchokes into thin rounds and drop them into the water to keep them from browning. Rinse and drain the sunchokes three times; then pat them very dry with paper towels.

Pour ½ inch of oil into a deep skillet. Set the pan over high heat and heat the oil until it shimmers (it should reach 375 degrees). Working in batches, fry the sunchoke slices, stirring occasionally, until they are golden brown, about 3 to 4 minutes. Using a skimmer or a slotted spoon, transfer the chips to paper towels to drain. Sprinkle them with salt and pepper. Serve the chips hot or at room temperature. They can be made about 2 hours ahead.

SUNCHOKES

Sun root is the name that early Native Americans gave to these nutty-tasting, slightly sweet tubers, which are the roots of a sunflower species. How *Jerusalem* and *artichoke* (sunchokes and Jerusalem artichokes are the same thing) came into play is anyone's guess—wind your way back to the Italians, Dutch, and French, who all had their say.

These crunchy, late-winter and early-spring roots are indigenous to our area. They store nicely. Those harvested late in the fall are available through the winter, while those left in the ground can be dug up when it thaws. The sunchokes that have wintered over are distinctly sweet. They are low in calories and a great source of iron and some protein. They may be peeled, but don't bother; just scrub them well. They are good raw for snacks and in salads. Toss them into stir-fries, soups, gratins, roasts, and sautés—anyplace you would use potatoes. Be warned, though, they do produce a fair amount of intestinal gas when eaten raw!

simple spring sauté

Just about any fresh vegetables will work splendidly in this recipe; vary them as spring blends into summer. Serve the sauté warm or at room temperature with the Pan-Roasted Lamb Chops with Fresh Mint–Cilantro Chutney (page 115) or the Potato and Sorrel Gratin (page 120). **SERVES 4**

2 tablespoons olive or hazelnut oil

1 leek or 2 ramps, white and tender green parts only, thinly sliced

5 garlic cloves, crushed

1 pound asparagus, trimmed and sliced diagonally

½ cup vegetable stock (page 110) or water

2 ounces fresh morel or other wild mushrooms, quartered

1 cup sliced sugar snap peas or shelled peas

½ cup chopped fresh mixed herbs (parsley, basil, thyme, chives, in any combination)

1 teaspoon lemon zest, or to taste

Juice of ½ to 1 lemon

Salt and freshly ground black pepper

In a large skillet set over medium heat, heat the oil and sauté the leek and garlic until the leek is soft, about 3 minutes. Add the asparagus and stock, cover the pan, and cook, tossing the vegetables. Add the morels and peas, and cook until they are just tender and the liquid has evaporated, about 2 minutes. Stir in the herbs, lemon zest, and lemon juice to taste. Season the sauté with salt and freshly ground black pepper.

cracked wheat tabouli with herbs

Cracked wheat—that is, wheat berries that have been broken into rough pieces—makes a nutritious alternative to bulgur in tabouli. Its distinctly wheaty flavor is delicious with crisp spring vegetables in a light vinaigrette. This is a great salad to make ahead. Add blanched veggies, such as asparagus and peas, and cooked chicken, turkey, or ham and call it a light meal. This is a terrific partner to the Turkey Cutlets with Spring Vegetables and Tangy Pan Sauces (page 113). **SERVES 4 TO 6**

3 cups water

1 teaspoon salt

1 cup cracked wheat

1 bunch scallions, white part only, thinly sliced

1 cup finely chopped mixed herbs (basil, cilantro, parsley, chives, in any combination)

2 tablespoons chopped fresh mint

Freshly ground black pepper and coarse salt

Vinaigrette

Juice of 2 lemons

¼ cup finely chopped mixed herbs (cilantro, mint, parsley in any combination)

1 clove garlic, minced

Pinch of sugar

⅓ cup hazelnut oil or olive oil

In a saucepan, bring the water and salt to a boil over high heat and add the cracked wheat. Reduce the heat to medium and simmer, uncovered, until tender, about 35 to 40 minutes. Drain the wheat and set it aside.

While the wheat is cooking, make the vinaigrette. In a small bowl, whisk together the lemon juice, herbs, garlic, and sugar to taste. Whisk in the oil.

In a large bowl, toss together the warm cracked wheat, the scallions, mixed herbs, and mint. Add enough vinaigrette to generously coat the salad, toss again, and season with salt and freshly ground black pepper to taste.

chocolate mousse with maple cream

―――――

Let's face it. During that muddy period of early spring, we all need chocolate. For this recipe, you'll want the best chocolate possible. Fair Trade chocolate, made from beans sourced from small, sustainable farms, is a good choice.

This elegant, easy dessert can be prepared a day or two before serving it. Serve this mousse with Maple Sugar Shortbread (page 136) or pile it into a baked Rich Tart Crust (page 207). **SERVES 6**

3 tablespoons unsalted butter

5 ounces bittersweet chocolate, chopped

3 eggs, separated

Pinch of salt

1 cup heavy cream

½ cup maple syrup

1 teaspoon vanilla

In a small saucepan set over low heat, melt the butter and chocolate together. Just before the chocolate is completely melted, remove the pan from the stove and stir briskly until the mixture is smooth.

Scrape the chocolate into a bowl and whisk in the egg yolks.

In a separate bowl, beat the egg whites with a pinch of salt until they are glossy and hold stiff peaks. In another bowl, beat the cream until it holds soft peaks, and then beat in the maple syrup and the vanilla.

Stir several tablespoons of the beaten egg whites into the chocolate; then gently but thoroughly fold in the remaining whites, alternating with ¾ of the maple cream. Turn the mousse into serving glasses or a serving bowl, top it with the remaining maple cream, and refrigerate. Garnish the mousse with a little shaved chocolate just before serving it.

MAPLE SYRUP: THE SWEET TASTE OF SPRING!

It may look like winter outside, but maple trees know when spring arrives. Their sap starts to run as the days lengthen and temperatures rise in a sweet farewell to winter. Toward the last of winter, my father would say, "One month after another gone by. Spring is near and we will get to our sweet work."
—NODINENS, MILLE LACS BAND OF OJIBWA (1910)

It's as much about the lovely sweet syrup as it is the chance to hang out all night with friends, telling stories, sipping coffee and hot toddies made with maple syrup, while stirring.
—KISHORI KOCH, AN AVID FORAGER AND COOK, ST. PAUL, MINNESOTA

Native Americans were the first to tap trees, inserting hollow reeds, letting the sap drip into troughs, and boiling it down over a wood fire. The process isn't much different today, except most people now use metal taps, plastic tubing, and buckets to catch the sap. It's still a lot of work; it takes 30 to 40 gallons of sap to make one gallon of syrup. Sugaring is worth the effort and gives us good reason to take advantage of sugar bush tours. In Minnesota alone, five state parks show people how to make their own syrup.

Maple Syrup Grades

Maple syrup is graded according to color, from light to dark. But the beauty and surprise of syrup made in small batches is that no one batch of syrup tastes the same as any other.

Grade A Fancy is light and delicately flavored with hints of vanilla; it's best served over pancakes or waffles that allow its subtle flavor to shine.

Grade A Medium Amber is a shade darker with a more pronounced maple flavor. Use it where you want that distinction to come through.

Grade A Dark Amber is hearty and robust, and assertive when used in baking. It can be smoky.

Grade B is especially good with strong-flavored foods such as winter squash, sweet potatoes, and roasted meats.

Look for syrup sold in glass containers, or bring your own to be filled. Glass is the best choice, as it will not impart any flavor to the syrup. Store unopened bottles in a cool, dark place; once opened, keep maple syrup in the refrigerator for up to six months.

When cooking, substitute an equal amount of maple syrup for the honey or corn syrup called for in a recipe. Maple sugar may be substituted for cane sugar, though its taste can be distinctive.

Here are some of the maple goods you may enjoy while turning sap into liquid gold:

Maple coffee and tea Maple sap is clear and mild and just a little sweet; syrupers use it in lieu of water to make coffee and tea as they wake and warm up for the day.

Maple whiskey As the sap boils down and starts to sweeten, it's great sipped with a shot of whiskey to chase the chills away.

Maple snow In the clean, clear woods, fresh snow, scooped up and topped with newly made syrup, beats snow cones any day.

Maple candy and maple sugar The maple crust left in the pot at the end of the syruping is the real reward for all this work. Maple candy is made by simply boiling down the syrup to reduce it into a firm state.

maple sugar shortbread

Rich, crumbly shortbread is a snap to make. Maple sugar gives it a distinct flavor, but light brown sugar will work as well. The dough comes together in seconds in a food processor and can be easily baked in a buttered tart pan before cutting it into wedges for a more traditional shortbread shape. Serve the shortbread with Strawberry Sorbet (page 139) or Chocolate Mousse with Maple Cream (page 134). **MAKES ABOUT 12 TO 16 WEDGES**

½ cup cold unsalted butter, cut into pieces
¼ cup maple sugar or light brown sugar, plus
    additional for topping
1 teaspoon vanilla

Pinch of salt
¾ cup unbleached all-purpose flour
2 tablespoons cornstarch

Preheat the oven to 350 degrees. Place a pie pan or a fluted metal tart pan in the freezer to chill while making the dough.

In a food processor fitted with a steel blade, process the butter, ¼ cup of maple sugar, vanilla, and salt until it is light, about 20 seconds. Sprinkle in the flour and cornstarch, and pulse 4 to 8 times until the dough begins to clump together.

Turn the dough into the chilled pan and press it out evenly. Sprinkle the dough with some additional maple sugar and prick the dough all over with a fork. Return the dough to the freezer and chill it for another 5 minutes.

Bake the shortbread until its edges begin to brown and the center is firm, about 25 to 30 minutes. Cool the shortbread on a wire rack for a few minutes. While the shortbread is still warm, cut it into wedges with a sharp knife. Let the shortbread cool completely before removing it from the pan.

pound cake with rhubarb-strawberry sauce

Pound cake is the first cake many bakers learn to make. It's almost foolproof and the recipe is easy to remember. Tart, assertive rhubarb sauce is delicious with the luxuriously rich old-fashioned pound cake. The trick to cooking rhubarb is to add the sugar after the rhubarb has softened in the pan. Added too soon, sugar toughens the plant. The sauce keeps nicely for several days in the fridge. The pound cake is especially good toasted. **SERVES 8 TO 10**

Pound Cake

1 cup unbleached all-purpose flour
1/8 teaspoon baking powder
3 eggs
1 cup sugar
2 teaspoons vanilla
1/8 teaspoon salt
1/4 cup heavy cream
1/2 cup unsalted butter, melted

Rhubarb-Strawberry Sauce

8 stalks rhubarb, trimmed and cut into 1/2-inch
    pieces (about 4 cups)
1/4 cup cranberry juice or apple cider
1 pint strawberries, stemmed and sliced,
    plus a few more for garnish
1 cup sugar, or to taste

Preheat the oven to 325 degrees. Butter an 8 1/2 × 4 1/2 × 2 1/2-inch loaf pan. Dust it with flour and tap out the excess.

Sift together the flour and baking powder. In a large bowl, beat together the eggs, sugar, vanilla, and salt until the batter is thick and pale, about 2 minutes. Add the flour in batches, alternating with the cream and butter, beginning and ending with the flour and mixing well after each addition. Scrape the batter into the prepared pan.

Bake the cake until the top is golden and a knife inserted into the center comes out clean, about 65 to 70 minutes. Transfer the pan to a rack to cool for 15 minutes; then remove the cake and allow it to cool completely on the rack.

To make the sauce, combine the rhubarb and juice in a pan, set it over medium heat, and cook, stirring constantly, until the rhubarb begins to soften. Stir in the strawberries and then the sugar, and continue cooking until the mixture begins to thicken, about 10 minutes. Taste the sauce and adjust the sugar. Remove the pan from the heat and allow the sauce to cool to room temperature. Slice the cake and serve it with the sauce and more berries.

once a year rhubarb pie

———

Late May and June is the best time to make this pie, a celebration of spring. Sweet and tangy, cuddled in a buttery shortbread crust, and topped with rich crumb topping, this rhubarb pie is worth the wait. **MAKES ONE 8- TO 9-INCH PIE**

1 Rich Tart Crust recipe (page 207)
1 pound rhubarb, cut into 1-inch pieces
1 tablespoon grated orange rind
½ cup sugar
2 tablespoons flour

Topping
¼ cup brown sugar
¼ cup butter
½ cup flour
½ cup toasted and chopped hickory nuts
(page 35) or pecans

Preheat the oven to 375 degrees.

Turn the chilled dough out onto a lightly floured surface. Using a lightly floured rolling pin, roll the dough out to fit an 8- or 9-inch pie pan. Gently lift the dough into the pan to line it, using your fingers to gently coax the dough to the edges of the pan and up its sides as necessary. Poke holes in the unbaked crust with a fork, cover it with a round of parchment paper or foil, and weigh it down with pie weights, dried beans, or rice. Bake the crust for about 15 minutes. Remove the crust from the oven and remove the paper or foil along with the weights. Reduce the oven to 350 degrees.

While the crust is baking, prepare the rhubarb and the topping. In a medium bowl, toss together the rhubarb, orange rind, sugar, and flour. In another bowl, use a pastry cutter, knives, or your fingers to work the brown sugar, butter, and flour into a mixture resembling small peas, and then work in the nuts.

Turn the rhubarb into the prepared crust and sprinkle the topping evenly over the top.

Bake the pie until the rhubarb is bubbly and the crust is golden brown, about 25 to 35 minutes.

strawberry sorbet

Use the tiny, wildly sweet local berries for the most robust flavor. **MAKES 1 QUART**

1 quart very fresh strawberries
Grated zest and juice of a Meyer lemon or
  a small orange

⅔ cup sugar

Rinse the berries, turn them onto a clean towel, and check them carefully, discarding any that are bruised or unripe. Remove the leaves and cores using a sharp knife or the tip of a vegetable peeler. Puree the berries in a food processor and set the puree side.

Combine the zest, juice, and sugar in a small saucepan, and set the pan over high heat. Bring the mixture to a boil, cooking and stirring until the sugar is dissolved. Set the syrup aside to cool.

Stir the syrup into the berries. Pour the mixture into an ice-cream maker and process according to the manufacturer's directions. Or, put it in a baking dish and set it in the freezer. Stir every 20 minutes until the sorbet is firm.

rhubarb lemonade

Rhubarb is loaded with vitamin C and makes an intriguing, refreshing drink. Steep it in water overnight; then sweeten it with honey or sugar to taste, and you have a refreshing elixir that will keep a week in the refrigerator. **MAKES 1 QUART**

2 pounds rhubarb

1 quart water, or enough to cover

½ to 1 cup sugar

Cut the rhubarb into 2-inch pieces and put them in a large pot or glass jug. Cover the rhubarb with the water. Let stand overnight. Strain off the liquid and discard the rhubarb. Sweeten to taste with the sugar. Serve chilled.

herbal elixirs

When your backyard herbs are at their peak, make these tonics. They are delicious additions to lemonade or plain soda water. Keep them in the fridge or freeze them in ice-cube trays to flavor drinks. **APPROXIMATELY 3 CUPS EACH**

Base In a saucepan, combine 2 cups of sugar and 2 cups of water with the herbs of your choice. Boil until the sugar has dissolved. Allow the syrup to cool; then strain it into a jar. Cover the jar and store it in the refrigerator.

Rosemary Syrup Add 3 sprigs of fresh rosemary.

Lemon Verbena Syrup Add 8 lemon verbena leaves.

Mint Syrup Add 6 sprigs of spearmint.

FRESH FARE

Fresh, crisp, light flavors and contrasting colors are dazzling in salads of crisp, bright radishes and dark, bitter watercress. Golden frittatas help bring our sleepy, winter-worn palates back to life. Young and new—field greens, tender asparagus, young lamb—are the foods we seek in spring.

LIVELY SPRING BRUNCH

Watercress Salad with a French Twist
Showy Spinach Soufflé
Pan-Roasted Radishes
Cracked Wheat Tabouli with Herbs
Pound Cake with Rhubarb-Strawberry Sauce

VEGETARIAN SUPPER
FOR A SOFT EVENING

Hot and Sour Vegetable Soup with Tofu
Spring Vegetable Curry
New Potato, Fiddlehead Ferns, and Arugula Salad
Strawberry Sorbet

APRIL SHOWER LUNCH

Rhubarb Lemonade
Minted Pea Soup
Buttermilk Scones, Sweet or Savory
Vegetable Frittata with Goat Cheese
Morels and Sunchokes with Toasted Hazelnuts
Maple Sugar Shortbread with Fresh Strawberries

GRADUATION GATHERING

Pizza with Arugula and Feta
Spring Greens and Strawberry Salad
    with Rhubarb Vinaigrette
Pork Tenderloin with Lemon and Herbs
Grilled Asparagus with Chive Vinaigrette
Potato and Sorrel Gratin
Chocolate Mousse with Maple Cream

SPRING FEAST

Sunchoke Chips
Light and Lemony Asparagus Soup
Butter Lettuce in Brown Butter Vinaigrette
Pan-Roasted Lamb Chops with Fresh
    Mint–Cilantro Chutney
Simple Spring Sauté
Once a Year Rhubarb Pie

spiced beet caviar

panzanella picnic salad

tomato, tomato, and tomato tart

watermelon gazpacho

sour cherry riesling soup

fresh tomato soup with basil ice cream

farmstand corn chowder

fresh tomato sauce for pasta

fourth of july brats

grilled tofu with spirited marinade

classic tarragon chicken salad

whole grilled whitefish or trout with warm tomato vinaigrette

planked whitefish

tomato, eggplant, zucchini, and potato bake

beer can chicken

barbecue ribs with honey jalapeño bbq sauce

pesto, presto trio

cool cucumber yogurt and mint salad

fennel kohlrabi slaw

melon, feta, and arugula salad

zucchini, summer squash, and lemon salad

grilled sweet corn with thyme butter

grilled cauliflower steaks

curried eggplant

green bean, corn, and fennel sauté

stuffed zucchini blossoms

slow-roasted tomatoes

fried green tomatoes

yogurt and crème fraiche

minted yogurt cream for summer fruit

meringue tart

upside down summer berry crisp

fresh blueberry ice cream

melon ice

zucchini spice cakes

concord grape tart

raspberry cordial

SUMMER

We've had ten days of warmer temperatures, and the crops are growing
like they have a bus to catch. It's amazing how they want to play catch-up.
The corn has tassels. Silks soon to follow. Later than last year but we'll take it
whenever it arrives. The cucumbers are plumping out; long, green, and crisp.
Melons and tomatoes are set and gaining weight like a hog at the trough.
So hang on to your bibs. The crops are coming.

—ATINA AND MARTIN DIFFLEY, FOUNDERS, GARDENS OF EAGAN, MINNESOTA

summer

DO THE BEANS TALK TO THE TOMATOES AND CORN? How is it that all of the best produce arrives at once? It's a conspiracy of ripeness. As soon as the peas are picked, the beets appear. Our midwinter dreams have become summer's dilemma, as we face mounds of glorious farmers' market produce or our burgeoning CSA boxes. Sort through the harvest, make a plan. Enjoy the ripest and most delicate things now, put some away, and then preserve the rest for a cold day.

Cooks can kick back this season, relying on crisp raw salads, light steamed and grilled foods, and cold meats, best prepared in the cool of the morning. Languid appetites need teasing forth. Icy gazpacho, cool grain salads, marinated vegetables, or freshly caught fish flipped on the grill. It's a time for picnics, barbecues, family reunions, ice-cream socials—casual, festive barefoot fare.

FIVE SUMMER DISHES IN FIVE MINUTES OR LESS

Tomato, Watermelon, and Feta Salad Chop 1 good-sized heirloom tomato and toss it with 1 cup of cubed watermelon, 1 small, mild Anaheim pepper (seeds and veins removed), a handful of chopped fresh basil, and several mint leaves. Dress the salad with extra-virgin olive oil, lime juice, salt and pepper, and 1/4 cup of crumbled feta cheese. Serve the salad on bruschetta or as a garnish for grilled chicken, fish, or steak.

Very Fresh Sweet Corn Salad Strip the kernels from freshly picked sweet corn, and toss them with chopped green onions and red bell pepper; chopped mint, basil, and parsley; and just enough heavy cream to lightly coat the salad. Season the salad with salt and pepper and a splash of vinegar or lemon juice.

Cool Fruit Soup In a blender, puree 1 cup of the berries of your choice, 1 cup of fruit juice, 1 cup of sweet wine (such as Riesling or ice wine), chopped fresh mint, and sugar or honey to taste. Serve ice cold.

Curried Melon Salad Cube a variety of fresh melons and toss it with a sprinkle of curry powder, chopped lime zest, and a little fresh lemon or lime juice. Serve the icy cold melon on dark greens as a starter salad, alongside chicken salad, or with grilled salmon.

Grilled Plums Halve the plums (or any other stone fruit), and then toss them on the grill for just a few seconds to char the fruit. Toss the grilled fruit into green salads, serve it as a side dish to meat, or slice and serve it with pound cake and whipped cream.

spiced beet caviar

Early summer beets are especially tender. For a remarkable presentation, use both gold and red beets and divide the remaining ingredients in half to create two contrasting caviars. Beet caviar is great as an appetizer served on bruschetta or as a garnish for a salad. It's a pretty side to the Beer Can Chicken (page 164). **SERVES 4 TO 6 AS AN APPETIZER OR PART OF A SALAD**

6 medium beets, 3 golden and 3 red for variation

2 large cloves garlic, unpeeled

4 whole cloves

4 allspice berries

2 large sprigs rosemary

1 tablespoon walnut oil

2 tablespoons Raspberry Vinegar (page 218) or fresh orange juice

1 teaspoon grated orange zest

Salt and freshly ground black pepper

Preheat the oven to 350 degrees. Place the beets, garlic, cloves, allspice berries, and rosemary on a large, doubled sheet of aluminum foil. Seal up the package and roast until the beets are tender, about 1½ hours.

Discard the cloves, allspice berries, and rosemary. Slip the beets from their skins. Dice the beets and garlic together (keeping the red and golden beets separated so the red beets don't bleed into the golden beets) and toss with the walnut oil, vinegar, zest, and salt and pepper to taste. Allow the salad to cool, and serve it in a pretty dish or on lettuce leaves.

panzanella picnic salad

This classic Italian bread salad makes nice use of the leftover odds and ends of good (but staling) bread. In this recipe, the bread is first crisped (like croutons), giving the dish crunch. The salad is great with cold chicken or sliced steak. Add some cubed mozzarella and call it a meal.

If you're transporting the salad, mix the croutons in just before serving so they don't get too soggy. This salad makes a wonderful partner to the Farmstand Corn Chowder (page 154). **SERVES 4 TO 6**

Croutons
3 tablespoons extra-virgin olive oil
1 (1-pound) loaf Italian bread, cut into large
    cubes (about 4 to 5 cups)
Salt

Vinaigrette
1 teaspoon Dijon mustard
1 small clove garlic, minced or crushed
2 tablespoons white wine vinegar or herb vinegar
¼ cup extra-virgin olive oil

Salad
1 red bell pepper, seeded and cut into
    1-inch pieces
1 cup cherry tomatoes, halved, or 2 medium
    tomatoes, cut into 1-inch pieces
1 cucumber, peeled, seeded, and cut into
    1-inch pieces
1 cup torn or chopped basil leaves, or to taste
Salt and freshly ground black pepper

To make the croutons, heat the oil in a large pan and add the bread cubes. Cook over medium heat, stirring frequently, until browned. Add more oil as needed and salt to taste. Set the croutons aside.

To make the vinaigrette, whisk together the mustard, garlic, and vinegar in a small bowl. Then whisk in the oil.

To complete the salad, toss the vegetables with the dressing, and then toss in the bread just before serving.

tomato, tomato, and tomato tart

Tomatoes, tomatoes, tomatoes ... We long for them in the winter, we lavish gorgeous oil on them in July, and by August, we are despairing as they race from blowsy ripeness to rot. How to enjoy the bounty? Try this gorgeous tomato tart.

The sturdy crust is loaded with nutty, flavorful Parmesan, and you can pile on any type of tomato you please. The world of heirloom tomatoes expands each year; don't hesitate to play with the different flavors and colors. Just pile them all on.

Play around with the cheese in this crust if you'd like (no need to stick to Parmesan, try an aged Gouda, Asiago, or cheddar). Baking the crust infuses the house with a lovely golden fragrance. It's the perfect foil for fresh, tangy, ripe tomatoes. The only trick is to assemble the tart right before serving (as you would a salad) so it doesn't get soggy. This makes a pretty starter to a dinner of Planked Whitefish (page 162) or a nice light lunch entrée. **MAKES ONE 9- OR 10-INCH TART OR SIX 3- OR 4-INCH TARTS**

6 perfect medium-sized heirloom tomatoes, or equivalent amount of cherry tomatoes, rinsed and sliced ⅛ to ¼ inch thick

1 teaspoon salt

½ cup unbleached all-purpose flour

½ cup whole wheat flour

½ cup chilled unsalted butter, cut into ¼-inch cubes

4 ounces Parmesan cheese, grated, plus a little more for garnish

2 tablespoons ice water

2 tablespoons extra-virgin olive or vegetable oil

¼ cup very thinly sliced basil

Salt and freshly ground black pepper

Drain the tomatoes by laying the slices on a platter or baking sheet lined with paper towels. Sprinkle the tomato slices with salt, place another layer of paper towels over the tomatoes, and press gently to absorb the moisture.

Put the flour, butter, and cheese into a food processor and cut the ingredients together by pulsing the processor, or cut the ingredients together in a medium bowl using knives or a pastry blender. Blend in the ice water to make a sticky dough. Turn the dough into a 9- to 10-inch tart pan. Working quickly, press the dough uniformly into the pan, over the bottom and up the sides to form a rim. Place the pan in the refrigerator and chill the dough for 15 minutes. Preheat the oven to 350 degrees.

Remove the tart pan from the refrigerator and poke a few holes into the dough with a fork. Cover the tart with a square of aluminum foil and fill it with pie weights or dry beans. Place the pan on a baking sheet and slide it onto the middle rack in the oven. Bake for 15 minutes, pull the crust out of the oven, and very gently peel back and remove the foil containing the weights. Place the uncovered crust back in the oven and continue baking until it is a deep golden brown, about 10 minutes. Remove the crust from the oven and sprinkle it with additional Parmesan cheese. Let the crust cool to room temperature before assembling the tart.

Just before serving, arrange the tomato slices in a concentric, overlapping pattern inside the crust. Drizzle the tomatoes with a little extra-virgin olive oil, and sprinkle on the slivered basil, salt, and freshly ground black pepper to taste. Serve immediately.

GOOD TOMATOES, WORTH THE WAIT

"Why would anyone eat tomatoes in January? They come here from China. They don't taste good. They leave an enormous carbon footprint. They're expensive. When the tomato crop is finished in October, I stop eating them so I can look forward to the next year's crop in July. When I've been waiting for them, when I'm hungry for them, they taste best."
—GREG REYNOLDS, RIVERBEND FARM, DELANO, MINNESOTA

watermelon gazpacho

Watermelon and cucumbers are a cool, refreshing combination in this icy soup for a blasting-hot day. Serve it in wine goblets with a shot of vodka for a festive summer starter. Enjoy this soup as a starter to Barbecue Ribs with Honey Jalapeño BBQ Sauce (page 166). **SERVES 4**

3 pounds watermelon, diced (about 3 cups)
1 small cucumber, peeled, seeded, and diced
1 red bell pepper, seeded, deveined, and diced
1 small jalapeño, seeded, deveined, and diced
1 shallot, diced
¼ cup finely chopped fresh mint

2 tablespoons finely chopped fresh basil
3 to 4 tablespoons fresh lemon juice
Salt and freshly ground black pepper
½ cup plain whole-milk yogurt (page 181)
   or sour cream

In a blender, puree 2 cups of the watermelon with the cucumber, bell pepper, jalapeño, shallot, mint, basil, and lemon juice. Stir in the remaining watermelon and season the soup with salt and pepper. Refrigerate the soup until it is very cold, 1 to 4 hours. Serve the soup garnished with yogurt or sour cream.

sour cherry riesling soup

Try this icy-cold soup on a hot summer night. It's not too sweet and is very light, just right for waking up sun-dazed appetites. Sour cherries are the pride of Michigan's Upper Peninsula and are in season for a fleeting two or three weeks in July. Distinctly tart and fragrant, they don't keep long and are most often sold frozen or dried. The fresh are best, of course, but the frozen work beautifully in this soup, as do the dried. Partner this soup with the Classic Tarragon Chicken Salad (page 159) on a steamy midsummer night. **SERVES 6**

2 cups dry Riesling

2 cups cherry juice

2½ pounds fresh sour cherries, pitted, or 2 pounds
    pitted frozen cherries

½ cup dried sour cherries

1 cinnamon stick

Pinch of freshly grated nutmeg

2 tablespoons honey, or to taste

¼ cup fresh orange juice

1 tablespoon cornstarch

1 tablespoon freshly grated orange zest

½ cup sour cream or plain whole-milk yogurt

Ground cardamom

In a large soup pot, mix together the wine, cherry juice, half of the fresh or frozen cherries, the dried cherries, cinnamon stick, and nutmeg and set the pot over medium-high heat. Bring the soup to a boil; then reduce it to a slow simmer and cook until the cherries are very soft, about 15 minutes. Remove the pot from the heat, and remove and discard the cinnamon stick.

In a blender or a food processor, puree the soup in batches, or use an immersion blender, until the cherries are finely chopped but retain their texture. Return the soup to the pot.

In a small bowl, whisk together the honey, orange juice, cornstarch, and orange zest to make a paste. Whisk the paste into the soup and place the pot over low heat.

Cook, stirring occasionally, until the soup begins to thicken, about 5 minutes. Stir in the remaining cherries. Transfer the soup to a bowl and allow it to cool to room temperature. Cover the bowl and refrigerate until the soup is thoroughly chilled. Chill the bowls or mugs in which you plan to serve the soup.

Ladle the soup into the bowls and top each with a dollop of sour cream and a dusting of cardamom.

SUMMER WINES

New Ulm, Minnesota, home to the state's oldest industry (brewing), is now the birthplace of an innovative, award-winning winery, Morgan Creek Vineyards. Not far from where August Schell built his brewery on the banks of the Cottonwood River, he planted vines from the Rhine valley of Germany. It is, perhaps, no surprise then that Schell's great-grandson Georg Marti established Morgan Creek Vineyards nearby. Morgan Creek Vineyards' wines have garnered medals at the International Slow Food show in San Francisco and been featured on menus at James Beard House. Morgan Creek's Riesling, Gewürztraminer, and ice wines are emblematic of their maker's German heritage and beautifully suited to Heartland climate and cuisine.

Alexis Bailly Vineyard (Hastings, Minnesota) produces a stunning ice wine, Isis, along with several table wines and award-winning ports. The vineyard's motto? "Where the Grapes suffer." Ice wines are made in the German eiswein style, where the grapes are not harvested until they are frozen. The ice is then removed, leaving behind a very sweet juice that will ferment into a wine reminiscent of ripe apricots, peaches, and honey.

Try any of the sweeter, German-style wines in the Sour Cherry Riesling Soup (page 151), and sip a little on the side.

fresh tomato soup with basil ice cream

This soup is the essence of summer tomatoes; it's ideal when you're faced with a large quantity of overripe, battered heirloom tomatoes. It is delicious warm or at room temperature and divine served icy cold with the basil ice cream. But if you're short on time, simply top the soup with sour cream or yogurt and chopped fresh herbs. Pair this soup with Grilled Cauliflower Steaks (page 174) and pasta tossed with pesto (page 167) for a festive summer meal. **SERVES 4 TO 6**

½ pound onions, chopped

¼ cup unsalted butter

2 pounds tomatoes, cored and roughly chopped

½ cup white wine, or to taste

1 tablespoon sugar, depending on the quality and freshness of the tomatoes

3 to 4 tablespoons torn basil, plus a few leaves for garnish

Salt and freshly ground black pepper

Vegetable stock (page 110) or water as needed

Heavy cream (optional)

In a large, deep pot, cook the onions in the butter over low heat until they're tender, about 5 minutes. Add the tomatoes, wine, and sugar and cook until the tomatoes are softened, about 10 minutes. Stir in the torn basil leaves. Working in batches, puree the soup in a blender (if you prefer a smooth soup, also pass it through a sieve or a food mill), or use an immersion blender, and put it back into the pot, adding vegetable stock or water if the soup seems too thick. Swirl in a little cream and serve warm, at room temperature, or chilled. It's amazing with the basil ice cream.

Basil Ice Cream

1 cup heavy cream

½ cup milk

1 cup finely chopped basil leaves

Pinch of salt

Pinch of sugar

In a medium bowl or a glass jug, mix all of the ingredients together and refrigerate for about 1 hour. Pour the mixture into an ice-cream maker and process according to the manufacturer's directions. Or, turn the mixture into a large flat dish and put it in the freezer. Stir the mixture every 20 minutes or so until it's the consistency of ice cream, about 2 hours or more. Eat it as soon as possible, as it doesn't keep long.

farmstand corn chowder

This soup is best when the corn is really, really fresh. Adding the cobs to the cooking water or broth intensifies its flavor. Serve this soup with Panzanella Picnic Salad (page 147) and Cool Cucumber Yogurt and Mint Salad (page 169) on a midsummer night. **SERVES ABOUT 6**

1 tablespoon unsalted butter
1 shallot, diced
1 stalk celery, diced
2 teaspoons chopped fresh thyme
12 to 14 ears corn, or enough to yield 8 cups
    corn kernels

6 cups corn water or vegetable stock
2 to 4 tablespoons whiskey (optional)
Salt and freshly ground black pepper
¼ cup crème fraiche (page 181) or heavy cream
Chopped chives

To remove the kernels from the cobs, lay each ear on its side and slice the kernels off with a large, sharp knife. Then stand each ear on the end and scrape it down with the back of your knife blade to remove the lovely juicy stuff that's hidden in the cobs.

To make the corn water, put the cobs in a large pot with enough water to just cover them. Bring the water to a boil, and then reduce the heat and simmer for about 15 to 20 minutes. Remove the cobs. Store any extra corn water in the refrigerator for several days or freeze it.

In a large soup pot, melt the butter and sauté the shallot, celery, and thyme until tender, about 3 minutes. Add the corn and corn water and cook until the corn is just tender. Puree the soup with an immersion blender or in a blender in batches until very smooth; then transfer it to a saucepan. Season the soup with the whiskey, salt, and freshly ground black pepper, and stir in the crème fraiche. Serve the soup warm, chilled, or at room temperature, garnished with the chives.

CORN!

"People have tried and tried, but sex is not better than sweet corn."
—HEARD ON GARRISON KEILLOR'S *A PRAIRIE HOME COMPANION*

Sweet corn, however, sure is easier to talk about. Come August, corn hangs on everyone's mind like summer haze. The yearly rite of husking ears, loosening silk, and letting the juices run free echoes ceremonies of our ancient ancestors. To the Chippewa and the Pawnee, corn was divine, notes David Shea, an environmentalist and food folklorist from Plymouth, Minnesota. "It could be eaten as fruit, vegetable, or cereal at every stage of growing."

The best corn is the freshest corn, harvested the day it's eaten. Look for farmers markets' and farmstands that sell heirloom varieties cultivated for their complex flavors, not their harvesting or storage qualities. Red, purple, and bicolor yellow-and-white varieties must be handpicked to ensure that the ears are fully mature and are not bruised or damaged in the process, as they are when harvested by machine. Some farmers grow popcorn and shockingly colored Indian corn, which they sell tied into bundles.

Most farmers dislike it when shoppers paw through ears and pull back husks that protect the kernels from drying out. "You peel it, you buy it," warns one sign at the Dane County Farmers' Market in Madison, Wisconsin.

The best way to cook corn? Get the ears from the corn patch into a pot of boiling water as quickly as possible, watch for the color to darken (about about 2 to 3 minutes after the water has return to a boil), then remove the corn. Never salt the water; it toughens the kernels. Don't add milk or sugar to the water—that's an old trick once used to revive overly mature ears.

fresh tomato sauce for pasta

This is the simplest tomato sauce, just the thing for robust, juicy garden tomatoes. Much of the tomato's flavor is in the seeds, so leave them in this rustic sauce. You can peel the tomatoes, but it's such a bother. This pasta is great paired with the Green Bean, Corn, and Fennel Sauté (page 176). **SERVES 4 TO 6**

2 pounds tomatoes

Coarse salt

2 tablespoons olive oil

3 cloves garlic, finely chopped

2 to 3 tablespoons red wine or balsamic vinegar

1 pound pasta

½ cup chopped basil

Grated Parmesan for garnish

Cut the tomatoes into chunks, toss them with a little salt, and set them in a colander to drain for about 5 minutes.

Heat the oil in a large saucepan over medium-low heat, and cook the garlic until it softens, about 2 minutes. Stir in the tomatoes and the vinegar and cook until just warmed through. Remove the pan from the heat and toss in the basil.

Cook the pasta in boiling salted water until it is tender but firm to the bite. Drain the pasta and immediately toss it into the tomatoes. Serve with a sprinkling of grated Parmesan cheese.

fourth of july brats

Sheboygan, Wisconsin, may be the official home of the brat, but every meat processor and many a farmer boasts distinctive sausages made with a variety of meat—heritage pork, turkey, beef, lamb, duck, goose, venison—seasoned with the flavors of Morocco, Asia, and South America, as well as Germany and Eastern Europe (see Sources). All are grill-worthy, but the classic brat is mildly spiced and snaps with sage-scented juice. To make the most of any brat, poach it in beer before putting it on the fire and serve it on a sturdy bun. Serve the brats with Fennel Kohlrabi Slaw (page 170) and Furious Mustard (page 219). **SERVES 4 TO 6 (EASILY DOUBLED)**

¼ cup unsalted butter

1 large yellow onion, sliced about ½ inch thick

Salt and freshly ground black pepper

1 (12-ounce) can of a beer you plan to drink with the meal

6 bratwurst

Melt the butter in a large pot over medium heat. Add the onions, toss to coat them with butter, and sprinkle them with salt and pepper. Reduce the heat, and sauté the onions until they are very soft and beginning to brown, about 15 minutes. Deglaze the pan with the beer, stirring up any of the browned bits on the bottom. Add the bratwurst and simmer (but do not boil) for about 15 minutes, or until they are nearly cooked, but still pink in the middle.

Heat the grill to about 500 degrees. If using a gas grill, turn off the center burner, arrange the brats in the middle, and turn the outer gas burners to low. On a charcoal grill, pile the hot coals in the middle and make a circle of brats along the outer edge, away from direct heat. Cover the grill and cook for 5 minutes. Turn the brats, replace the cover, and cook another 5 minutes. Then, transfer the brats back to the pot.

Serve the brats on sturdy buns with the onions and plenty of mustard.

grilled tofu with spirited marinade

Tart, salty, tangy, and just a little sweet, this marinade is also great over grilled fish. Garnish the tofu with cilantro pesto (page 168) and serve it while still hot on a bed of buckwheat noodles and dark greens (mizuna, watercress, sorrel), which you want the heat to wilt a little. **SERVES 4 TO 6**

2 (14- to 16-ounce) blocks extra-firm tofu, rinsed and drained
4 cloves garlic, minced
1 tablespoon grated fresh ginger
1 tablespoon honey or brown sugar
2 tablespoons toasted sesame oil

2 tablespoons rice or cider vinegar
¼ cup soy sauce
½ cup apple cider
Pinch of crushed red pepper
2 tablespoons whiskey (optional)

Prepare a charcoal grill for cooking over indirect heat or preheat a gas grill to medium. Cut each tofu block crosswise into 6 slices about 1½ to 2 inches thick. Arrange the sliced tofu on a layer of paper towels. Top the tofu with another layer of towels and weight it with a baking sheet to remove excess liquid, about 10 minutes.

In a large, flat bowl, whisk together the garlic, ginger, honey, sesame oil, rice vinegar, soy sauce, cider, crushed red pepper, and whiskey (if using). Set the tofu in the marinade and let it sit, turning occasionally, at least 10 minutes. Grill the tofu, carefully turning once with a spatula, until it's charred and heated through, about 6 to 7 minutes total.

While the tofu is grilling, thicken the marinade by boiling it in a saucepan until it becomes syrupy. Serve the tofu drizzled with some of the sauce and pass additional sauce on the side.

HEARTLAND TOFU

When it comes to tofu, there is an enormous difference between those made with organically raised and processed soybeans and those made with conventional products. The good news is that we're in a hotbed of organic soy. The downside is that one of the country's largest processors is in California, so our soybeans are shipped there to be processed before being shipped back here. Rosewood Tofu of Ann Arbor, Michigan, however, uses local organic soybeans in its tofu and makes its soy products with traditional methods. Its products are available throughout the region. Keep an eye out.

classic tarragon chicken salad

Tarragon and chicken are a classic duo, and this salad is a versatile standby. Serve it mounded on fresh greens or sandwiched between two thick slices of bread. Toss it with cooked or chilled pasta, or stuff it into tomatoes.

This recipe makes great use of leftover chicken or turkey, whether it's roasted, grilled, or poached. Present this on a bed of greens with warm Buttermilk Scones, Sweet or Savory (page 196) for a pretty lunch or a light dinner. **SERVES 4 TO 6**

1 tablespoon Dijon mustard
1 tablespoon vinegar or fresh lemon juice, or to taste
½ cup mayonnaise
½ cup plain whole-milk yogurt or sour cream
1 to 2 tablespoons chopped fresh tarragon

2 tablespoons chopped parsley
Milk, as needed to thin the dressing
1 pound cooked chicken meat, cut into 1-inch cubes or shredded (about 2 cups)
1 small red onion, chopped
Salt and freshly ground black pepper

In a large bowl, whisk together the mustard, vinegar, mayonnaise, yogurt, tarragon, and parsley. Thin the dressing with a little milk if it seems too thick. Add the chicken and onion and toss to coat. Salt and pepper to taste. Refrigerate the salad until you are ready to serve.

whole grilled whitefish or trout
with warm tomato vinaigrette

Shore lunch is the best way to cook fish. It goes straight off the hook into a frying pan, or roasts in the fire on the beach. But if you're not on the lake, try cooking a whole walleye, trout, or whitefish on the grill. Pair the fish with Grilled Sweet Corn with Thyme Butter (page 173) and pasta tossed with Traditional Basil Pesto (page 167). **SERVES 4**

1 whole walleye, trout, or whitefish, about 10
    to 15 inches long, cleaned
2 tablespoons butter
1 small onion, thinly sliced

2 sprigs rosemary
Salt and freshly ground black pepper
1 whole lemon, cut into wedges

Prepare a charcoal grill for medium heat or preheat a gas grill to medium.

Place the cleaned whole fish on a lightly buttered piece of aluminum foil large enough to fold over the fish several times. Fill the fish with chunks of butter, onion slices, and the rosemary sprigs. Add salt, pepper, and any other spices you like. Sprinkle the fish with a little lemon.

Wrap the fish tightly. Place the wrapped fish right on the grill and turn it every 5 minutes. Cook until the flesh is opaque and flakes easily, about 25 to 30 minutes. Be careful opening the foil. Serve the fish with Warm Tomato Vinaigrette and lemon wedges.

Warm Tomato Vinaigrette

Warming the ingredients first intensifies the tomato flavor and sweetens the shallot. This vinaigrette is great on whitefish, tilapia, and walleye. Spoon it over the fish just before serving. **MAKES ABOUT 1 CUP**

½ cup chopped fresh tomatoes
Salt and freshly ground black pepper
1 small shallot, minced

¼ cup olive oil or vegetable oil
1 tablespoon Dijon mustard
2 tablespoons red or white wine vinegar

Toss the tomatoes with a little salt and pepper and let them stand while you proceed.

In a medium skillet set over medium-high heat, sauté the shallot in the olive oil until it is translucent. Add the tomatoes with their liquid, stirring for a minute until they're warm. Turn the tomatoes into a medium bowl and whisk in the mustard and vinegar. Season with salt and pepper to taste. Spoon the vinaigrette over the cooked fish right before serving.

WISCONSIN STURGEON

The primitive sturgeon enjoys an iconic status in Wisconsin. Ron Bruch, a fisheries manager for the Wisconsin Department of Natural Resources, says, "There are hundreds, sometimes thousands of people watching the sturgeon spawn each spring." The lake sturgeon populations are on the rebound after being nearly wiped out at the turn of the twentieth century. Still, overfishing and environmental dangers threaten many sturgeon populations around the world, which explains why caviar from the Caspian Sea goes for nearly $5,000 per pound.

In Lake Winnebago, the sturgeon population has reached 40,000, equaling that of the 1800s. "Some people say they're awfully homely, awful bad looking ... but to me they are beautiful fish, just like a beautiful blonde," says 75-year-old Pat Wudtke. He has speared sturgeon for 50 years during the state's annual season in the winter on Lake Winnebago. Wudtke is among many hundreds of volunteers who protect the fish from poachers. "I'll do everything I can to preserve them."

"People love the animals because of their unique look and their size," Bruch says. "This is the only place in the world you can see them to this extent."

CARP-ING. CAN'T BEAT THEM? EAT THEM!

The common carp is a favorite of those who know their "rough fish," like Rob Buffler and Tom Dickson, authors of *Fishing for Buffalo: A Guide to the Pursuit and Cuisine of Carp, Suckers, Eelpout, Gar, and Other Rough Fish* (see Sources). These are the fish most anglers toss back, but advocates argue that these fish are not only tasty but a much better choice than many of the overfished species and those from poorly managed farms.

One solution to the surging Asian carp population is to find a use for them. Having escaped from aquaculture farms into the Illinois and Mississippi Rivers, they are threatening the native catfish. Still, the bony, oily Asian carp is a tough sell to American diners, so companies such as Big River Fish Corporation and Schafer Fisheries, both of Illinois, are shipping record tons of this carp to China.

According to Mike Schafer, owner of Schafer Fisheries, the carp have a mild flavor and are popular in Chinese markets. To appeal to American palates, Schafer Fisheries is developing a ground carp product to substitute for hamburger in tacos, chili, and other dishes.

planked whitefish

Planking, or roasting a fish on an unfinished plank, is considered the best way to cook whitefish; the subtle flavor from the wood enhances the taste of this delicate, firm fish. The original recipe dates back to the Native people who planked fish by lashing the bigger ones to wet driftwood and set it upright in the sand next to the fire on the beach, cooking the fish vertically in the heat of the flames. Today, the plank is first soaked in tap water before the fish is cooked in a hot oven or on a hot grill.

You can make your own plank by cutting a 14-inch length from an untreated cedar, maple, or oak 2 × 8, or purchase one ready to go at any number of cookware shops or gift stores (see Sources). Planked white fish is traditionally served with mashed potatoes (page 37). **SERVES 4**

1 cooking plank, soaked in hot water for about an hour

1 (3-pound) whitefish, split and backbone and head removed

¼ cup melted butter

¼ cup fresh lemon juice

Several sprigs parsley

Salt and freshly ground black pepper

Lemon wedges for garnish

Chopped fresh parsley for garnish

Preheat the oven to 400 degrees. Set a baking sheet on a low shelf to catch drips.

Place the fish skin-side down in the middle of the plank.

In a small bowl, mix together the butter and the lemon juice; then brush the fish with it. Lay the parsley sprigs on the fish. Bake, basting occasionally with the lemon butter, until the fish flakes when tested with a fork, about 20 minutes. Present the fish on the plank, garnished with lemon wedges and chopped parsley. To serve, carefully lift the fillets from the bone and divide them among four plates.

To grill whitefish, heat a grill to medium-high (the coals should be white) and set the grate about 2 to 4 inches above the coals. Place the fish on the soaked plank, brush the fish with the butter and lemon, and lay the parsley sprigs on top. Grill about 5 minutes for each half-inch thickness of fish.

GREAT LAKES FISHING

"Fishing is in the blood," says Mike Peterson of Apostle Island Fish Company in Red Cliff, Wisconsin. Peterson, like so many Great Lakes commercial fishermen, was born into this business.

Peterson and his business partner, Keith Bresette, have fished together since they were kids, learning from their fathers in a family profession that goes five generations back. "Lake Superior fish, especially whitefish, make very clean, healthy eating," he says.

Today's Lake Superior fishing industry is healthy, sustainable, and scientifically managed and strictly regulated by tribal, state, federal, and Canadian authorities. Peterson and Bresette fish throughout the year, even when the bays turn solid with ice. Then they snowmobile out to the stakes that mark their nets, pulling the catch through the holes they've chopped through to the water. Superior is the deepest and coldest of the Great Lakes, which is why its fish have very high levels of omega-3 oil. The meat of Lake Superior fish is firm and delicate, with a steely taste that comes from swimming in pure, fresh northern waters.

tomato, eggplant, zucchini, and potato bake

Easier to make than ratatouille, this simple bake makes a lovely vegetarian dinner. Use a local feta or any flavorful local cheese. The trick is to bake the gratin long enough for the vegetables to melt together in the pan. This makes a nice side dish to Grilled Tofu with Spirited Marinade (page 158). **SERVES 4 TO 6**

2 to 3 tablespoons extra-virgin olive oil

1 large heirloom tomato, cut into ¼-inch slices

2 small or 1 large zucchini, cut into ¼-inch slices

1 small eggplant, cut into ¼-inch slices

3 potatoes, sliced

1 large onion, cut into ¼-inch slices

2 cloves garlic, minced

¼ cup chopped Kalamata olives

1 cup fresh basil leaves

½ cup chopped fresh parsley

Salt and freshly ground black pepper

¼ cup crumbled feta cheese

Preheat the oven to 350 degrees. Use a little of the oil to grease a 9 × 13-inch baking dish or a 2- to 3-quart casserole dish.

Layer the tomato, zucchini, eggplant, potato, and onion slices alternately with the garlic, olives, basil, and parsley, adding a sprinkling of salt and freshly ground black pepper as you go.

Drizzle on the oil and sprinkle the cheese on top. Lightly cover the pan with aluminum foil, and bake until the vegetables are softened, about 30 minutes. Remove the foil and continue baking until the cheese is bubbly.

beer can chicken

Beer can chicken is nothing new, but this recipe has been tweaked to turn out a mahogany-skinned, soy-lacquered bird. Serve this with the Fennel Kohlrabi Slaw (page 170) or the Zucchini, Summer Squash, and Lemon Salad (page 172). **SERVES 4**

1 can beer or ginger ale
1 tablespoon honey
3 cloves garlic, crushed
1 tablespoon grated ginger
2 tablespoons soy sauce

2 tablespoons lime juice
2 tablespoons vegetable oil
1 (3½- to 4-pound) chicken, seasoned inside
    and out with salt and pepper

Open the beer can by removing the entire top with a can opener. Pour ¼ cup of beer into a mixing bowl; then drink or discard all but half of the rest (leave that in the can).

Whisk the ¼ cup of beer with the honey, garlic, ginger, soy, lime juice, and vegetable oil. Marinate the chicken in this mixture for at least 1 hour, or overnight in the refrigerator.

Prepare the grill for indirect heat or, if using a gas grill, heat it to medium. Lower the chicken over the can so that the can is inside the cavity and the chicken is upright.

Put the chicken on the cooler side of the grill, cover, and cook until the chicken is golden and the juices in the thigh meat run clear when poked with a knife, about 1½ to 1¾ hours.

When the chicken is done, carefully remove the can. Let the chicken rest for about 5 minutes before serving.

DAVE'S BREWFARM

Dave Anderson brews beer with the wind near Wilson, Wisconsin, about 60 miles east of the Twin Cities. Using the hops, herbs, and fruit he grows on his farm, and the energy generated by "Jake," the 20-kilowatt wind generator, he's creating award-winning brews in his onsite LaBrewatory. Visitors may visit the brewery and taste his latest creations, such as the seasonal Harukaze (which is Japanese for "spring wind"), an ancient gruit-style ale brewed primarily with herbs and spices that Dave describes as "refreshing, spry, and dry." Or Matacabras, a rye-tinged strong Belgian ale, which is brewed for production at Sand Creek Brewing Company in Black River Falls, Wisconsin. His BrewFarm Select golden lager is produced and canned at Steven's Point Brewery in Steven's Point, Wisconsin. Both beers are available in specialty stores throughout the area.

Perfect for Fourth of July gatherings, BrewFarm Select (BFS) is, according to Anderson, "an easy-drinkin' beer that will appeal to beer geeks and non-geeks alike. It's full-flavored and full of character, yet smooth and crisp. It comes across as a hoppy pils—medium to full-bodied, lingering bitterness, a hint of malt sweetness, but finishes dry. I envision it as a staple in many refrigerators across the region. That go-to beer before or after those triple IPAs, Russian Imperial Stouts, and other taste bud rearrangers."

Dave's BrewFarm sits atop a ridge on the rolling rural landscape, and Jake the windmill, a beacon of brewing's possible future, generates most of the farm's electricity. Geothermal and solar thermal panels supply the rest. "I don't consider myself a tree-hugger," Anderson says, "but breweries are one of the largest users of energy and water, so trying to minimize those outlays with renewable just made environmental and economic sense. This is also a demonstration project, a vision of how a sustainable business can operate."

barbecue ribs with honey jalapeño bbq sauce

This is one of those reliable recipes that doesn't require much from the cook except time. Pair these finger-licking ribs with Grilled Sweet Corn with Thyme Butter (page 173) and Real Cornbread (page 197) for a homey backyard dinner. **SERVES 4 TO 6**

3 racks baby back pork ribs (about 3 pounds total); do not cut apart

2 large onions, peeled and cut into ½-inch rings

2 (12-ounce) bottles beer

Salt and freshly ground black pepper

1 cup Honey Jalapeño BBQ Sauce (page 216)

Preheat the oven to 325 degrees. Put the baby back ribs into a deep roasting pan, layer the slabs with the onions, add the beer, and sprinkle lightly with salt and pepper. Cover the pan with aluminum foil and bake until the meat becomes tender, about 1½ hours. Remove the foil and continue baking, brushing with the sauce every 20 minutes or so until the meat is very tender.

Remove the ribs from the oven. Prepare a charcoal grill, preheat a gas grill, or light the broiler. Arrange the ribs on the grill or a broiler pan and brush them liberally with the sauce. Cook until the sauce is bubbling.

PORK RIBS

Spareribs come from the pig's belly, right next to the area used for bacon. The ribs are sold in slabs, or racks, of about 13 bones each; the smaller the slab, the more tender the meat.

Baby back ribs are smaller, tapered bones from the blade and center section of the pork loin (the back of the hog). They're more tender but less flavorful than spareribs, and they cook more quickly.

Country-style ribs are found near the baby back ribs but farther forward, right behind the shoulder. The meatiest of the ribs, they're sold individually, not in racks, more like chops.

No matter which ribs you choose, know that buying heritage pork makes a tremendous difference in flavor (page 114).

pesto, presto trio

Pesto *is the Italian word for a pounded sauce made with herbs and oil. It's fresh, it's fast, and it makes delicious use of too many backyard herbs. Think beyond basil and pound out fabulous pestos of parsley, mint, cilantro; all are great tossed with pasta, on top of pizza, or with grilled meat and fish. Stir pesto into mayonnaise for a swell sandwich condiment or shake it into a vinaigrette.*

Note While pounding herbs by hand releases their aromatic oils, along with pent-up tension, a food-processor will speed the process without compromising the flavor. Just be careful not to overprocess. It's nice to have a rough, rustic texture.

Traditional Basil Pesto

Make this pesto thick or thin it to taste. It's great on sliced tomatoes or tossed with pasta, and wonderful slathered on bruschetta. **MAKES ABOUT 1 CUP**

2 cups fresh basil leaves

1 to 2 cloves garlic, crushed

2 tablespoons toasted pine nuts or walnuts

½ cup good-quality extra-virgin olive oil

Salt and freshly ground black pepper

¼ to ½ cup freshly grated Parmesan cheese (optional)

Salt and freshly ground black pepper

Put the basil, garlic, nuts, and about half of the oil in a food processor or a blender and whir until you have a thick paste. Thin with the remaining oil to the desired consistency. Just before using, stir in the Parmesan by hand.

To make this by hand, put the basil, garlic, and nuts into a mortar and pound into a paste, adding oil until you have the desired consistency. Add salt and pepper to taste. Just before using the pesto, stir in the Parmesan.

Note This pesto will keep up to 3 days in the refrigerator, or it can be frozen.

Parsley and Walnut Pesto

This pesto is lovely on broiled chicken, fish, burgers, and steak. Try it tossed with grilled mushrooms or swirl it into chilled tomato soup. **MAKES ABOUT 1 CUP**

2 cups parsley leaves

1 clove garlic, crushed

Zest and juice of 1 medium lemon

¼ cup lightly toasted walnuts

¾ cup extra-virgin olive oil

Salt and freshly ground black pepper

Put the parsley, garlic, zest, lemon juice, and nuts along with half the oil into a food processor or a blender. Blend into a thick paste, and add additional oil to reach the consistency desired.

To make this pesto by hand, put the parsley and garlic into a mortar and then pound in the lemon zest and juice along with the nuts. Slowly pound in the oil until you reach the consistency desired. Add salt and pepper to taste.

Note This pesto will keep in the refrigerator for about 5 to 7 days covered with a thin layer of oil and plastic wrap. It also freezes beautifully.

Cilantro, Mint, and Cashew Pesto

Cilantro pesto is terrific on grilled fish or tossed with buckwheat (soba) noodles.
MAKES ABOUT ½ TO ¾ CUP

1 cup fresh cilantro leaves
¼ cup fresh mint leaves
1 clove garlic, crushed
¼ cup unsalted cashews, chopped

1 tablespoon lime juice, or to taste
¼ cup vegetable oil, or more as needed
Salt and freshly ground black pepper

Put the cilantro, mint, garlic, cashews, lime juice, and about half of the oil into a food processor or a blender. Blend into a thick paste, and add additional oil to reach the consistency desired. Add salt and pepper to taste.

To make this pesto by hand, put the cilantro, mint, garlic, cashews, and lime juice into a mortar and pound into a paste. Slowly add the oil, pounding as you go. Taste and adjust the seasoning.

Note Use this pesto immediately; it doesn't keep more than one or two days.

cool cucumber yogurt and mint salad

This is so easy to make that it hardly needs a recipe. It's just the kind of effortless salad you want for a blasting-hot day. Vary the herbs depending on what you have in the garden and what you like. It's terrific on lamb or alongside grilled trout (page 160) or Classic Tarragon Chicken Salad (page 159). **SERVES 4**

1 pound cucumbers
½ cup plain whole-milk yogurt, preferably
 strained or Greek-style yogurt
1 clove garlic, minced

2 tablespoons chopped fresh mint, or to taste
1 tablespoon chopped fresh basil, or to taste
Salt and freshly ground black pepper
Pinch of sugar (optional)

Peel, seed, and thinly slice the cucumbers. Put them in a colander to drain, about 10 minutes. Whisk together the yogurt, garlic, mint, and basil. Turn the cucumbers into a large bowl, toss in the yogurt, and season with salt, pepper, and sugar to taste. Serve the salad right away.

fennel kohlrabi slaw

Fennel has the texture of celery and a mild anise flavor. Here it pairs with assertive kohlrabi in a refreshing salad that keeps beautifully. Serve it with the Barbecue Ribs with Honey Jalapeño BBQ Sauce (page 166) or Beer Can Chicken (page 164). Substitute red cabbage for the kohlrabi, if you prefer. **SERVES 4 TO 6**

1 medium kohlrabi

1 medium fennel bulb

2 carrots, scrubbed

1 bunch scallions, white parts only

1 tablespoon capers

Juice of 1 large lemon

1 teaspoon whole-grain mustard

2 to 4 tablespoons extra-virgin olive oil

Salt and freshly ground black pepper

Thinly slice the kohlrabi, fennel bulb, and carrots, and chop the scallions. Put the vegetables into a large bowl with the capers.

In a small bowl, whisk together the lemon juice, mustard, and enough oil to make an emulsion. Season the dressing with salt and pepper to taste, and add more oil if necessary. Lightly dress the vegetables, cover the bowl, and allow to stand a few minutes before serving.

This salad can be made a day ahead and kept in the refrigerator.

melon, feta, and arugula salad

Sweet melon and peppery arugula partner beautifully in this salad. It makes a wonderful side to Barbeque Ribs with Honey Jalapeño BBQ Sauce (page 166) or Grilled Tofu with Spirited Marinade (page 158). **SERVES 4**

2 tablespoon raspberry vinegar (page 218)
    or lemon juice
2 tablespoons olive oil
Pinch of sugar
Pinch of crushed red pepper

1 small ripe melon, such as cantaloupe, honeydew, or watermelon, quartered, seeded, and cut into 2-inch chunks (about 4 cups)
Large bunch of arugula
1 red onion, thinly sliced
Salt and freshly ground black pepper
4 ounces feta cheese, crumbled (optional)

In a large bowl, whisk together the vinegar and olive oil with sugar and crushed red pepper to taste. Add the melon and toss to lightly coat it with the dressing. Arrange the arugula on a platter with the onions. Arrange the melon over the arugula and onions, season to taste with salt and freshly ground black pepper, and scatter the cheese, if using, over the salad.

GROWING POWER

Will Allen, founder of Growing Power and recipient of a prestigious fellowship, or "genius grant," from the John D. and Catherine T. MacArthur Foundation, believes that to grow good food one needs good soil. In his work creating urban gardens in abandoned areas, he and Growing Power activists create new vegetable beds by laying down several feet of nutrient-rich compost created through vermiculture (raising worms). Discarded and spoiled vegetables from warehouses and grocery stores provide the material for the compost. The worm castings are sifted, bagged, and sold as fertilizer.

Allen, in his 60s and a six-foot-seven former college and pro basketball hero, is introducing Growing Power and its composting system to urban communities throughout the United States. Growing Power's Milwaukee headquarters is just two acres, but has six greenhouses; eight hoop houses (for herbs, vegetables, and greens); pens for goats, ducks, chickens, and turkeys; beehives; and a system for raising tilapia and perch. There's more. Allen and his team hope to create a learning center in a five-story building that uses renewable energy.

Growing Power provides good food such as microgreens, herbs, edible flowers, and heirloom tomatoes, but it also brings people in the community together for a common purpose. The organization is run by community residents who understand their area's needs. Growing Power includes a 40-acre farm outside Milwaukee and gardens in neighborhoods throughout the city. In Chicago, there is a garden at the Cabrini Green housing project and farms in Grant and Jackson Parks. In Minneapolis, the Little Earth Native American housing project garden provides traditional herbs, plus squash, corn, and beans to residents at affordable prices.

Allen contends that instead of talking about the problems with our food system, we ought to be out in our backyards and in urban community gardens. By growing good food and sharing it with everyone, we may be able to grow change.

zucchini, summer squash, and lemon salad

This pretty, pale green-and-yellow salad is light and fresh, the essence of summer. It's wonderful with pasta tossed with any of the pestos (page 167) or with the Tomato, Tomato, and Tomato Tart (page 148). **SERVES 4**

2 zucchini

2 yellow summer squash

Grated zest and juice of 1 lemon

2 tablespoons olive oil

2 tablespoons chopped savory

Pinch of sugar

Salt and freshly ground black pepper

Using a potato peeler, cut the zucchini and yellow squash very thin lengthwise, and put the slices in a shallow dish. Sprinkle the grated lemon zest over them.

In a small bowl, whisk together the lemon juice, olive oil, savory, sugar, and salt and pepper. Pour the dressing over the zucchini and yellow squash and toss gently.

GREAT ZUKES!

No doubt, zucchini grows like a weed in our Northern Heartland gardens, but some varieties are better suited to our extreme summers, whose temperatures swing from bouts of 100-degree heat to weeks of cool, damp rain.

Eight Ball, a tasty new zucchini variety, is the easiest to grow. It can be seeded directly in the ground and takes about 50 days to mature. It's hardy and cold tolerant, and less likely to succumb to mold. The fruit is just a little sweet and firm, not as mushy or soft as others. It's best harvested when the fruit is about 3 inches across (like a billiard ball, hence the name). If they get away from you before harvest (leaving you a vine full of softballs instead of eight balls), just scoop out and discard the seeds and innards and proceed with your recipe. Their shape makes them perfect for stuffing. They make wonderful pickles too.

Also look for heirloom varieties such as Costata Romanesco, a distinctive Italian variety that is pale gray-green with green flecks and prominent ribs. Its firm, dense flesh is nutty and delicious raw or cooked.

grilled sweet corn with thyme butter

Grilling corn caramelizes its sugars and intensifies its flavor. Corn has an affinity for fresh thyme. Pair the grilled corn with the Tomato, Tomato, and Tomato Tart (page 148) and pasta tossed with Traditional Basil Pesto (page 167) or with the Fourth of July Brats (page 157).

SERVES 4 (EASILY DOUBLED)

4 ears corn

4 tablespoons unsalted butter, softened

2 teaspoons finely minced fresh thyme leaves

2 teaspoons lemon juice

Lemon zest to taste

Salt and freshly ground black pepper

Chopped fresh basil

Prepare a moderately hot charcoal fire or preheat a gas grill to medium-high.

Peel back the cornhusks without removing them; then pull out and discard the silk. Replace the husks and twist the tops closed. Soak the corn in cold water for about 20 minutes. Meanwhile, smash together the butter, thyme, lemon juice, and lemon zest in a small bowl.

Place the corn over the coals or flames, cover the grill, and roast, turning the ears about every 5 minutes, until the husks are brown and the corn kernels seem tender, about 15 minutes.

Strip the husks and slather the corn with the thyme butter, season with salt and pepper, and sprinkle on the basil. Serve right away.

Note Grill several extra ears of corn to use in a corn salad the next day. Remove the kernels from the cobs, and toss them with chopped tomatoes, diced onions, cooked green beans (or whatever you have on hand), a little extra-virgin olive oil, fresh lemon or lime juice, fresh thyme, a little fresh mint, and salt and pepper to taste. Serve well chilled.

grilled cauliflower steaks

Cut the cauliflower into thick steaks by slicing from the top to the bottom near the center so that the florets are held together by the core. Serve cauliflower steaks with pasta tossed with any of the pestos (page 167) or with Curried Eggplant (page 175) and toasted pita bread. **SERVES 4**

2 to 3 medium heads cauliflower

Extra-virgin olive oil

Coarse salt

Chopped cilantro

Lemon wedges

Prepare a moderate charcoal fire for indirect grilling or preheat a gas grill to medium.

Trim each cauliflower, removing any leaves and cutting the stem flush with the base. Set a cauliflower upright on a cutting board and cut two to three 1-inch "steaks" from the center of each cauliflower. The core will hold the florets together. Repeat with each cauliflower. Save the outer parts of the heads and any florets you lose in the process to toss into salads and sautés.

Brush the cauliflower with oil and season it with coarse salt. Place the steaks on the grill and cook, turning once, until they are charred and tender when pierced with a knife, about 15 minutes.

Transfer the grilled cauliflower to a platter and serve it garnished with chopped cilantro and lemon wedges.

curried eggplant

Curried eggplant is a simple, satisfying, and low-fat dish. It is like baba ghanoush and can be served as a side dish, as a dip, or as a filling for pita bread. Serve it alongside Grilled Tofu with Spirited Marinade (page 158) or Whole Grilled Whitefish or Trout with Warm Tomato Vinaigrette (page 160). **SERVES 4 TO 6**

2 to 3 eggplants (about 2½ to 3 pounds total)
3 tablespoons extra-virgin olive oil
2 cups chopped onions
3 cloves garlic, crushed
3 tablespoons grated fresh ginger, or to taste
1 to 2 tablespoons good-quality curry powder

Pinch of cayenne pepper
Salt and freshly ground black pepper
Lime juice
2 medium tomatoes, chopped
¼ cup chopped fresh cilantro
½ cup plain whole-milk yogurt, or to taste

Preheat the oven to 400 degrees. Prick the eggplants with a fork, place them on a baking sheet, and roast until tender, about 30 to 40 minutes. Allow the eggplants to cool. Cut the eggplants in half, remove the flesh to a bowl, and mash it with a fork.

Heat the oil in a medium skillet over medium heat. Sauté the onions until they are translucent, about 10 minutes; then add the garlic, ginger, curry powder, and cayenne pepper and continue cooking about 5 more minutes. Add the eggplant and season it with salt, pepper, and lime juice to taste. Stir in the chopped tomatoes and cilantro. Turn off the heat and add yogurt to taste. Serve the eggplant garnished with additional cilantro and a little more yogurt on the side.

CONSIDERING EGGPLANT

Like tomatoes, eggplants appear in early August in a stunning array of colors, shapes, and sizes: scarlet Rosita, streaked Sicilian zebra, pure white Casper, skinny lavender Farmers' Long, pretty Rosa Biancas, purple-and-white striped Purple Rain, short Japanese and egg-shaped Indian eggplants, and those wacky Hmong purple-and-yellow baseball-size and green marble-size eggplants. Whether hybrids or heirlooms, these eggplants are beautiful enough to set out on a table as a display. Because farmers' market eggplant is fresh and hasn't been stored or subjected to the cold, it's not bitter or tough.

green bean, corn, and fennel sauté

Serve this sauté as a side dish or toss it with wild rice. It's great hot or at room temperature and will keep several days in the refrigerator. Pair it with Beer Can Chicken (page 164) or, for a vegetarian dinner, the Tomato, Eggplant, Zucchini, and Potato Bake (page 163). **SERVES 4 TO 6**

3 tablespoons vegetable oil or hazelnut oil

1 large shallot, chopped

1 fennel bulb, diced

1 pound green beans, ends snapped, cut into
    1-inch pieces

1 cup fresh corn kernels

1 tablespoon fresh thyme

1 teaspoon chopped fresh mint

2 tablespoons chopped fresh parsley

2 to 4 tablespoons cider vinegar or lime juice

Salt and freshly ground black pepper

Heat the oil in a large skillet, add the shallot and fennel, and cook until soft, about 3 minutes. Add the green beans and corn and just enough water to cover the bottom of the pan; then shake the pan to coat the vegetables. Cover the pan, reduce the heat to low, and cook until the beans are tender, about 10 minutes. Toss in the thyme, mint, and parsley, remove the pan from the heat, and season with vinegar, salt, and pepper to taste. Serve warm or at room temperature.

stuffed zucchini blossoms

Our gardens are often overrun by zucchini; if you pick the female blossoms, this recipe makes great use of the tender blossoms while eliminating some potential baseball bats. Don't let the idea of frying dissuade you. These are far easier, and way faster, to make than you might think. They make a lovely side to Whole Grilled Whitefish or Trout with Warm Tomato Vinaigrette (page 160) or a festive appetizer. **SERVES 4 TO 6**

Batter
¾ cup unbleached all-purpose flour
Salt and freshly ground black pepper
1 egg
¾ cup cold beer
Flowers
8 to 10 zucchini or summer squash blossoms
4 ounces ricotta

1 ounce shredded Parmesan
2 tablespoons chopped chives
1 tablespoon chopped fresh parsley
2 tablespoons chopped fresh basil
Grating of nutmeg
Salt and freshly ground black pepper
Oil for frying

In a medium bowl, stir together the flour with a little salt and pepper. Make a well in the center and add the egg; then whisk in the beer to make a batter the consistency of heavy cream. Refrigerate the batter until you're ready to use it.

Remove the stigma from the center of the blossoms (along with any bugs). In a small bowl, mix together the ricotta, Parmesan, chives, parsley, and basil, and season the filling with nutmeg, salt, and pepper to taste.

With your fingers, gently open the blossom, leaving one finger inside to hold it open. Gently stuff the blossom with a teaspoon of the filling, and then seal it with a little twist.

Pour about 4 inches of oil into a deep skillet and heat it until it reaches about 325 degrees (or until a cube of bread dropped into the oil turns golden brown in less than a minute). Dip each stuffed blossom into the batter and fry it in the hot oil, being careful not to crowd the skillet. Turn the blossoms occasionally (about every 30 seconds) until they're golden, about 2 to 4 minutes. Remove the blossoms from the oil and drain them on paper towels. Sprinkle with salt and freshly ground black pepper and serve immediately.

GARDENS OF EAGAN

Exemplary organic vegetable farmers and innovative marketers, Martin and Atina Diffley are pioneers in the organic movement. Gardens of Eagan, in Farmington, Minnesota, is one of the oldest certified organic operations in the United States, having first been certified in 1975. It is one of the few farms in the region to survive devastating urban sprawl. Before purchasing their own land, they leased a fifth-generation Eagan farm from Martin's family, which was later sold to a developer of suburban houses. They then farmed twelve different locations within a thirty-mile radius while their own newly purchased land completed the transition process to qualify for certification. The 140 acres is now certified organic by International Certification Services.

Vivacious advocates for organic methods, the Diffleys have promoted awareness of land preservation in urban areas, created a documentary, *Turn Here Sweet Corn*, and published widely. They were instrumental in establishing organic standards in Minnesota and nationally. They've helped launch fledgling organic farmers through their on-farm intern program, the first in the Midwest.

In 2001 the Diffleys sold Gardens of Eagan to the Wedge Natural Foods Co-op in Minneapolis. They continue to live on the property and consult widely throughout the country.

slow-roasted tomatoes

This is a great way to save the last of summer's tomatoes before the frost. Make a big batch for the freezer, and when the first snow hits, you can add summer's bright flavor to soups and stews. Serve these tomatoes on top of grilled steak or chicken, or toss them with pasta sprinkled with cheese. They're terrific on sandwiches, bruschetta, and pizza. **MAKES ABOUT 2 CUPS**

4 pounds ripe tomatoes (use a mix of cherry, plum, and slicing tomatoes)

1 to 2 tablespoons olive oil

1 teaspoon sugar

Coarse salt

Freshly ground black pepper

Preheat the oven to 350 degrees. Cut the tomatoes so that all are in ½-inch pieces and turn them into a large bowl. Coat the tomatoes with the oil, and sprinkle them with the sugar, salt, and black pepper. Spread out the tomatoes on a baking sheet, and roast until most of the tomatoes' liquid has evaporated and they have begun to brown, about 2 to 2½ hours. Remove the pan from the oven and cool to room temperature. Store the roasted tomatoes in a covered container in the refrigerator for about a week, or freeze them.

GARLIC—A ROSE BY ANY OTHER NAME

Silver Rose garlic is very pretty and smells great. The succulent cloves have a warm flavor. It can be chopped into salsa and tastes fresh even when cooked, yet it is mild enough not to dominate a dish. Use it raw in salads and dressings; flash it in stir-fries and sautés. It is great roasted.

Find Silver Rose garlic at farmers' markets or grow your own—it's not hard. Plant individual cloves as you would flower bulbs, in a sunny spot, and next summer you will have your own garlic to harvest. Silver Rose is a softneck variety that is pretty when braided and hung.

fried green tomatoes

A tad messy, but well worth the effort, these tangy nibbles are best eaten right out of the pan. Serve them for appetizers with beer or chilled wine; pair them with the Tomato, Tomato, and Tomato Tart (page 148) for fun. **SERVES 4 TO 6**

3 medium green tomatoes
Salt and freshly ground black pepper
¼ cup milk
½ cup unbleached all-purpose flour

2 eggs, lightly beaten
⅔ cup cornmeal
¼ cup vegetable oil

Cut the tomatoes into ½-inch slices and sprinkle them with salt and pepper. Place the milk, flour, eggs, and cornmeal in separate low-sided dishes. Film a skillet with about 2 tablespoons of the oil and set it over medium heat. Dip the tomato slices first in the milk, then the flour, then the eggs, then the cornmeal. Fry half of the coated tomato slices at a time until they are brown, flipping once, about 4 to 6 minutes per side. Repeat with the remaining tomato slices, adding more oil to the skillet as necessary. Season with additional salt and pepper before serving.

VICTORY GARDEN

The Dowling Community Garden, in Minneapolis, is one of two remaining victory gardens established in the mid-1940s in the United States to support the war effort. (The other is the Fenway Garden in Boston.) Rose Hayden-Smith, a historian and Food and Society Fellow at the Institute for Agriculture and Trade Policy, headquartered in Minneapolis, says, "The victory garden program, run through the Department of Education and the War Department, was designed to save fuel, improve family nutrition, and secure food safety." Today, Dowling serves more than two hundred gardeners. The old victory garden mission is still remarkably relevant.

yogurt and crème fraiche

───

It is especially easy to make yogurt and crème fraiche using fresh, local, organic milk. Because they don't contain commercial stabilizers or thickeners, they are naturally tangy, clean tasting, and refreshing.

Yogurt

Delicious in smoothies, on top of berries, or mixed with granola, this will keep a week in the refrigerator. Save a little to start the next batch. Use unhomogenized, organic whole milk for the creamiest, smoothest yogurt. **MAKES 1 QUART**

1 quart milk

½ cup plain organic whole-milk yogurt that does not contain sugar or stabilizers

In a large saucepan, heat the milk to 180 to 190 degrees (it will be steaming). Pull it from the stove just as bubbles are beginning to form. Allow it to cool to about 115 or 120 degrees (it will still be very warm). Remove ½ cup of milk from the pot, stir the yogurt into it, and return it to the steamed milk.

Put the milk into a warm jar or several containers, cover, and keep the milk still and warm until it sets, usually about 4 to 6 hours. You can set it on top of a refrigerator, on the back of the stove, or wrap it with several kitchen towels. Once the yogurt sets, refrigerate it so that it becomes firm. It will keep in the refrigerator 5 to 7 days.

Crème Fraiche

This lush, tangy cream is milder than sour cream and wonderful spooned over fresh berries or folded into whipped cream to top shortcakes. Use it in place of sour cream when making dips or thickening sauces. Be sure you do not use ultra-pasteurized heavy cream; unhomogenized organic cream works best. **MAKES 1 PINT**

1 pint heavy cream

¼ cup buttermilk

In a medium saucepan, heat the cream to between 180 and 190 degrees (it will be steaming). Pull it from the stove just as bubbles are beginning to form. Allow it to cool to about 115 degrees. Stir in the buttermilk and transfer to a clean glass jug. Set in a warm spot—on top of the refrigerator, on the back of the stove—or wrap it with several kitchen towels. Once it has set, store it in the refrigerator. It will keep in the refrigerator for 5 to 7 days.

minted yogurt cream for summer fruit

Minted yogurt cream is wonderful on any summer fruit as well as on the Meringue Tart (page 183). Try this on blueberries, raspberries, black raspberries, or a mix of all of them. **MAKES 2 CUPS**

¼ cup sugar

⅓ cup shredded mint leaves

¼ cup water

1½ cups yogurt, preferably plain whole-milk yogurt

½ cup heavy cream

Place the sugar, mint, and water in a small saucepan, set it over medium heat, and simmer, stirring occasionally, until the sugar has dissolved. Reduce the heat to low and continue cooking until you have a thick syrup. Cool the syrup and strain out the mint.

Stir the mint syrup into the yogurt. Whip the cream in a small bowl until soft peaks form. Fold the whipped cream into the yogurt. Chill well before serving over sliced fruit or berries.

KIWIFRUIT?

Cold-hardy fruit advocate, geologist, and environmental scientist Bob Guthrie has devoted the past two decades to cultivating kiwi vines able to withstand our long, cold, and unpredictable winters. Working with Jim Luby, fruit-breeding professor at the University of Minnesota, Guthrie has crossed different kiwifruit species that don't look much like the fuzzy brown-coated, green-fleshed fruits we know. These are grape-sized, fuzz-free varietals with smooth skins that turn from green to orange or red and purple as they ripen. They're sweeter than the big kiwis and can be dried, like raisins, and made into a sweet wine. It will be a while before cooks can get their hands on the new fruit unless they grow them themselves. Linder's Nursery (St. Paul), among others, will be carrying vines in the near future. The University of Minnesota has in-depth information on its Web site about growing kiwifruit at home (see Sources).

meringue tart

Fill this lovely light meringue shell with just about anything you dream up—fresh fruit and whipped cream, ice cream and chocolate sauce. It's great with the Minted Yogurt Cream (page 182) and fresh fruit. The Germans called it Schaum Torte, and the Australians know it as Pavlova. **SERVES 4 TO 6**

4 egg whites

1 cup superfine sugar

1 teaspoon strawberry vinegar or fresh lemon juice

½ teaspoon vanilla

Preheat the oven to 300 degrees. Line a baking sheet with parchment paper.

Beat the egg whites, adding in the sugar a tablespoon at a time. When the whites begin to stiffen, beat in the vinegar and vanilla. Continue beating until the egg whites are very stiff. Mound the egg whites onto the parchment paper and spread it into a 2-inch-thick circle.

Reduce the oven temperature to 275 degrees. Bake the tart in the middle of the oven until it is slightly browned and crisp, about 1 hour. Remove the tart from the oven, gently invert it on a plate, peel off the paper, and then turn the tart right-side up. Allow it to cool before filling.

upside down summer berry crisp

The "crisp" layer is baked first, then topped with the berries as it comes hot from the oven. The heat from the crisp softens the berries and releases their juices. Because the berries do not cook through, they retain their fresh texture and taste. Serve the upside down crisp with Spirited Whipped Cream (page 46) or Minted Yogurt Cream (page 182) or top it with Fresh Blueberry Ice Cream (page 186). **MAKES A 9 × 9-INCH CRISP**

1 stick unsalted butter, softened
1 cup confectioners sugar
1 cup unbleached all-purpose flour

2 pints mixed raspberries and blackberries
2 tablespoons lemon juice
2 teaspoons honey

Preheat the oven to 350 degrees. Lightly grease a 9 × 9-inch pan or a 2-quart casserole or baking dish. In a medium bowl, work together the butter, sugar, and flour to make a crumbly dough. Pat it evenly over the prepared pan. Bake until golden brown, about 15 to 20 minutes.

While the "crisp" is baking, toss the berries with the lemon juice and honey.

Remove the pan from the oven and scatter the berries with any juices they have released evenly over the hot crisp. Enjoy right away.

WILD BERRY LOVE

Here's a guide to picking the jewels of summer.

Blackberries Nicknamed "black caps," the blackberry and its kin, the smaller dewberry, can be tough to find, hiding on low, scrubby bushes along wooded paths. When not quite ripe, the berry is astringent, but when ready, it's fragrant and memorably sweet. The blackberry root makes a tea used to cure digestive ailments and was a tonic that Civil War soldiers used as a cure for dysentery.

Blueberries Tinier and sweeter than their plump high-bush cousins, wild blueberries grow on low, scrubby bushes, most often near the beach and along rough shores.

Chokecherries Chokecherries resemble small, dark blue-black cherries and grow on short trees in clearings in the woods. Though astringent when fresh, they cook up into excellent syrup, jelly, and wine.

Currants Sweet-tart and delicious, black, red, and golden currants are found in thickets that grow along the borders of fields, woods, and streams in early and late summer. They are great in pies and tarts or tossed in with other fruits when making a crumble.

Elderberries Find elderberries throughout our land in sunny spots with rich soil: along the edges of farm fields and wooded lots, in ditches, and by streams and ponds. They are ripe in late summer. They will stain your fingers purple. Use them in pies with other fruit, and add them to muffins and cakes. They are delicious with raspberries and strawberries in a fresh fruit sauce or simply folded into cream.

Gooseberries These prickly berries are sometimes called dogberries. Their spines soften during cooking, so they can be used in jams and jellies. Cooked, they taste a little like rhubarb.

Mulberries Mulberry trees are everywhere, and the fruit is slightly sweet and musty. Mulberries don't keep, so use them right away as you would fresh raspberries or blackberries in jams, jellies, pies, muffins, and sauces.

Pin Cherries The tiny brilliant-red fruit of low trees, pin cherries are tart but delicious in jellies, jams, pies, and syrups.

Raspberries and Black Raspberries These berries grow on prickly canes that are hard to reach, tucked along paths in the woods and scrub. The wild berries, seedier and tinier than the domesticated berries, are very sweet.

Rosehips These pretty, tart berries take over the rose plant after the petals have fallen. They're delicious and good for you too. They're great in jellies and jams. Toss them into applesauce, where they'll add color, create a lovely perfume and tang, and give a great dose of Vitamin C.

Serviceberries Also known as Saskatoon berries, serviceberries resemble crab apples (although they grow on shrubs, not trees) and, like crab apples, are tart. So toss them with sweeter fruit into pies, tarts, and crumbles.

fresh blueberry ice cream

This ice cream is especially good with blueberries, but any fresh berry will certainly do. Serve this over the Upside Down Summer Berry Crisp (page 184) as it comes hot from the oven or use it to fill the Meringue Tart (page 183). **MAKES 1 QUART**

2½ cups heavy cream
1 cup whole milk
1 cup sugar

1 vanilla pod, split lengthwise, or 2 teaspoons
    vanilla extract
4 large egg yolks
2 pints fresh berries, picked through

Place the cream, milk, and sugar in a heavy saucepan. Using a dull knife, scrape the vanilla seeds into the milk; then put the entire pod into the pan, or simply add the vanilla extract. Set the pan over medium heat and stir until the sugar dissolves and the mixture is hot. Remove the vanilla pods.

In a medium bowl, whisk together the egg yolks. Carefully and slowly, gradually whisk the cream into the yolks. Then pour the mixture back into the saucepan, stirring to blend.

Cook over medium-high heat, whisking constantly, until the temperature of the mixture reaches about 140 degrees on an instant-read thermometer, about 10 minutes. Remove from the heat, stir in the berries, and let stand until cool. Strain the mixture if you wish to remove the seeds. Cover and refrigerate until cold, at least 2 hours, or overnight.

Pour the mixture into an ice-cream maker and process according to the manufacturer's instructions. Serve immediately.

NORTH SHORE BLUEBERRIES

These tiny flavor-packed blueberries we find on scrubby bushes along the North Shore are low bush berries, quite different from their bigger highbush cousins. Most often found in the wild, they are unique to our cold-hardy climate and sandy or rocky soil. (They're related to but not the same as huckleberries that grow in the Northwest.)

ORGANIC MILK

Organic Valley, in LaFarge, Wisconsin, is the largest organic milk co-op in the country. Co-op members Loretta and Martin Jaus, of Jaus Farm, in southern Minnesota, wildlife researchers by training, returned to Martin's dad's farm in the 1990s and decided to convert the dairy to organic milk production. That they've been able to make a good living is, to them, as rewarding as living well. Since they began, they've seen over 200 species of birds return to the property, including the rare orchard oriole, not seen in this area for at least a generation. Their well-managed land has withstood several droughts and floods that have devastated nearby conventional farms. But despite their success, they are concerned about the drift from neighboring farmers who plant genetically modified organism (GMO) seeds, fearing that this will compromise their crops and harm the local wildlife.

Organic Valley was founded in the national farm-debt crisis of 1988 when eight southwest Wisconsin farmers met to create a co-op that allowed them to connect more directly with consumers by marketing their milk differently. Today, the milk of over 1,341 farmer-members is dispersed throughout the country, yielding over six hundred million dollars in annual sales. The co-op is governed by a farmer-member board of directors.

Independent organic dairies, like Cedar Summit Farm in New Prague, Minnesota, are marketing their unhomogenized milk and cream in returnable glass bottles. "When you buy milk from a single farm, you'll appreciate how its flavors change through the season depending on what the cows eat in the field," says Florence Minar, Cedar Summit Farm's co-owner. The best thing about Cedar Summit Farm's whole milk is the top layer of sweet cream.

melon ice

This is the coolest, most refreshing dessert. For an extra kick, add a splash of vodka before serving it. You can make the ice with red watermelon, but try it with golden watermelon too. **SERVES 4**

3 cups cubed cantaloupe or watermelon

¼ cup chopped fresh mint

1 tablespoon sugar, or to taste

1 tablespoon fresh lime juice

Pinch of salt

¼ cup vodka (optional)

Put the cubed melon in the freezer until it becomes icy hard. Just before serving, put the melon, mint, sugar, lime juice, salt, and vodka (if using) into a food processor and process until it is smooth.

DEATH'S DOOR SPIRITS

The six-mile passage connecting Green Bay with Lake Michigan, known as "Death's Door," is legendary in Native American and French voyageur lore. It's the graveyard of French traders, fishermen, and the cargo ships that stopped to restock at Washington Island, located in the middle of this narrow passage at the tip of Wisconsin's Door County. Eighteenth-century sea captains who survived the passage retreated to the elegant Washington Island Inn, now the Washington Hotel. The inn has been lovingly restored and now functions as a bed and breakfast, with a restaurant serving vegetables from its garden and bread and pasta made with flour ground from the island's wheat.

That wheat is also brewed into Capital Brewery's Island Wheat Beer and distilled into vodka, gin, and whiskey by Death's Door Spirits. Death's Door Vodka has a pure, clean taste. Its gin, seasoned with the island's juniper berries and locally sourced coriander, is great as is, straight up. Death's Door Whiskey is aged in steel barrels so that it's clear and bright as moonlight on winter's snow.

zucchini spice cakes

Inspired by the breakfast breads served up at the Firelight Inn in Duluth, Minnesota, this simple cake is not at all heavy or dense. It makes quick use of overabundant zucchini and freezes beautifully. **MAKES 2 LOAVES**

3 cups unbleached all-purpose flour

2 teaspoons ground ginger

2 teaspoons ground cinnamon

1 teaspoon ground allspice

1 teaspoon baking soda

1/4 teaspoon baking powder

1 teaspoon salt

1/2 cup chopped toasted walnuts

3 large eggs

1 cup vegetable oil

2 cups sugar

2 teaspoons vanilla extract

2 cups grated zucchini

Preheat the oven to 325 degrees. Coat two 8½ × 4¼ × 2¾-inch loaf pans with vegetable oil and lightly dust them with flour. Shake out the excess flour

In a small bowl, whisk together the flour, ginger, cinnamon, allspice, baking soda, baking powder, salt, and nuts.

In a large bowl, whisk together the eggs, oil, sugar, and vanilla, and beat until the sugar is dissolved. Stir in the zucchini. Turn the wet ingredients into the dry ingredients and stir with a wooden spoon just until blended. Divide the batter between the two prepared pans.

Bake until the bread is firm and a toothpick inserted in the center comes up clean, about 1 hour. Set the pans on a rack to cool for about 10 minutes; then invert them to move the loaves from the pans. Allow the loaves to cool right-side up.

Note To toast walnuts, spread them on a baking sheet and roast them in a preheated 350-degree oven until they start to brown and smell nutty, about 3 to 5 minutes.

concord grape tart

___

This is an updated version of a very old recipe that makes use of the Concord grapes that grow in profusion in backyards. Concord grapes have seeds and skins but are not difficult to work with as long as you have a food mill. Serve this tart with Spirited Whipped Cream (page 46) or top it with Fresh Blueberry Ice Cream (page 186). **MAKES ONE 9-INCH TART**

2½ pounds Concord grapes, washed
½ cup sugar, or more to taste
2 tablespoons flour

Grated zest and juice of 1 lemon
9-inch, prebaked Rich Tart Crust (page 207)

Squeeze the grapes to slip them from their skins into a saucepan, and then put the skins into a bowl. Bring the skinned grapes to a boil, and cook until they turn white and soft, about 5 minutes. Pass the cooked grapes through a food mill to separate out the seeds, working the pulp into the bowl with the skins.

Put the grape pulp and skins in a saucepan. Stir in the sugar, flour, lemon zest, and lemon juice, and simmer until the mixture has thickened, about 10 minutes. Taste the filling and add more sugar if needed. Allow the filling to cool while preheating the oven to 400 degrees.

Turn the filling into the prepared tart shell and set it on a sheet pan. Bake until the filling is set, about 35 minutes. Let the tart cool before serving.

raspberry cordial

Make this cordial when the raspberries are at their very peak. Blackberries and black raspberries work beautifully too. **MAKES 1 QUART**

1 quart fresh raspberries

1 quart vodka

1 cup sugar

Put the raspberries, vodka, and sugar into a large, nonreactive saucepan and heat gently until the sugar melts. Cover the pan and allow the cordial to steep at room temperature for at least a day.

Strain off the raspberries and pour the cordial into decorative bottles.

SUNSHINE AND MOONLIGHT

It's almost as though nature herself is saying take a break. Don't fuss in the kitchen; come outside and play. Everything you need for a gorgeous salad can be gathered right from the garden or in a swoop through the farmers' market or by tossing together the contents of your CSA box. Jewel-toned and cooling sour cherry soup, sunny corn, bright and juicy tomatoes (in any and every way imaginable), and the light char of food right off the grill—summer's splendors, indeed.

SUMMER BBQ

Sour Cherry Riesling Soup
Whole Grilled Whitefish or Trout with
    Warm Tomato Vinaigrette
Fourth of July Brats
Grilled Sweet Corn with Thyme Butter
Grilled Cauliflower Steaks
Mixed Tomatoes and Pasta Tossed with Basil Pesto
Meringue Tart with Summer Berries

PICNIC IN THE PARK

Panzanella Picnic Salad
Classic Tarragon Chicken Salad
Cool Cucumber Yogurt and Mint Salad
Zucchini Spice Cakes

SUNSET CRUISE ON THE LAKE

Spiced Beet Caviar
Tomato, Tomato, and Tomato Tart
Pasta with Basil Pesto and Slow-Roasted Tomatoes
Melon, Feta, and Arugula Salad
Concord Grape Tart
Raspberry Cordial

COOL MEATLESS MIDSUMMER MEAL

Curried Eggplant with Bruschetta
Fresh Tomato Soup with Basil Ice Cream
Grilled Tofu with Spirited Marinade
Zucchini, Summer Squash, and Lemon Salad
Melon Ice and Fresh Blueberry Ice Cream

DINNER ON THE DECK

Farmstand Corn Chowder
Beer Can Chicken
Fried Green Tomatoes
Garden Lettuces with Apostle Island Dressing
Fresh Berries with Minted Yogurt Cream

The smell of baking bread was my mother's greeting to us as we came through the door after school, and later arrived home from college, and later still, when we brought our friends and then partners through the kitchen door to meet her. That wheaten aroma, the slices warm enough to melt butter, simply meant we were home.

—ERIK OLSEN, GREEN BAY, WISCONSIN

THE NORTHERN HEARTLAND
HEARTH

THESE recipes are meant for today's kitchens and today's lives. They are simple and forgiving, yet will fill the home with the old-fashioned scent of freshly baked bread.

many muffins—one recipe

Light, tender muffins are the quintessential breakfast treat in the North Country, where summer's wild low-bush blueberries sprawl along the shore and in backwoods bogs. Muffins are best warm, right out of the oven. After that, slice and toast them and slather them with plenty of butter and jam. When the blues are gone, toss in chopped apples or pears or both; after that, use dried cherries and fresh cranberries; come spring, chopped rhubarb and strawberries.

Handle the batter as little as possible. Whip the butter along with the sugar and eggs, but fold the dry ingredients in just until they are barely mixed. Muffins freeze well. **MAKES 18 MUFFINS**

1¾ cups unbleached all-purpose flour
2 teaspoons baking powder
1 teaspoon salt
½ cup unsalted butter, at room temperature
⅔ cup sugar

2 eggs
1 cup buttermilk
2 cups fresh fruit (sliced strawberries, pitted cherries, chopped apples, pears, cranberries, diced rhubarb)

Preheat the oven to 400 degrees. Lightly grease or butter 18 muffin cups, or line them with paper liners.

In a large bowl, whisk together the flour, baking powder, and salt. In a separate bowl, beat the butter until it is light and fluffy; then beat in the sugar, eggs, and buttermilk. Gently fold the wet ingredients into the dry ingredients until just mixed; then carefully fold in the fruit.

Spoon the batter into the prepared muffin tins, filling each at least two-thirds full. Bake until the tops are golden and spring back when lightly pressed, about 18 to 20 minutes. Turn the muffins out onto a cooling rack and allow them to cool about 15 minutes before serving.

Note Out of buttermilk? Simply mix 1 cup of milk with 1 teaspoon of white wine vinegar and let it stand for 5 minutes before using.

muesli

Muesli is uncooked granola, so it is quicker and less messy to make than granola. It is great heated like oatmeal and good sprinkled into pancakes or muffins. **MAKES 10 CUPS**

5 cups rolled grains

3 cups mixed seeds and nuts (such as sunflower seeds, chopped walnuts, hickory nuts, hazelnuts, pecans)

2 teaspoons cinnamon

Salt to taste

2 cups dried fruit (cranberries, apples, pears, blueberries), larger pieces chopped

In a large bowl, toss all of the ingredients together. Store the muesli in an airtight container in the refrigerator.

buttermilk scones, sweet or savory

The Scots and Welsh who came here seeking mining jobs brought a hankering for scones along with their taste for tea. Like the South's biscuits, these scones double as shortcakes when loaded with whipped cream and fresh berries. They are terrific for breakfast with a little butter and lots of jam. Add shredded cheese and herbs for a savory treat. **MAKES 12**

2¼ cups unbleached all-purpose flour

2½ teaspoons baking powder

¾ teaspoon baking soda

1 teaspoon sugar

1 teaspoon salt

6 tablespoons cold unsalted butter, cut into pieces

1 cup buttermilk

Preheat the oven to 450 degrees. Butter a large baking sheet.

Whisk together the flour, baking powder, baking soda, sugar, and salt in a medium-size bowl. Blend in the butter with your fingertips or a pastry cutter until the mixture resembles small peas. Gently stir in the buttermilk until the ingredients are just combined.

Drop 12 equal-sized rounds of the dough about 2 inches apart onto the buttered baking sheet. Bake until golden, about 18 to 25 minutes.

Cheddar Chive Scones

Add 1 ½ cups of grated Cheddar cheese and ¼ cup of chopped chives to the flour mixture before working in the buttermilk.

MARY ECKMEIER MAKES REAL SCONES

"Buttermilk is the key ingredient in making the lightest, most tender scones," says Mary Eckmeier, Brett Laidlaw's wife and partner in Real Bread. She uses unbleached all-purpose flower, real butter, and her hands. "Don't overhandle the dough," she says. "Despite what the books say, I use room temperature butter (not cold butter) because I can work it in quickly. It doesn't take long to get the feel for making scones."

real cornbread

Cornbread is the iconic marriage of Native ingredients and European flour. Use the fresh stone-ground cornmeal that tastes like corn: nutty and buttery, with a fine grassy kick (use cornmeal ground from Mandan Bride corn, if possible). Stone grinding doesn't heat the corn as the faster steel rollers do, so the kernels don't get scorched and those fresh, corny flavors remain intact. Whole-grain cornmeal is not uniform in shape or color; it's mottled, often grayish, and it should be kept in the refrigerator or frozen if not used within a few weeks. **MAKES A 9 × 9-INCH PAN OF CORNBREAD OR 12 MUFFINS OR CORN STICKS**

Softened butter to grease pan
1 cup unbleached all-purpose flour
1 cup coarse yellow cornmeal
1½ teaspoons baking powder
¼ teaspoon baking soda

½ teaspoon salt
¼ cup honey
1 cup buttermilk
1 egg, lightly beaten
¼ cup corn oil

Preheat the oven to 375 degrees. Lightly butter a 9 × 9-inch pan, mini-muffin tins, large-muffin tins, or corn stick molds. (Depending on the type of pan and how many you have, you may need to bake in batches.)

Whisk together the flour, cornmeal, baking powder, baking soda, and salt.

In a separate bowl, whisk together the honey, buttermilk, egg, and oil. Stir the wet ingredients into the flour mixture until just combined. Fill the prepared pan about two-thirds full. Bake until the top is golden and a toothpick inserted into the center comes out clean, about 20 to 25 minutes for the bread and 10 to 15 minutes for the muffins or corn sticks, depending on their size and depth.

Transfer the pan to a wire rack, and let the cornbread cool in the pan for about 5 minutes. Turn the muffins out of the tin. Serve warm or at room temperature.

rich brown soda bread

This quick bread pairs beautifully with stews and soups and is great toasted for breakfast. It doesn't keep, so enjoy it the night you make it, right out of the oven. **MAKES 1 ROUND LOAF**

2 cups unbleached all-purpose flour

2 cups whole wheat flour

2 teaspoons salt

¾ teaspoon baking soda

¾ teaspoon baking powder

¼ cup unsalted butter, melted, plus some for greasing the pan

1½ cups buttermilk

½ cup dried cranberries (optional)

Preheat the oven to 375 degrees. Butter a baking sheet.

In a large bowl, stir together the flours, salt, baking soda, and baking powder. Add the melted butter and then enough buttermilk to make a soft but not overly sticky dough, and then work in the dried cranberries. Turn the dough onto a lightly floured board and knead it for about 3 minutes. The dough should be smooth and elastic.

Shape the dough into a round loaf on the prepared baking sheet. Slash the top with a sharp knife. Bake until the loaf is golden brown and sounds hollow when thumped on the bottom, about 45 minutes. Set the loaf on a rack to cool.

DAILY BREAD—CRESS SPRING BAKERY

There's a bread line every Saturday morning for Cress Spring Bakery bread at the Dane County Farmers' Market in Madison, Wisconsin. Jeff Ford, Cress Spring's owner and baker, grinds local wheat, kamut, spelt, barley, and rye at his tiny operation in Blue Mounds, Wisconsin. Ford claims that the old-fashioned strains of wheat are more nutritious and easier to digest than commercial grains that have been bred to withstand machine harvesting and require chemical fertilizers and pesticides. Many of Ford's customers who are sensitive to gluten claim that they can enjoy this bread. He credits his success to the great flavor of freshly milled grain and his wood-fired oven, which produces crisp, chewy loaves. Ford has said that while he may never get rich, the queue of happy customers is pay-off for his hard work.

a daily loaf

This is the kind of bread our grandmothers made, straightforward and forgiving. Vary the proportions of white to whole wheat flour, shape the dough into dinner rolls or bread sticks, bake it off as a loaf or a boule. **MAKES 1 LOAF**

1 ¼ cups very warm (120 degrees) water
1 tablespoon honey
1 package (2 ¼ teaspoons) active dry yeast
2 cups unbleached all-purpose flour or bread
    flour, plus a little more for kneading

1 cup whole wheat flour
1 teaspoon salt
2 tablespoons butter, softened

In a large bowl, stir together the water, honey, and yeast and allow it to stand a few minutes. Gradually beat in the white and the whole wheat flour, the salt, and the butter. Continue beating until you have an elastic dough.

Turn the dough onto a lightly floured surface and knead until the dough is smooth and springy, about 5 minutes. Grease a large bowl with butter or oil. Place the dough in the bowl and turn it to grease all sides. Cover the bowl with plastic wrap or a towel and allow it to rise in a warm place until it has doubled in size, about 40 to 50 minutes. The dough is ready if an indentation remains when you touch it.

(If you don't have time to allow the dough to rise fully, cover the dough and put it in the refrigerator or a very cool spot in the kitchen. When you're ready, simply allow it to rise at room temperature until just about doubled and then proceed with the recipe.)

Gently punch your fist into the dough to deflate it. Shape the dough and place it on a lightly greased baking sheet. Cover and let it rise in a warm spot until it has doubled again, about 35 to 50 minutes. Preheat the oven to 350 degrees.

Bake the loaf until it is golden brown and sounds hollow when tapped, about 30 to 40 minutes. Place the loaf on a wire rack to cool.

FRESH FLOUR

Think flour is just, well, flour? Try tasting bread made with conventional bleached all-purpose flour alongside bread made with freshly milled local wheat. No, flours are not all alike.

Small mills, like Sunrise Flour Mill in North Branch, Minnesota, source grain from local organic farms, grind it themselves, and sell it right away. It is so fresh that they recommend storing it in the freezer. The wheat they mill is naturally higher in protein and makes terrific bread. The fresher the flour, the more distinctive the flavor of the wheat will be.

Whole Grain Milling in Welcome, Minnesota, is one of the region's largest organic mills, processing every kind of local grain, including wheat, rye, buckwheat, and a high-lysine corn that contains more protein than most corn flours. "My father tried to use chemicals early on, but things just didn't seem right," says Doug Hilgendorf, who, with his family, now farms and runs the mill. "The birds went away and it became too quiet, so he returned to his traditional ways and I've been farming this way ever since."

It stands to reason that fresh flour is more nutritious. Processing strips the wheat not just of its flavor but of the fiber, vitamins, and proteins. Many commercial brands attempt to return these natural properties by "enriching" flour.

Flours differ depending on the amount of protein in the wheat they are milled from. These gluten-forming proteins determine how the flour will perform in baked goods. A higher percentage of protein means a stronger flour that will yield chewy crusts. These are labeled bread flour. A soft, or low-protein, flour known as cake flour is best suited to tender cakes and pastries. All-purpose flour falls right between these two. All-purpose flour is versatile enough for everything from cakes to breads; to a casual baker, differences will be slight. Unbleached flour has not been treated with whitening agents. The primary difference between bleached and unbleached flour is looks.

whole wheat bread

This dense and wheaty loaf is terrific sliced for sandwiches and toast. Feel free to replace one cup of the whole wheat flour with white flour to lighten the texture and flavor of the bread. **MAKES 1 LOAF**

About 1 tablespoon vegetable oil
2½ cups whole wheat flour
½ cup coarse cornmeal

1 teaspoon active dry yeast
1 teaspoon salt
1½ cups warm water

Combine the whole wheat flour, cornmeal, yeast, and salt in a large bowl and stir in the water, mixing until you have a dough that is rough and shaggy. Set the bowl in a warm spot and allow the dough to rise for about 4 hours.

Lightly oil a standard loaf pan. Shape the dough into a rectangle and then lay it in the pan, pressing the edges to the side. Let the dough rise another hour.

Preheat the oven to 350 degrees. Bake the bread until it sounds hollow when tapped, about 45 to 50 minutes. Allow the loaf to cool completely before slicing it.

BAKING REAL BREAD WITH BRETT

"Don't fear the yeast," says Brett Laidlaw, a master baker who sells Real Bread at the Midtown Farmers Market in Minneapolis. "Time is on your side." Using freshly milled local flour, Brett and his wife, Mary Eckmeier, turn out about one hundred loaves each Friday, using a fifteen-year-old sourdough starter to leaven all but his baguettes. Here's his advice, born of experience:

- Kneading is important, but I find myself kneading for a shorter time than most books recommend— it just isn't necessary. Five minutes is fine.
- Proofing is key. Longer, frequent proofing makes better loaves. Let the dough rise and punch it down, rise again and punch it down. Let it proof in the refrigerator, especially in the summer. The cooler temperatures help the gluten develop more slowly and that helps develop the flavor.
- Put a few ice cubes on a baking tray and set that in the oven shortly after you put the loaves in to bake. The steam makes for a terrific crust.
- Use filtered water. City water includes chlorine, which hurts the yeast and alters the flavor. Yeast is alive, and its vigor is dampened by chlorine.
- The best place to learn to make bread is in your own kitchen. Start with a good recipe and after you've made it a couple of times, play around.

FORGOTTEN BREAD

No one likes to throw bread away (especially the baker). Here are a few tips for using up those last heels and lonely slices:

- **Bread pudding** Bread pudding (page 99) is delicious made with a mix of bread, quick breads, muffins, and scones.
- **Fresh bread crumbs** Tear the bread into pieces and drop it into a food processor or a blender for 30 seconds to a minute. Store the bread crumbs in the freezer.
- **Dried bread crumbs** Spread out bread slices on a baking pan. Bake in a low oven (220 degrees) until the bread is dry and hard. Pulverize it in a food processor or blender and store the bread crumbs in airtight containers.
- **Buttered bread crumbs** Sometimes called poor man's cheese, these make a terrific topping to any casserole or buttered noodles. Simply melt enough butter to cover the bottom of a skillet. Scatter the breadcrumbs over the butter, toss to coat, then cook until the crumbs are nicely brown and nutty. Allow the bread crumbs to cool; then store them in an airtight container. (Note that this also works well with hazelnut or walnut oil instead of butter.)

pizza dough

This simple pizza dough can be baked now or kept a day or two in the fridge. It's best to allow the dough to rise for six hours in a cool spot, but if you're really in a hurry, let the dough rise while you're preparing the topping ingredients and then proceed with the recipe. **MAKES A 12- TO 14-INCH PIZZA OR 4 TO 6 MINI-PIZZAS**

1 ½ cups warm water
¼ teaspoon active dry yeast
3 ⅓ cups unbleached all-purpose flour or
    bread flour

½ teaspoon salt
Cornmeal for dusting the dough

In a large bowl, stir together the water, yeast, flour, and salt to make a rough dough. Let the dough rest, covered, for about 15 minutes.

Turn the dough onto a floured board and knead it for 5 minutes. Shape the dough into a disk (for mini pizzas, cut the dough into 4 pieces and shape 4 disks) and set it on surface sprinkled with cornmeal or flour. Cover the dough and let it proof for 6 hours in a cool area.

When you're ready to make your pizza, roll out the dough and then allow it to rest a few minutes before adding toppings. Bake at 425 degrees for 15 to 20 minutes.

simply granola

You can eat granola as is for a snack, top off yogurt with it, toss it into cookies, or douse it with milk for breakfast. Most packaged varieties are cloyingly sweet, but this one, chock-full of nuts and dried fruit, strikes a balance. **MAKES 10 CUPS**

5 cups rolled grain (such as oats, wheat, rye, or barley)

1 cup sunflower seeds

2 cups mixed chopped nuts (such as hickory nuts, hazelnuts, and walnuts)

2 teaspoons ground cinnamon, or to taste

1 tablespoon hazelnut, walnut, or vegetable oil

2/3 cup honey or maple syrup, or to taste

Salt

2 cups dried fruit (cranberries, apples, pears, blueberries), larger pieces chopped

Preheat the oven to 350 degrees. Lightly grease a rimmed baking sheet.

In a large bowl, toss together the rolled grain, seeds, nuts, cinnamon, oil, honey, and a little salt to taste. Spread out the mixture on the baking sheet. Bake, stirring occasionally, until the granola is toasty and evenly browned, about 30 minutes.

Place the pan on a rack and allow the granola to cool on the pan. Add the dried fruit. Store the granola in an airtight container. It's best kept refrigerated.

ROLLED GRAINS 101

The most familiar rolled grain is oatmeal, but rye, wheat, and barley make wonderful morning cereal too. The grains are steamed and then flattened, and they all cook in about the same amount of time. They are all highly nutritious, and their flavors are subtly different. Here's the basic formula for cooking rolled grains.

Use 1/4 cup of the rolled grain per serving. To cook the grain, use about 2 parts water to 1 part grain, and add a pinch of salt to the water. Bring the water to a boil, reduce the heat, and simmer until the mixture is cooked to your liking. Turn off the heat and allow the cereal to stand for about 1 minute before serving it. Top the cereal with milk (or a splash of cream), dried or fresh fruit, yogurt, honey, maple syrup, or maple sugar.

comfort lodge buttermilk pancakes

The name says it all. Be sure to serve these with lots of pure maple syrup. **MAKES ABOUT 18 PANCAKES, SERVES ABOUT 4 TO 6**

1⅓ cups unbleached all-purpose flour

2 teaspoons baking powder

¾ teaspoons salt

2 eggs, separated (see note)

1¼ cups buttermilk

3 tablespoons honey or sugar

1 cup fresh berries, in season if available

3 tablespoons vegetable oil

In a large bowl, toss together the flour, baking powder, and salt (omit the baking powder if you use self-rising flour). Beat the egg yolks with the buttermilk and honey until just blended; then stir the wet ingredients into the dry ingredients. Beat the egg whites until they form stiff peaks, and fold them into the batter. Stir in the berries.

Drop about 2 tablespoons of batter onto a hot, lightly greased griddle set over medium-high heat and cook until bubbles appear on the surface, about 1 to 2 minutes. Flip the pancakes and continue cooking another 30 seconds.

Serve with warm real maple syrup.

Note Beating the egg whites separately yields a light, fluffy pancake. If you're in a hurry, omit this step. They'll still taste great.

flaky butter crust

This is the classic, rich butter crust—great for just about any pie, savory or sweet. This crust works nicely with the Honey Pumpkin Ginger Pie (page 46). **MAKES ONE 9- OR 10-INCH SINGLE-CRUST PIE**

1 ½ cups unbleached all-purpose flour

1 teaspoon sugar

½ teaspoon salt

6 tablespoons cold unsalted butter, cut into small pieces

3 tablespoons ice water, or more as needed

In a food processor fitted with a steel blade, process the flour, sugar, and salt. Pulse in the butter until the mixture resembles coarse cornmeal. Drizzle in the water one tablespoon at a time, pulsing, until the mixture begins to clump. Turn the dough onto a sheet of parchment paper or plastic wrap and flatten it into a disk. Wrap the dough in the plastic wrap or parchment paper, and chill it for at least 30 minutes before rolling it out (or refrigerate it overnight).

Roll out the dough on a lightly floured surface with a lightly floured rolling pin or roll it out between two pieces of parchment paper or plastic wrap. Once you have a circle about 10 inches across and ⅛ inch thick, lift it into the pie pan and trim off the excess dough. Chill the dough while you prepare the filling.

PIE CRUST PRIMER

Great pastry relies on one key ingredient—butter. Margarine and shortening may make an acceptable crust, but it will never be as flavorful, or as flaky, as one made with butter. Use good-tasting unsalted butter. (You have more control of salt levels by adding your own.) Look for local butter made in small batches (such as that made by Hope Creamery). It often costs less than imported brands and is certainly better tasting than large commercial brands.

For a flaky crust, use cold butter and work it into the flour quickly. A food processor fitted with a steel blade, a pastry cutter, or two knives are best, but don't overprocess the dough. If the butter becomes too soft, chill it for a few minutes. Finally, let the dough rest in the refrigerator before rolling it out. This not only gives you a chance to clean up and prepare the filling; it makes rolling out the dough easier. Refrigerated dough will keep for several days, or freeze the dough for another time.

rich tart crust

This is a shortbread cookie crust that is best baked ahead for cream or cooked-fruit fillings. This crust works beautifully with the Concord Grape Tart (page 190), or fill it with the Chocolate Mousse with Maple Cream (page 134). Fill the crust shortly before serving so it stays crisp. **MAKES ONE 9-INCH PIE OR 10-INCH TART**

1 large egg yolk
1 teaspoon vanilla extract
1 ¼ cups unbleached all-purpose flour, plus more as needed
1 cup confectioners sugar

¼ teaspoon salt
¾ cup (12 tablespoons) chilled unsalted butter, cut into pieces
1 to 2 tablespoons heavy cream or milk, if needed

Whisk the egg yolk and the vanilla together in a small bowl. In a food processor fitted with a steel blade, process the flour, confectioners sugar, and salt; then add the butter, pulsing until the mixture is the texture of cornmeal. Add the egg mixture, pulsing until the dough clings to itself. (If the dough seems too dry, add a drizzle of cream or milk, but no more than 1 to 2 tablespoons.) Turn the dough out onto a sheet of parchment or plastic wrap and flatten into a 6-inch round. Wrap the disk in parchment paper or plastic wrap and refrigerate it for at least 30 minutes, or overnight, before rolling it out.

Remove the dough from the refrigerator and roll it out on a lightly floured surface with a lightly floured rolling pin, or roll it out between two large sheets of parchment paper or plastic wrap. When the dough is about 15 inches across and ⅛ inch thick, transfer the dough to a 10-inch tart pan with a removable bottom. Ease the dough into the pan and press the dough against the sides of the pan with your fingers. Don't worry if it tears or if the edges are too thin; just repair them with some excess dough. (Any excess dough can be rolled out and cut into shapes to bake alongside the crust. Use them to garnish the tart.) Set the pan on a baking sheet and put it in the freezer for about 30 minutes to firm up the dough.

Preheat the oven to 375 degrees. Line the chilled dough with aluminum foil and fill it with pie weights, dried beans, or rice. Bake until the dough dries out and begins to blister, about 30 minutes. Remove the pan from the oven and carefully lift off the aluminum foil and weights. Return the pan to the oven and continue baking until the crust begins to turn golden, another 5 minutes. Set the pan on a wire rack and allow the crust to cool before filling it.

sweet cornmeal crust

This is one of the easiest, quickest, and sturdiest crusts, a golden foundation for fresh fruit. It's lovely with the Cranberry Tartlets (page 96) and the Once a Year Rhubarb Pie (page 138). Or, simply bake the crust and fill it with fresh berries and whipped cream. **MAKES ONE 9-INCH PIE, ONE 10-INCH TART, OR 6 TARTLETS**

1 cup cornmeal
1 cup unbleached all-purpose flour
½ teaspoon salt

2 tablespoons honey
½ cup unsalted butter, softened
1 to 2 tablespoons milk

In a food processor fitted with a steel blade or in a large bowl, combine the cornmeal, flour, and salt. Work in the honey and butter, by pulsing or with a wooden spoon, until the mixture is the consistency of small peas. Then quickly work in some of the milk until the dough gathers into a ball, adding a little bit more milk if the dough is too dry. Turn the dough onto a sheet of parchment paper and flatten it into a large disk. Refrigerate the dough until it becomes firm but not too stiff, about 10 minutes.

On a floured surface with a floured rolling pin, or between two sheets of parchment paper, roll the dough out into a circle to fit the size of the pan you're using. Don't worry if the dough splits or crumbles; just keep working it back together. Lift the dough and fit it into the pan, pressing it against the sides. If the dough cracks or falls apart as you're putting it into the pan, just patch and press it back together once it is in the pan. Trim the top.

A meal is a good time for mindfulness and grace, because it is at least potentially a time for transformations. A meal represents a place where sunshine becomes sustenance, where the free gift of photosynthesis comes home, where nature becomes culture. Grace is thanks for nourishment. But mindfulness is also nourishment for soul *and* society. It is a private practice of commitment, a habit that keeps both head and heart in the whole web of life, and if we act on our understandings, such mindfulness can help us think about how to heal the wounds of industrial agriculture.

—JAMES FARRELL, *THE NATURE OF COLLEGE*

STOCKING THE
CUPBOARD

vinaigrettes, dressings, and sauces

KEEP these vinaigrettes, dressings, and sauces on hand to spark up dishes quickly. They are far more flavorful than anything on the supermarket shelves and far less expensive. They make terrific gifts too.

honey mustard vinaigrette

This vinaigrette is versatile. It is a great salad dressing; a terrific sauce for roasted vegetables, poultry, and pork; and a wonderful basting sauce or glaze for grilled meats and roasted root vegetables. **MAKES ABOUT 1½ CUPS**

¼ cup white wine vinegar
3 small shallots, diced
2 tablespoons coarse Dijon mustard

½ cup honey
¾ cup vegetable oil

Put the vinegar, shallots, mustard, and honey into a blender and blend on high. Then add the oil in a slow, steady stream.

Note For maple mustard vinaigrette, simply substitute maple syrup for the honey.

VINEGARY

Farmstead fruit vinegars were once a staple throughout the Northern Heartland. Every farm brewed its own using leftover wine made from orchard fruit. Leatherwood Vinegary, in Long Prairie, Minnesota, is the first (if not the only) to revive this tradition. Apples, cherries, plums, grapes, and rhubarb are fermented into wines, then inoculated with mother of vinegar (the bacteria culture used to make vinegar) and brewed. Unlike the commercial varieties, Leatherwood does not add artificial flavors or colors to its vinegar. Instead, Ron and Nancy Leasman, the owners of the vinegary, let nature take its time. "We don't rush it. When it's ready, we bottle," Ron says.

Use fruit vinegars as you would use citrus juice or wine to perk up flavors in a pan sauce or a stew. Keep them on hand for ready seasoning.

the real buttermilk ranch dressing

Is there a more popular dip and dressing at picnics and potlucks? Buttermilk adds tang and creaminess, more flavor, and less fat. This will keep, covered and refrigerated, up to a week. **MAKES 2 CUPS**

1 cup buttermilk

½ cup mayonnaise

1 tablespoon cider vinegar or white vinegar

2 tablespoons chopped fresh chives

2 tablespoons chopped fresh parsley

Salt and freshly ground black pepper

Whisk all of the ingredients together or whir them in a blender.

apostle island dressing

This riff on Thousand Island dressing is standard fare along Lake Superior's Wisconsin shores. Though the basic recipe originated in a resort on the St. Lawrence Seaway, it traveled to the Great Lakes, where it was perked up with a little horseradish sauce. Chopped dill pickles add the requisite sour note. **MAKES 1 GENEROUS CUP**

¾ cup mayonnaise

¼ cup ketchup

1 teaspoon grated fresh horseradish

1 tablespoon diced dill pickle, or to taste

Salt and freshly ground black pepper

Whisk together the mayonnaise, ketchup, and horseradish, and then stir in the chopped pickle. Add salt and pepper to taste.

brown butter vinaigrette

You won't think that Brown Butter Vinaigrette sounds odd once you taste it on room-temperature vegetable salads, grain salads, steamed vegetables, and sautés. **MAKES ¾ CUP**

¼ cup good-quality unsalted butter (such as
    Rochdale Farms, Hope Creamery,
    or PastureLand)

4 tablespoons malt, balsamic, or sherry vinegar
¼ cup extra-virgin olive oil
Salt and freshly ground black pepper

Melt the butter in a small saucepan set over low heat. Cook it until the foam subsides and the milk solids begin to turn a nutty brown and smell of toasted nuts. Turn the butter into a small bowl, and quickly whisk in the vinegar and olive oil. Season to taste with salt and pepper.

juniper–gin marinade

Given the juniper bushes that grow like weeds throughout the region, it's a wonder that there aren't more distilleries making the gin that relies on juniper berries for its distinctive flavor. This peppery marinade puts both to work seasoning red meat and game. It's an especially good marinade for venison and bison cuts. **MAKES ABOUT 1½ CUPS**

⅓ cup gin (preferably Death's Door Gin)
   or vodka
¼ cup lime juice
¼ cup honey
2 tablespoons freshly ground black pepper
¼ cup olive oil

3 large cloves garlic, minced
1 teaspoon juniper berries, crushed
¼ teaspoon salt
2 tablespoons chopped parsley
1 tablespoon chopped fresh thyme

In a small bowl, whisk together all of the ingredients.

rosemary-mint marinade

This is the marinade that Prairie Grass Farms of New Florence, Missouri, recommends for grilling lamb. They raise seven hundred of them, so they should know. Don't limit its use to lamb; this marinade is wonderful on dark meat chicken and pork chops too. **MAKES ¾ TO 1 CUP**

1 tablespoon minced shallot
2 teaspoons Dijon mustard
¼ cup raspberry or white wine vinegar
¼ cup chopped fresh mint

2 tablespoons chopped fresh parsley
½ cup vegetable oil
Salt and freshly ground black pepper

In a small bowl, whisk together the shallot, mustard, vinegar, mint, and parsley; then whisk in the oil in a slow, steady stream. Season the marinade with salt and pepper to taste.

honey jalapeño bbq sauce

This is great on chicken but even better on pork, especially barbeque ribs (page 166). Make the sauce hotter or milder by varying the quantity of jalapeños. **MAKES 2 CUPS**

1 cup ketchup (page 235)

½ cup honey

2 jalapeños, seeded and diced, or to taste

¼ cup Dijon mustard

¼ cup apple cider vinegar

½ to 1 teaspoon hot sauce

3 cloves garlic, crushed

3 teaspoons Worcestershire sauce

Salt and freshly ground black pepper

Combine all of the ingredients in a small saucepan set over medium heat. Bring the sauce to a boil; then reduce the heat and simmer until the sauce is thick and smooth, about 10 to 15 minutes.

maple mustard basting sauce

This sweet, rough sauce works nicely on chicken and pork, whether roasted or grilled. **MAKES 1 ¼ CUPS**

2 tablespoons Dijon mustard

½ cup maple syrup

¼ cup cider vinegar

¼ cup vegetable oil

Combine all of the ingredients in a medium saucepan and set over medium-high heat. Bring the sauce to a simmer and cook until it is slightly reduced. The sauce will be thin.

raspberry vinegar (fruit vinegar)

This vinegar is terrific in salad dressings but also makes a refreshing summer drink when cut with soda water. **MAKES 4 PINTS**

2 cups white wine vinegar or champagne vinegar   6 pounds raspberries

Put the fruit in a nonreactive container, cover it with the vinegar, and stir well. Allow the fruit to macerate for three days in the refrigerator. Strain out the crushed raspberries. Pour the vinegar into sterilized bottles.

HERB VINEGAR

Make your own herb vinegar, and you'll never pay for pricey gourmet vinegar again. Simply stuff a few sprigs into clean bottles, and cover completely with good-quality, mild, white wine vinegar. Cork or seal the bottle tightly, and leave it to stand at least one week before using the vinegar.

furious mustard

Surly Furious beer, brewed in Minneapolis, is a very serious ale. It comes in big cans that some just can't finish. Turn the leftovers (or any other good brown ale) into seriously furious, potent mustard. Like the brew, this mustard is not for the faint of taste. **MAKES ABOUT 2 CUPS**

¼ cup brown mustard seeds

¼ cup yellow mustard seeds

¾ cup flat dark beer

2 tablespoons Dijon mustard

½ cup malt vinegar

1 teaspoon salt

1 teaspoon ground black pepper

Soak the mustard seeds in the beer overnight. Stir the Dijon mustard into the soaked seed mix and allow it to sit for about 20 minutes. Pour the soaked seeds into a blender along with the vinegar, salt, and pepper. Grind until the mixture becomes a paste but still has some seeds visible. Transfer the mustard to a glass container, cover it, and refrigerate at least 4 to 5 days before using.

Note This mustard keeps for a long time and makes a terrific house gift if you're headed out of town to spend a summer weekend with friends.

roasted tomato vodka sauce

Roasting tomatoes deepens their flavor, and this is an especially rich-tasting sauce, just the thing to bring warmth months down the road, when summer and sunshine are just memories. The vodka adds just enough acid to the tomatoes to keep the sauce from becoming too sweet. This recipe was inspired by Leah Caplan, former chef at the Washington Hotel in Door County, Wisconsin, and a co-founder of Death's Door Spirits. **MAKES ABOUT 1 QUART**

2 pounds very ripe tomatoes, cored and quartered
¼ cup extra-virgin olive oil
1 large onion, peeled and diced
1 carrot, diced
1 head garlic, cut in half horizontally

½ cup vodka
2 sprigs oregano
2 sprigs thyme
1 cup chopped basil leaves

Preheat the oven to 350 degrees. Toss the tomatoes with half of the olive oil. Spread out the tomatoes on a baking dish and roast them, uncovered, until the flesh is very soft and the skin separates easily from the flesh, about 30 minutes.

Heat the remaining oil in a nonreactive pot, add the onion, carrot, and garlic, and cook over medium heat until the vegetables are very soft, about 10 minutes. Add the vodka and then the roasted tomatoes, oregano, thyme, and basil. Simmer, stirring frequently to prevent scorching, until the tomatoes are very soft and the flavors have melded, about 40 minutes. If you prefer a smooth sauce, pass it through a food mill. This sauce will keep about a week in the refrigerator and freezes well.

Note Oven-roasted tomatoes are also wonderful served on their own as a side dish, in salads, or on top of pizza or bruschetta.

sweet bell pepper sauce

Here's how to turn all those sweet peppers into a terrific sauce. Delicious on pasta, it's also great tossed into rice or spooned over grilled eggplant. **MAKES 2 CUPS**

2 tablespoons unsalted butter

5 cloves garlic, smashed

1 large onion, chopped

3 large bell peppers, stemmed, seeded, and chopped

1 ½ pounds tomatoes, coarsely chopped

Salt and freshly ground black pepper

½ cup chopped basil

¼ cup chopped parsley

Heat the butter in a large, deep saucepan. Add the garlic and the onion and cook until the onion is translucent, about 5 to 7 minutes. Add the peppers and the tomatoes and simmer until tender, about 20 minutes. Working in batches, puree the sauce in a food processor or a blender, or with an immersion blender, until it reaches the consistency you desire (it's great rough and rustic or finely pureed). Serve tossed with pasta or spooned onto grilled eggplant, chicken, or fish.

Note This sauce will keep up to three days in the refrigerator and freezes well.

compound butters

These compound butters spark meat, poultry, and vegetables; polish a sauce; and are great spread on homemade bread. They will keep up to a week in the refrigerator.

Lemon–Parsley Butter

Enjoy on steamed vegetables, broiled fish, and baked or steamed new potatoes. **MAKES ½ CUP**

½ cup unsalted butter, softened
½ teaspoon grated lemon zest
1 tablespoon fresh lemon juice

2 tablespoons chopped parsley
½ teaspoon salt, or to taste

In a small bowl, mash the butter and all of the other ingredients together with a fork until blended. Transfer the butter to a sheet of waxed paper or parchment paper and roll it into a 6-inch log. Refrigerate for at least 1 hour.

Thyme Butter

Try this on steamed corn or toss it with steamed new potatoes. **MAKES ½ CUP**

½ cup unsalted butter, softened
2 tablespoons dry white wine

1 tablespoon chopped fresh thyme
½ teaspoon salt, or to taste

In a small bowl, mash the butter and all of the other ingredients together with a fork until blended. Transfer the butter to a sheet of waxed paper or parchment paper and roll it into a 6-inch log. Refrigerate for at least 1 hour.

BEST BUTTER

Not all butter is alike. Small producers, like Hope Creamery, do not freeze their butter (something the larger dairies do to ride out market dips). Freezing imparts an off or burned flavor to the butter, noticeable when you taste a frozen butter against one that's truly fresh.

The flavor of fresh local butter will vary depending on the time of year and what the cows were eating. "The flavor may vary depending on the season," says Victor Mrotz, owner of Hope Creamery, located in Hope, Minnesota. "In spring, it tends to be just a little grassy, when the cows return to pasture." Locally made butters also tend to have higher butterfat content, making for richer, creamier sauces.

Blue Cheese Butter

This is absolutely luscious on a thick grilled steak or on chicken. Try it spread on rye bread and topped with sliced radishes. **MAKES ½ CUP**

½ cup unsalted butter, softened

4 tablespoons crumbled blue cheese, or to taste

Salt and freshly ground black pepper

In a small bowl, mash the butter and all of the other ingredients together with a fork until blended. Transfer the butter to a sheet of waxed paper or parchment paper and roll it into a 6-inch log. Refrigerate for at least 1 hour.

Maple Nut Butter

Slather this butter on warm scones, biscuits, toast, pancakes, and waffles. **MAKES ½ CUP**

½ cup unsalted butter, softened

2 tablespoons maple syrup

Pinch of salt

2 tablespoons chopped toasted black walnuts

In a small bowl, mash the butter and all of the other ingredients together with a fork until blended. Transfer the butter to a sheet of waxed paper or parchment paper and roll it into a 6-inch log. Refrigerate for at least 1 hour.

Honey Cinnamon Butter

Vary the spices in this. Try adding a pinch of nutmeg, cardamom, or both. It's terrific on toast or melted over cornbread. **MAKES ½ CUP**

½ cup unsalted butter, softened

1 teaspoon cinnamon

Pinch of nutmeg

Pinch of salt

In a small bowl, mash the butter and all of the other ingredients together with a fork until blended. Transfer the butter to a sheet of waxed paper or parchment paper and roll it into a 6-inch log. Refrigerate for at least 1 hour.

HEARTLAND
PRESERVES AND CONDIMENTS

PRESERVING fresh local food is the surest way to guarantee that you're eating the best food all year long. Making pickles, preserves, jams, and jellies means the food we're eating does not contain artificial ingredients. In the midst of winter, a taste of sunny corn relish can bring back an August afternoon. Once considered an art of survival, canning is now an artful way to ensure we have the best local flavors throughout the year.

pickle this

Sweet Garden Crunchers, pickles made famous by Gedney, are the result of a happy accident. Leslie Grant, a University of Minnesota professor, was putting up his garden pickles and, by accident, doubled the quantity of sugar. They ended up being his best pickles ever, winning him first place at the Minnesota State Fair that year and an award from Gedney Pickle Company, which now produces Sweet Garden Crunchers for sale in grocery stores. Here's a recipe similar to Grant's, along with his tips for making great pickles.

"Start with the best cucumber," Grant told Chaska Herald *reporter Mollee Francisco. "Good ingredients make for good product." Grant also recommends using good water. "I don't use Minneapolis water," he said. "I buy it at the grocery store." Presentation counts as well. Grant cuts his cucumber slices by hand and has even been known to arrange them in the jar. Beyond that, Grant encourages cooks to get creative. After all, one never knows when an extra heap of sugar might just be the key to winning it all.* **MAKES 1 QUART**

1 cup apple cider vinegar

2 tablespoons salt

1 cup sugar

1 teaspoon mustard seed

2 pounds firm young cucumbers, thinly sliced

2 sweet onions, peeled and thinly sliced

5 cloves garlic, peeled

In a small saucepan set over medium-high heat, combine the vinegar, salt, sugar, and mustard seed. Bring the vinegar to a boil; then reduce the heat and simmer for 5 minutes. Loosely pack the cucumbers, onions, and garlic into a quart-sized canning jar. Pour in the hot liquid. Allow the pickles to cool before covering the jar. Refrigerate for 24 hours before eating.

YES WE CAN

Canning isn't hard, but there are a few details to keep in mind. Follow these simple steps, and you can't go wrong.

1. Wash the jars, lids, and bands in hot soapy water and rinse them well. Keep the jars warm until they are ready to use. This will help prevent them from breaking when they're filled with hot liquid. Keep them in a pot of simmering water or a heated dishwasher, or in the oven at the lowest temperature.
2. Fill a stockpot or a canner with enough water to cover the jars by at least 1 inch and heat it to a simmer (180 degrees).
3. Follow the recipes for the recommended amount to fill the jars. Each jar needs space between the food and the jar rim (called headspace) to allow the food to expand. Most recipes specify ½ inch of headspace.
4. After you've filled the jar, remove the air bubbles by sliding a small, nonmetallic spatula inside the jar and gently pressing the food against the opposite side of the jar. Air bubbles inside the jar can affect the canning process, resulting, for example, in unsealed jars or discolored food.
5. Wipe any food from the rims of the jars. Center a new, clean lid on the jar; then twist on the band until it is finger tight. Do not screw the tops on too tightly because the air inside the jar must be able to escape during processing.
6. Place the filled and sealed jars into a canning rack; then lower them into the pot of boiling water, making sure they're covered by at least an inch of water.
7. After processing the jars for the amount of time recommended in the recipe, turn off the heat and let the jars stand in the water for at least 5 minutes. Remove the rack and the jars from the water and allow the jars to cool for 12 hours. Do not retighten or overtighten bands that may have come loose during canning, as that will interfere with the sealing process.
8. Press on the center of the cooled lid. If the jar is sealed, the lid will not flex up or down.
9. Store the sealed jars in a cool, dark pantry for up to a year.

Check with your local university extension service for more information about canning, or check out Web sites such as www.vegetablegardener.com. See Sources for additional books and resources on canning.

Note Some recipes call for canning salt. This is pure salt that does not contain anticaking agents or iodine that might make the canning liquid cloudy. You may substitute pure sea salt for canning salt.

EXTENDING THE SEASONS

"Think of sweet cherries, peaches, artichokes, all being grown locally," says Jim Riddle, University of Minnesota's organic outreach coordinator, who is working with researchers and farmers to extend our short growing season. Hoop houses, high tunnels, and greenhouses help harness today's technologies to a delicious future by protecting crops from the wind and capturing the sun with solar panels. Riddle works with organic farmers and those transitioning to organic practices, connecting them to the latest in research and production methods. "We are a young country, a country of immigrants with a variety of food traditions. We have an opportunity to develop a cuisine rooted in place, in the soil." Such advances in sustainable practices will provide us with food that tastes fresher and is healthier than anything being shipped in from other parts of the country and the world.

pickled cherry peppers

This has become a favorite at backyard barbecues and on picnics. **MAKES 1 QUART**

10 to 15 cherry peppers

2 cloves garlic, peeled

¼ teaspoon black peppercorns

1 small bunch parsley

1 small bay leaf

1½ cups white wine vinegar

1 cup water

1 teaspoon coarse salt

1 tablespoon sugar

Wash and dry the peppers and put them in a quart-sized canning jar. Add the garlic, peppercorns, parsley, and bay leaf.

In a saucepan, combine the vinegar, water, salt, and sugar and turn the heat to high. Bring the mixture to a boil and cook for 1 minute. Pour the liquid over the peppers; then let the jar and its contents cool completely to room temperature. Cover and refrigerate for at least 1 week. The pickled peppers will keep up to 2 months, refrigerated.

pickled carrots

These carrots perk up hearty winter soups and stews with their intense color and bright, sharp flavors.

MAKES ABOUT 1 PINT

½ pound carrots, cut into 2-inch matchsticks

1 tablespoon coarse salt

1 cup champagne vinegar or fruit vinegar

¼ cup honey or brown sugar

Crushed red pepper flakes to taste

Place the carrots in a bowl and toss them with the salt. Allow the carrots to sit for 1 hour; then rinse and drain them well. Put the carrots into a canning jar or a glass bowl.

In a small saucepan, combine the vinegar, honey, and crushed red pepper. Bring the vinegar to a boil, stirring. Pour the vinegar over the carrots and let cool to room temperature. Cover the jar and store it in the refrigerator overnight to allow the flavors to marry before serving. It keeps for up to 1 month.

dilly beans

Dilly Beans are great served with a selection of cheeses, as a side to grilled burgers and chicken, and to garnish Bloody Marys. **MAKES ABOUT 4 PINTS OR 2 QUARTS**

2 pounds green beans
1 teaspoon cayenne pepper
4 cloves garlic
4 heads dill

¼ cup canning salt
2½ cups white wine vinegar
2½ cups water

Prepare a stockpot or canner and jars (see page 227).

Trim the ends off the beans. Pack the beans lengthwise into the hot jars, leaving ¼ inch of headspace. Add ¼ teaspoon of cayenne pepper, 1 clove of garlic, and 1 head of dill to each pint jar. Or, add ½ teaspoon of cayenne pepper, 2 cloves of garlic, and 2 heads of dill to each quart jar.

Combine the salt, vinegar, and water in a large saucepan set over high heat and bring it to a boil. Ladle the hot liquid over the beans, leaving ¼ inch of headspace. Remove the air bubbles and check the headspace again. If needed, add more hot pickling liquid to meet the recommended headspace.

Wipe the jar rim, place a lid on the jar, and screw on the band until it is just finger tight. Process the jars for 10 minutes in boiling water that covers the jars by 1 inch.

Turn off the heat and allow the jars to stand in the hot water for 5 minutes before removing them. Allow the jars to cool for at least 12 hours before storing them in a cool, dark place.

spiced pickled beets

These magenta beets add a pretty, sweet-spicy note to the relish tray. **MAKES ABOUT 4 PINTS**

4 pounds beets

2 cups sugar

4 cinnamon sticks

1 tablespoon whole cloves

1 tablespoon cardamom seeds

1 teaspoon salt

2½ cups cider vinegar

1½ cups water

3 medium onions, sliced 1 inch thick

Preheat the oven to 350 degrees. Wash the beets, wrap them in foil, and place the packet on a baking sheet. Roast until the beets are tender, about 50 minutes to 1 hour. After the beets have cooled, peel them and cut them into 1-inch slices.

Prepare a stockpot or canner and jars (see page 227).

Put the sugar, cinnamon sticks, cloves, cardamom seeds, salt, vinegar, and water in a saucepan set over high heat. Bring it to a boil; then reduce the heat and simmer for about 5 minutes.

Tightly pack the beets and onions into sterilized canning jars. Remove the cinnamon sticks, cloves, and cardamom seeds from the liquid. Pour the hot liquid over the vegetables, leaving ¼ inch of headspace. Remove the air bubbles and check the headspace again. Wipe the rims, center the lids on the jars, and screw on the bands until they are just finger tight.

Process the filled jars in boiling water for about 30 minutes. Turn off the heat, remove the canner lid, and let the jars remain in the hot water for 5 minutes before removing them. Let the pickled beets cool, and then store them in a cool, dark place.

pickled eggs with horseradish and beets

This timeless bar snack is brightened by beets and a kick of horseradish. The eggs and beets make a nice alternative to deviled eggs and are great in egg salad. Serve them with the Spiced Beet Caviar (page 146). The recipe comes from International Falls, Minnesota, where pickled eggs are standard picnic fare and toted in coolers in fishing boats. (For a particularly special twist, try tiny quail eggs.) **MAKES 6 EGGS**

6 hard-boiled eggs, peeled

1½ cups cider vinegar

¼ cup grated fresh horseradish or 2 tablespoons prepared horseradish

2 teaspoons coarse salt

1 tablespoon sugar

1 small white onion, thinly sliced

2 medium beets, thinly sliced

5 cloves garlic, peeled

Put the eggs in a roomy glass jar with a tight-fitting lid. Put the remaining ingredients and 1½ cups of water into a nonreactive pot set over medium-high heat. Bring it to a boil; then reduce the heat so the mixture bubbles gently. Cook until the onion and beets are soft. Carefully remove the beets and add them with the garlic to the jar of eggs; then pour the hot liquid over the eggs. (Discard the onion.) Let the jar and its contents sit at room temperature for an hour or so until cool. Cover the jar tightly and refrigerate the eggs for at least 24 hours before eating. The eggs will keep about a week in the refrigerator.

roasted tomato–chipotle salsa

The time for tomatoes is the height of summer, when they are juice-splitting perfect and easy to can. Our farmers' markets are burgeoning then with peppers, hot and sweet, as well. **MAKES 3 PINTS**

9 dried chipotle chili peppers, stemmed
9 dried cascabel chili peppers, stemmed
1 ½ cups hot water
2 ¼ pounds Italian plum tomatoes
2 small green bell peppers

1 large onion
1 clove garlic
1 ½ teaspoons sugar
¾ teaspoon salt
¾ cup white wine vinegar

Prepare a stockpot or canner and jars (see page 227).

Toast the chipotle and cascabel chilies on both sides in a large, dry skillet over medium heat until they release their aroma and are pliable, about 30 seconds per side. Transfer the chilies to a large glass or stainless steel bowl and add the hot water. Weight the chilies with a bowl or other weight to ensure they remain submerged, and soak until they have softened, about 15 minutes. Working in batches, transfer the chilies and their soaking liquid to a blender or a food processor fitted with a metal blade and puree until smooth. Set aside.

Roast the tomatoes, bell peppers, onion, and garlic under a broiler, turning to roast on all sides, until the tomatoes and peppers are blistered, blackened, and softened and the onion and garlic are blackened in spots, about 15 minutes. Set the onion and garlic aside until they are cool. Place the tomatoes and bell peppers in paper bags. Secure the openings and set aside until they are cool enough to handle, about 15 minutes. Peel and chop the tomatoes, peppers, onion, and garlic.

Combine the chili puree, roasted vegetables, sugar, salt, and vinegar in a large stainless steel saucepan. Bring to a boil over medium-high heat, stirring constantly. Reduce the heat and boil gently, stirring frequently, until slightly thickened, about 15 minutes.

Ladle the hot salsa into the warm jars, leaving ½ inch of headspace. Remove the air bubbles and check the headspace again. If needed, add more salsa to meet the recommended headspace. Wipe the rims, center the lids on the jars, and screw on the bands until they are just finger tight.

Process the filled jars in boiling water for 45 minutes. Turn off the heat, remove the canner lid, and let the jars remain in the hot water for another 5 minutes. Remove the jars, let them cool, and then store them in a cool, dark place.

fresh corn relish

About this time of year, we're all getting a little weary of corn, but come January, we'll be counting the months until it is back in town. Here's a quick way to capture corn's sunny flavor. **MAKES 3 PINTS**

4 cups (about 9 ears) corn kernels

2 cups (about ½ head) chopped green cabbage

½ cup chopped onion

½ cup chopped green bell pepper

½ cup chopped red bell pepper

½ cup sugar

1 tablespoon dry mustard

1½ teaspoons celery seed

1½ teaspoons mustard seed

1½ teaspoons salt

1½ teaspoons turmeric

2 cups vinegar

½ cup water

Prepare a stockpot or canner and jars (see page 227).

Combine all of the ingredients in a large saucepan. Bring the mixture to a boil; then reduce the heat and simmer for 20 minutes.

Ladle the hot relish into the jars, leaving ¼ inch of headspace. Remove the air bubbles and check the headspace again. If needed, add more relish to meet the recommended headspace. Wipe the jar rims, center the lids on the jars, and screw on the bands until they are just finger tight.

Process the filled jars in boiling water for 15 minutes. Turn off the heat, remove the canner lid, and let the jars sit in the hot water for another 5 minutes. Remove the jars, let them cool, and then store them in a cool, dark place.

real ketchup

This richly spiced ketchup is far tastier than anything on the grocery store shelves, and it is lower in sugar and salt too. Unlike commercial ketchup, homemade ketchup is thickened by cooking rather than by artificial thickeners or stabilizers. You'll need a big nonreactive saucepan or soup pot, about 12 quarts, to hold all the tomatoes. **MAKES ABOUT 7 PINTS (IT'S GOOD TO STOCK UP)**

2 tablespoons celery seed

1 tablespoon whole cloves

3 cinnamon sticks

2 teaspoons allspice berries

3 cups cider vinegar

24 pounds (about 72 medium) tomatoes,
    quartered, with their juices

4 cups chopped onions

1 teaspoon cayenne pepper

1¼ cups sugar

¼ cup kosher or sea salt

Prepare a stockpot or canner and jars (see page 227).

Tie the celery seed, cloves, cinnamon sticks, and allspice berries into a square of cheesecloth or a spice bag.

Put the vinegar and the spice bag in a large stainless steel saucepan. Bring the vinegar to a boil over high heat. Turn off the heat and let the vinegar stand for about 30 minutes; then remove and discard the spice bag.

In a large stainless steel pot, stir together the tomatoes and their juices, onions, and cayenne, and mash the tomatoes to release even more juice. Set the pan over high heat and bring to a boil. Reduce the heat and simmer for about 20 minutes, stirring occasionally. Add the infused vinegar and continue simmering until the vegetables are soft and the mixture begins to thicken, about 30 minutes.

Working in batches, transfer the mixture to a sieve set over a glass or stainless steel bowl and press with the back of a spoon to extract all the liquid. Or, put the mixture through a food mill. Discard the solids.

Return the strained liquid to the saucepan, add the sugar and salt, and set the heat to medium-high. Bring the ketchup to a boil; then reduce the heat and simmer, stirring frequently, until the liquid is reduced by half and the mixture is as thick as commercial ketchup, about 45 minutes.

Ladle the hot ketchup into the warm jars, leaving ½ inch of headspace. Remove the air bubbles and check the headspace again. If needed, add more ketchup to meet the recommended headspace. Wipe the jar rims, center the lids on the jars, and screw on the bands until they are just finger tight.

Place the jars in the canner, ensuring they are completely covered with water. Bring to a boil and process for 15 minutes. Turn off the heat, remove the canner lid, and let the jars remain in the hot water for another 5 minutes. Remove the jars, let them cool, and then store them in a cool, dark place.

watermelon rind pickles

Easy! **MAKES 3 PINTS**

1 large watermelon

2 quarts water

½ cup canning salt

3 cups sugar

2 cups white wine vinegar

4 thinly sliced lemons

5 cinnamon sticks

3 tablespoons allspice berries

10 whole cloves

Remove the skin and any remaining pink flesh from the watermelon rind and cut the rind into 1-inch chunks. (You should have about 8 cups.) Stir together the 2 quarts of water and the salt in a large, nonreactive container. Add the rind and let it soak overnight.

Prepare a stockpot or canner and jars (see page 227).

Drain the rind, rinse it, and drain it again. Put the rind into a large pan, cover it with water, and turn the heat to high. Bring the water to a boil; then reduce the heat and simmer until the rind is tender, about 10 to 15 minutes. Drain the rind.

In a large saucepan, stir together the sugar, vinegar, and lemons. Add the cinnamon sticks, allspice berries, and cloves. Set the pan over high heat, bring it to a boil, then reduce the heat and simmer for about 5 minutes. Add the rind and cook until it is clear, about 15 minutes.

Pack the rind into hot, sterilized 1-pint jars. Pour in the syrup, leaving about ½ inch of headspace. Wipe the jar rims, center the lids on the jars, and screw on the bands until they are just finger tight. Process the jars for 10 minutes in enough boiling water to cover the jars by 1 inch. Turn off the heat, remove the canner lid, and allow the jars to stand in the hot water for 5 minutes before removing them. Cool the pickles for at least 12 hours before storing them in a cool, dark place.

rhubarb chutney

Put up pints of spring's first rhubarb to give at the holidays. It's wonderful with turkey or served over mild cheese with crackers. **MAKES 7 TO 8 PINTS**

4 cups chopped rhubarb

2 cups honey

½ cup molasses or sorghum

2 cups dried fruit (cherries and cranberries)

¼ cup golden raisins

1 teaspoon freshly grated ginger

Zest of 1 orange

½ cup white wine

¼ cup white wine vinegar

1 teaspoon ground allspice

1 teaspoon ground cloves

2 teaspoons ground cinnamon

Prepare a stockpot or canner and jars (see page 227).

Place all the ingredients in a large heavy-bottomed saucepan set over high heat. Bring it to a boil, stir, and cook, uncovered, for about 30 minutes, stirring occasionally. Taste and adjust the seasonings, adding more vinegar or a little more honey if necessary. Ladle the chutney into the hot, sterilized jars, leaving ½ inch of headspace. Wipe the jar rims, center the lids on the jars, and screw on the bands until they are just finger tight. Process the jars for 10 minutes in enough boiling water to cover the jars by 1 inch. Turn off the heat, remove the canner lid, and allow the jars to stand in the hot water for 5 minutes before removing them. Cool the jars for at least 12 hours before storing them in a cool, dark place.

green tomato marmalade

This spicy sweet puts those end-of-season green tomatoes to good use. **MAKES 6 HALF-PINT JARS**

3 pounds green tomatoes

Finely grated zest and juice of 1 organic orange

5 cups sugar

1 whole jalapeño, seeded, deveined, and chopped

Wash and dice the tomatoes and put them in a bowl with the orange zest and orange juice. Cover the tomatoes with the sugar and let them stand overnight.

Transfer the mixture to a big saucepan and add the jalapeño. Set the pan over medium heat and cook to dissolve the sugar; then bring the mixture to a gentle boil and cook until the jam begins to set, or will coat the back of a spoon, about 45 minutes.

Meanwhile, prepare a stockpot or canner and jars (see page 227).

Spoon the marmalade into sterilized jars, leaving ½ inch of headspace. Wipe the jar rims, center the lids on the jars, and screw on the bands until they are just finger tight. Process the jars for 10 minutes in enough boiling water to cover the jars by 1 inch. Turn off the heat, remove the canner lid, and allow the jars to stand in the hot water for 5 minutes before removing them. Cool the jars for at least 12 hours before storing them in a cool, dark place.

cranberry ginger salsa

Serve this fresh, tangy salsa with chips, on top of a mild creamy cheese, or alongside a roast. It will keep for several weeks in the refrigerator. **MAKES ABOUT 3 CUPS**

1 large orange

3 cups fresh cranberries, rinsed and sorted

¼ cup crystallized ginger, chopped

2 teaspoons grated fresh ginger

½ cup sugar, or to taste

Using a vegetable peeler or a zester, remove the zest from the orange, avoiding the bitter white pith, and place it in a food processor fitted with a steel blade. Slice the orange in half and squeeze the juice into the food processor. Add the cranberries along with the crystallized ginger, fresh ginger, and sugar. Process until the mixture is chunky, about 15 to 30 seconds. Taste the salsa and add more ginger or sugar, if desired. This will keep in the refrigerator, covered, up to one month.

apple jelly, savory and sweet

Make apple jelly with mint for lamb dishes and with sage or rosemary for chicken or pork. Steep it with cinnamon, add some additional sugar, and you have a lovely breakfast spread. **MAKES 5 TO 6 HALF-PINT JARS**

3 pounds tart apples or crab apples, peeled, cored, and chopped

1 cinnamon stick or 1 small bunch fresh mint, rosemary, or sage, chopped

1 tablespoon cider vinegar

Sugar (see instructions for amount)

Put the apples into a large heavy-bottomed pot with 4 cups of water. Add the cinnamon stick, if using, and the vinegar (herbs, if used, are added later). Bring the water to a boil; then reduce the heat and simmer until the fruit is very tender, about 40 to 50 minutes.

Turn the apple mixture into a jelly bag or cheesecloth, and allow it to drip into a large, nonreactive bowl for several hours or overnight. Do not squeeze the bag or the jelly will cloud.

When the fruit has stop dripping, measure the juice in the bowl and then pour it into a pan. For every 2½ cups of liquid, add 2½ cups of sugar.

Set the pan over low heat, and heat the liquid until the sugar is completely dissolved. Raise the heat and bring the liquid to a boil. When the mixture has reached the softball stage (about 235 degrees on a candy thermometer) and thickly coats the back of a spoon, about 25 minutes, remove the pan from the heat. Skim the scum off the surface. Once the jelly has rested for 10 to 15 minutes, stir in the chopped herb, if using.

Meanwhile, prepare a stockpot or canner and jars (see page 227).

Pour the jelly into warm, sterilized jars, leaving ¼ inch of headspace. Wipe the jar rims, center the lids on the jars, and screw on the bands until they are just finger tight. Process the jelly for 10 minutes in enough boiling water to cover the jars by 1 inch. Turn off the heat, remove the canner lid, and allow the jars to stand in the hot water for 5 minutes before removing them. Cool the jelly for at least 12 hours before storing it in a cool, dark place.

grandmother's strawberry jam

Jam made with fresh strawberries sets easily when the strawberries are left to stand overnight, allowing time for the berries to slowly release their juices along with some of their natural pectin. **MAKES 4 PINTS**

4 cups unblemished, tiny sweet strawberries

Juice of 1 lemon

3 cups sugar

Put the strawberries and lemon juice in a stainless steel saucepan and cover them with the sugar. Let the berries stand overnight.

Prepare a stockpot or canner and jars (see page 227).

Put the saucepan containing the berries and the accumulated juices on the stove. Bring it to a boil and stir until the sugar is dissolved. Mash some of the berries with the back of a fork. Continue to boil until the jam begins to set and thickly coats the back of a spoon, about 30 minutes.

Pour the jam into sterilized jars, leaving ¼ inch of headspace. Wipe the jar rims, center the lids on the jars, and screw on the bands until they are just finger tight. Process the jars for 10 minutes in boiling water that covers the jars by 1 inch. Turn off the heat, remove the canner lid, and allow the jars to stand in the hot water for 5 minutes before removing them. Cool the jam for at least 12 hours before storing it in a cool, dark place.

backyard grape jelly

This is the tangy jelly our grandmothers made that truly tasted of fresh grapes. To make it, you'll need a jelly cone, which is a muslin sleeve that filters the grape juice from the skins and seeds. A strainer lined with a double thickness of cheesecloth will work too. **MAKES 8 CUPS**

5 cups fresh grape juice (recipe follows)　　1 box pectin or Sure-Jell
7 cups sugar

Prepare a stockpot or canner and jars (see page 227).

Pour the juice into a saucepan. In a small bowl, stir together the sugar and pectin and set it aside. (Stirring the pectin into the sugar before adding it to the juice helps prevent the pectin from clumping into sandy nubs.) Bring the juice to a full, rolling boil, stirring constantly; then quickly stir in the sugar and pectin. Return the juice to a boil and cook for 1 minute, stirring all the while. Remove the pan from the heat and skim off the foam.

Quickly ladle the jelly into the jars, filling them to within 1/8 inch of the top. Wipe the jar rims, center the lids on the jars, and screw on the bands until they are just finger tight. Process the jars for 10 minutes in enough boiling water to cover the jars by 1 inch. Turn off the heat, remove the canner lid, and allow the jars to stand in the hot water for 5 minutes before removing them. Cool the jelly for at least 12 hours before storing it in a cool, dark place.

Grape Juice
MAKES ABOUT 8 TO 10 CUPS

15 cups Concord grapes (approximately)

Put the grapes in a large pot and add enough water to just cover the grapes. Bring the water to a boil, reduce the heat, and simmer until the grapes have burst their skins and cooked down. Turn the juice into a jelly bag and allow it to drip into a large pot. Alternately, strain it twice through a strainer lined with a double layer of cheesecloth.

acknowledgments

WHEN IT COMES TO WRITING A COOKBOOK, no one can do it alone. Every recipe and story is shared in person or on the page. I am ever grateful to friends and family who joined me in creating this work. Kevin, my husband, is a deep well of encouragement, good humor, and sound advice, and our sons, Matt, Kip, and Tim, have cheered me on for years in the kitchen.

Warm thanks to my editor, Todd Orjala, for his enthusiasm, insight, clarity, and guidance; to Pam Price for her accuracy and grace in copyediting this manuscript; and to Kristian Tvedten for his patience and care in expediting its production.

Cooks need eaters and writers need readers. Lucky me to have friends willing to be both. Kathy Coskran, a fine writer, helped wrestle the first full draft into shape with kindness and wit. Martha Brand's keen eye, culinary experience, and advice helped me reach the finish line. Thanks to Larkin McPhee and Barbara Coffin for their company as we barnstormed and brainstormed over blue highways researching our respective projects. Elly Grace was a valiant and spirited traveling companion to farms near and far.

How can I repay friends who read pages and tested recipes: Mary O'Brien, Martha McLaughlin, Sally Spector, Kishori Koch, Adam Jensen, and Julie Coskran. To Leslie Bush, Patty Hoolihan, Angie Lillihei, Mary Reyelts, Randi Lebedoff, and Sarah Evert, thanks for your endless interest and support. Bonnie Blodgett inspired many of the recipes that first appeared in her *Garden Letter*.

I owe much to the farmers, purveyors, chefs, writers, and researchers who shared their knowledge of our local foodshed. Many are named throughout the book, but special thanks to Atina Diffley, Audrey Arner, Mary Jo Forbord, Loretta and Martin Jaus, Florence Minar, Meg Moynihan, Jim Riddle, Keith Adams, Greg Reynolds, Jack Hedin, Tim Fischer, Steven Read and Jodi Ohlsen Read, Mary Falk, Ken Meter, Todd Churchill, Tom Nuessmeier, Brett Laidlaw and Mary Eckmeier, Doug and Lin Hilgendorf, Leah Caplan, Phil Rutter, Brian DeVore, Barth Anderson, Victor Mrotz, Lisa Lindberg, Regi Haslett-Marroquin, and Nick Vander Puy.

This book continues the work begun with *Savoring the Seasons of the Northern Heartland*, coauthored with Lucia Watson, a dear friend and wise, accomplished chef and restaurateur from whom I have learned so much through these many years.

sources

IT IS IMPOSSIBLE to track all of the wonderful artisan products coming into market. This list, by no means complete, attempts to present a sense of the range of enterprises that use sustainable practices and produce astonishingly good food.

Alemar Cheese
622 North Riverfront Drive
Mankato, Minnesota 56001
(507) 385-1004
www.alemarcheese.com
Bent River Camembert-style cheese from single-source milk

Alexis Bailly Vineyard
18200 Kirby Avenue
Hastings, Minnesota 55033
(651) 437-1413
www.abvwines.com
Outstanding Isis (ice wine) and fortified orange-infused Ratafia

Ames Farm
Main Street
Watertown, Minnesota 55388
(952) 955-3348
www.amesfarm.com
Single-source honey from the surrounding prairie

Badgersett Research Farm
18606 Deer Road
Canton, Minnesota 55922
(507) 743-8570
www.badgersett.com
Chestnuts, hazelnuts

Bar 5 Meat and Poultry
23160 441st Avenue
Arlington, Minnesota 55307
(507) 964-5612
Fresh and smoked chicken, duck, turkey, and pork

Bay Fisheries
207 Wilson Avenue
Bayfield, Wisconsin 54814
(715) 779-3910
Fresh and smoked fish

Big Woods Bison
12220 190th Street East
Nerstrand, Minnesota 55053
(507) 789-5880
All manner of cuts, plus burger, jerky, and sausage

Bodin Fisheries
208 Wilson Avenue
Bayfield, Wisconsin 54814
(715) 779-3301
www.bodinfisheries.com
Fresh and smoked fish

Bushel Boy Farms
215 32nd Avenue Southwest
Owatonna, Minnesota 55060
(507) 451-5692
www.bushelboy.com
Hydroponic tomatoes, lettuces, herbs, and greens

Callister Farm
52237 170th Avenue
West Concord, Minnesota 55985
(507) 527-8521
www.callisterfarm.com
Free-range heritage chickens (Poulet Rouge),
turkeys, and eggs

Capital Brewery
7734 Terrace Avenue
Middleton, Wisconsin 53562
(608) 836-7100
www.capital-brewery.com
Island Wheat Beer brewed from Washington Island wheat

Cedar Summit Farm
25830 Drexel Avenue
New Prague, Minnesota 55047
(952) 758-6886
www.cedarsummit.com
Farmstead organic, free-range, single-source milk, yogurt,
and ice cream

Crave Brothers Farmstead Cheese
W11555 Torpy Road
Waterloo, Wisconsin 53594
(920) 478-4887
www.cravecheese.com
Range of farmstead cheeses, including fresh mozzarella
and mascarpone

Cress Spring Bakery
4035 Ryan Road
Blue Mounds, Wisconsin 53517
(608) 767-3875
Artisan bread from local, freshly ground wheat, baked on-site

Dakota Growers Pasta Company
One Pasta Avenue
Carrington, North Dakota 58421
(701) 652-2855
www.dakotagrowers.com
Assorted pastas from locally grown wheat

Dakota Harvest Farm
33565 Dakota Road
Jefferson, South Dakota 57038
(605) 966-5490
www.dakotaharvestfarm.com
Lamb from long-haired (not fleece) meat sheep

Dave's BrewFarm
2470 Wilson Street
Wilson, Wisconsin 54027
(612) 432-8130
www.davesbrewfarm.blogspot.com
A rare farmstead brewery

Death's Door Spirits
220 West Lakeside Street
Madison, Wisconsin 53715
(608) 441-1083
www.deathsdoorspirits.com
Vodka, gin, and white whiskey made from
Washington Island wheat and herbs

Dockside Fish Market
418 West Highway 61
Grand Marais, Minnesota 55604
(218) 387-2906
www.docksidefishmarket.com
Fresh and smoked fish

Dragsmith Farms
1301 16th Avenue
Barron, Wisconsin 54812
(715) 537-3307
Greenhouse greens, lettuces, herbs, and microgreens

Eichten's Hidden Acres
16440 Lake Boulevard
Center City, Minnesota 55012
(651) 267-1566
www.theeichtensbistro.com
www.specialtycheese.com
European-style cheeses and American bison meat

Faribault Dairy Company, Inc.
222 Third Street Northeast
Faribault, Minnesota 55021
(507) 334-5260
www.faribaultdairy.com
Cave-aged blue cheeses and Gorgonzola cheese

Featherstone Farm
43090 City Park Road
Rushford Village, Minnesota 55971
(507) 459-5209 (CSA information)
(507) 864-2400 (main)
www.featherstonefarm.com
CSA and vegetable farm

Ferndale Market
31659 County 24 Boulevard
Cannon Falls, Minnesota 55009
(507) 263-4556
www.ferndalemarketonline.com
*Farmstead free-range turkeys and assorted locally
produced foods*

Fischer Family Farms Pork
37784 100th Street
Waseca, Minnesota 56093-4501
(866) 524-7623
www.fischerfamilyfarmspork.com
Pork cuts, sausage, and bacon

Forest Mushrooms
14715 County Road 51
St. Joseph, Minnesota 56374
(320) 363-7956
www.forestmushrooms.com
*Fresh and dried shiitake, chanterelle, and oyster
mushrooms plus grow-your-own kits*

Future Farm Food and Fuel
2047 County Road E
Baldwin, Wisconsin 54002
www.afuturefarm.com
Tilapia, salad greens, and herbs

Gardens of Eagan
25494 Highview Avenue
Farmington, Minnesota 55024
(952) 985-7233
www.gardensofeagan.com
*One of the area's first organic vegetable farms,
with a farm school*

Halvorson Fisheries
Bell Marina
22690 Siskiwit Parkway
Cornucopia, Wisconsin 54827
(715) 742-3402
www.halvorsonfisheries.com
Fresh and smoked fish

Harmony Valley Farm
S3442 Wire Hollow Road
Viroqua, Wisconsin 54665
(608) 483-2143
www.harmonyvalleyfarm.com
CSA vegetables and organic meat

Hickory Nut Heaven
65 Parkview Circle
Columbus, Wisconsin 53925
(920) 623-3145
hickoryheaven@charter.net
Hickory nuts and other wild-gathered items

Hillside Farmers Cooperative
Rural Enterprise Center
105 East Fourth Street, Suite 300
Northfield, Minnesota 55057
(952) 201-8852
Main Street Project
2104 Stevens Avenue
Minneapolis, Minnesota 55404
(612) 879-7578
www.ruralec.com
*Hillside Farmers Cooperative is a project of the Rural
Enterprise Center, which is a program of the Main Street
Project. Co-op members produce free-range poultry. The co-op
connects Latino immigrants with established farmers.*

Hoch Orchard
32553 Forster Road
La Crescent, Minnesota 55947
(507) 643-6329
www.hochorchard.com
Organic heritage apples, berries, and cider

Hodgson Mill
1100 Stevens Avenue
Effingham, Illinois 62401
(800) 347-0105
www.hodgsonmIllinoiscom
Range of organic flours, baking ingredients, and mixes

Hook's Cheese Company, Inc.
320 Commerce Street
Mineral Point, Wisconsin 53565
(608) 987-3259
www.hookscheese.com
Award-winning Gorgonzola, blue, and Colby cheeses,
plus cheddar and other cheeses

Hope Creamery
9043 Southwest 37th Avenue
Hope, Minnesota 56046
(507) 451-2029
Fresh high-fat, small-batch butter

J & L Bison Ranch
5650 41st Avenue Northwest
Willmar, Minnesota 56201
(320) 235-8465
www.jlbison.com
Bison cuts

La Quercia
400 Hakes Drive
Norwalk, Iowa 50211
(515) 981-1625
www.laquercia.us/home
Artisan cured-pork products such as prosciutto, pancetta,
coppa, speck, lonza, guanciale, and lardo

Leatherwood Vinegary
20395 County 86
Long Prairie, Minnesota 56347
(320) 732-2879
www.leatherwoodvinegary.com
The region's oldest (perhaps only) farmstead vinegary

Lorentz Meats
705 Cannon Industrial Boulevard
Cannon Falls, Minnesota 55009
(507) 263-3618
www.lorentzmeats.com
Small, artisan processor of fresh and processed meat;
sausage maker

Lou's Fish House
1319 Highway 61
Two Harbors, Minnesota 55616
(218) 834-5254
www.lousfish.com
One of the first to smoke fish on the North Shore

LoveTree Farmstead Cheese
12413 County Road Z
Grantsburg, Wisconsin 54840
(715) 488-2966
www.lovetreefarmstead.com
Artisan farmstead cave-aged sheep milk cheeses

Maytag Dairy Farm
2282 Eighth Street North
Newton, Iowa 50208
(641) 792-1133
www.maytagdairyfarm.com
Handmade, small-batch blue cheese

Miesfeld's Meat Market
4811 Venture Drive
Sheboygan, Wisconsin 53083
(920) 565-6328
www.miesfelds.com
Brats and more

Morel-Farms.com

600 Mor-Land Drive

Lafayette, Indiana 47903

(800) 522-6550

www.morel-farms.com

Elm saplings inoculated with morel fungus for
establishing morel plantations

Morgan Creek Vineyards

23707 478th Avenue

New Ulm, Minnesota 56073

(507) 947-3547

www.morgancreekvineyards.com

Riesling, ice wine, and other wines made from
Minnesota grapes

Native Harvest

607 Main Avenue

Callaway, Minnesota 56521

(888) 274-8318

www.nativeharvest.com

Native American foods such as hominy, hand-harvested wild
rice, maple syrup, dried berries, and herb teas

Neuske's

1390 East Grand Avenue

Wittenberg, Wisconsin 54499

(715) 253-4059 (store)

(800) 392-2266 (phone orders)

www.neuskes.com

Applewood-smoked country-style ham and bacon

Newago Fish Market

707 Old Military Road

Bayfield, Wisconsin 54814

(715) 779-2388

www.lakesuperiorwhitefish.com/NewagoFisheries.html

Fresh and smoked Lake Superior fish

Northern Waters Smokehaus

394 Lake Avenue South, Suite 106

Duluth, Minnesota 55802

(218) 724-7307

www.nwsmokehaus.com

Range of smoked fish and meat, including bacon, salami, and pate

Organic Valley Family of Farms

CROPP Cooperative

One Organic Way

LaFarge, Wisconsin 54639

(888) 444-6455

www.organicvalley.coop

Organic dairy products and eggs

Pastures A Plenty

4075 and 4077 110th Avenue Northeast

Kerkhoven, Minnesota 56252

(320) 367-2061

www.pasturesaplenty.com

Free-range meats

PastureLand Dairy

26889 County 9 Boulevard

Goodhue, Minnesota 55027

(612) 331-9115

www.pastureland.coop

Organic butter and artisanal cheese

Pepin Heights

1753 South Highway 61

Lake City, Minnesota 55041

(651) 345-2305

www.pepinheights.com

Honey Crisp, SweeTango, Zestar, and other apples—
plus lots of cider

Peterson Fisheries

87770 State Highway 13

Bayfield, Wisconsin 54814

(715) 779-5023

Fresh and smoked fish

Peterson's Fish Market
49813 Highway U.S. 41
Hancock, Michigan 49930
(906) 482-2343
exploringthenorth.com/Petersons/fish.html
Fresh and wonderful smoked whitefish

Phillips Distilling
25 Main Street Southeast
Minneapolis, Minnesota 55414
(612) 362-7500
www.prairievodka.com
Makes Prairie Organic Vodka, a locally made spirit

Red Lake Nation Foods, Inc.
P. O. Box 547
Highway 1 North
Red Lake, Minnesota 56671
(218) 679-2611
www.redlakenationfoods.com
Walleye and other freshwater fish, wild rice, and jams

Reichert's Dairy Air
1022 Quebec Street
Knoxville, Iowa 50138
(641) 218-4296
www.reichertsdairyair.com
Farmstead chèvre and feta

Rochdale Farms
K & K Creamery
110 Eagle Drive
Cashton, Wisconsin 54619
(608) 654-7444
Hand-rolled butter and artisan cheeses

Rosewood Tofu
738 Airport Boulevard, #6
Ann Arbor, Michigan 48108
(734) 665-2222
www.rosewoodproducts.com
*Variety of small-batch, handmade, and organic tofu
and soy-based products*

Sandhill Farm
Rural Route 1, Box 155
Rutledge, Missouri 63563
www.sandhillfarm.org
Organic Sandhill sorghum

Seed Savers Exchange
3094 North Winn Road
Decorah, Iowa 52101
(563) 382-5990
www.seedsavers.org
Seed bank, great source for information and heirloom seeds

Shepherd's Way Farms
Nerstrand, Minnesota 55053
(507) 663-9040
www.shepherdswayfarms.com
Artisan farmstead sheep's milk cheeses and lamb sausage

Smude Enterprises
25804 173rd Avenue
Pierz, Minnesota 56364
(320) 468-6925
www.smudeoil.com
Cold-pressed virgin sunflower oil

Stickney Hill Dairy
15371 County Road 48
Kimball, Minnesota 55353
(320) 398-5360
www.stickneydairy.com
Goats' milk cheese

Sunrise Bakery and Gourmet Foods
2810 Diane Lane
Hibbing, Minnesota 55746
(800) 782-6736
www.sunrisegourmet.com
Potica, strudel, and other specialty baked goods

Sunrise Flour Mill
35624 Grand Avenue
North Branch, Minnesota 55056
(651) 674-8050
www.sunriseflourmill.com
Small-batch, hand-milled flour

Superior Planks
Eco Wood Company
La Pointe, Wisconsin 54850
www.superiorplanks.com
Planks for cooking fish

Surly Brewing Company
4811 Dusharme Drive
Brooklyn Center, Minnesota 55429
(763) 535-3330
www.surlybrewing.com
Craft beer in big bold cans

Thousand Hills Cattle Company
6492 318th Street, Suite A
Cannon Falls, Minnesota 55009
(507) 263-4001
www.thousandhillscattleco.com
Grass-fed beef, burgers, and hot dogs

Tiny But Mighty Popcorn (formerly K & K Popcorn)
3282 62nd Street
Shellsburg, Iowa 52332
(319) 436-2119
tinybutmightyfoods.com
Heirloom popcorn—tiny kernels that pop big

Uplands Cheese
5023 State Road 23 North
Dodgeville, Wisconsin 53533
(888) 935-5558
www.uplandscheese.com
Artisan cheeses, including award-winning Pleasant Ridge Reserve

Usinger's Sausage
1030 North Old World Third Street
Milwaukee, Wisconsin 53203
(414) 276-9105
www.usinger.com
European-style wurst, including brats

Whole Grain Milling Company
1579 120th Avenue
Welcome, Minnesota 56181
(507) 728-8489
www.wholegrainmilling.net
Range of organic flours and grain products

Wild Acres Game Farm
7047 Wild Acres Road
Pequot Lakes, Minnesota 56472
(218) 820-1257 (game orders)
(218) 568-5024 (hunting)
wildacresmn.com
Hunting preserve and game farm

Wild Idea Buffalo
P. O. Box 1209
Rapid City, South Dakota 55709-1209
(866) 658-6137
www.wildideabuffalo.com
Cuts of free-range buffalo

Zingerman's Deli and Bakehouse
422 Detroit Street
Ann Arbor, Michigan 48104
(734) 663-3354
www.zingermansdeli.com
An astounding emporium of Northern Heartland fare

FOOD WEB SITES

apples: www.apples.umn.edu
beer: www.midwestmicrobrews.com
bison meat: www.eatbisonmeat.com
grass-fed meat, poultry, eggs: www.eatwild.com

BOOKS

Abundantly Wild: Collecting and Cooking Wild Edibles in the Upper Midwest, Teresa Marrone (Adventure Publications, Inc.)

The Flavor of Wisconsin: An Informal History of Food and Eating in the Badger State, Harva Hachten and Terese Allen (State Historical Society of Wisconsin)

The Fresh Girls Guide to Easy Canning and Preserving, Ana Micka (Voyageur Press)

Land of Amber Waters: The History of Brewing in Minnesota, Doug Hoverson (University of Minnesota Press)

The Minnesota Homegrown Cookbook: Local Food, Local Restaurants, Local Recipes, Renewing the Countryside (Voyageur Press)

The Minnesota Table: Recipes for Savoring Local Food throughout the Year, Shelley N. C. Holl and B. J. Carpenter (Voyageur Press)

Taste of the Midwest, Dan Kaercher (Globe Pequot)

Tastes from Valley to Bluff: The Featherstone Farm Cookbook, Mi Ae Lipe (Featherstone Farm)

Wisconsin Cheese: A Cookbook and Guide to the Cheeses of Wisconsin, Martin Hintz and Pam Percy (Globe Pequot)

NEWSLETTERS AND MAGAZINES

Edible Communities publications covering
the Northern Heartland:
Iowa River Valley: *Edible Iowa River Valley*,
www.ediblecommunities.com/iowarivervalley/
Madison, Wisconsin, and metro area: *Edible Madison*,
www.ediblecommunities.com/madison/
Southeastern Michigan: *Edible WOW*,
www.ediblecommunities.com/wow/
Twin Cities and metro area: *Edible Twin Cities,*
www.ediblecommunities.com/twincities/

The Heavy Table
http://heavytable.com
An e-zine and blog that covers food from roots to table in the Upper Midwest

Simple, Good, and Tasty
www.simplegoodandtasty.com
An e-zine and blog about healthy, sustainably produced food: what it is, where to find it, how to cook it. Membership includes discounts from various vendors.

GENERAL RESOURCES

Crossroads Resource Center
www.crcworks.org
Initiates research and disseminates information to support community self-determination

Food Alliance Midwest
foodalliance.org
Certifies sustainable agriculture practices for farms, ranches, and processors

Institute for Agriculture and Trade Policy
www.IATP.org
Policy and information resource

The Land Institute
www.landinstitute.org
Researches natural systems agriculture and provides information on topics related to sustainability

Land Stewardship Project
www.landstewardshipproject.org
Great source for information about local food in Minnesota. Publishes a yearly CSA directory.

Leopold Center for Sustainable Agriculture
www.leopold.iastate.edu
A think tank that shares the latest research and information

Local Foods
localfoods.umn.edu
Information about local foods

Midwest Organic and Sustainable Education Service (MOSES)
www.mosesorganic.org
Hosts an annual gathering of farmers, producers, researchers, cooks, chefs, and anyone else interested in sustainable food. Works with sustainable farming organizations such as Practical Farmers of Iowa and Sustainable Farming Association of Minnesota (SFA)

Minnesota Grown Program
www.minnesotagrown.com
Statewide partnerships to support local food; produces free Minnesota Grown directory listing farmers' markets, CSA farms, and more

Natural Foods Co-op Directory
www.coopdirectory.org
Online national guide to natural food co-ops

Renewing the Countryside
www.renewingthecountryside.org
Provides information and resources to support the growth of a healthy local food system

University of Minnesota College of Food, Agriculture and Natural Resource Sciences
http://fruit.cfans.umn.edu
Information about growing fruit

University of Minnesota Regional Sustainable Development Partnerships
www.regionalpartnerships.umn.edu
Encourages production and use of locally grown foods

University of Minnesota Southwest Research and Outreach Center
organicecology.umn.edu
Great source of information about local foods and organic farming practices

index

*Numerals in **boldface** indicate recipe titles.*

a

Alexis Bailly's Ratafia, 95, 100
Allen, Will, 171
Amboy Cottage Café, 65
American chestnuts, 7
Anderson, Dave, 165
Anderson, Lynn, 114
Anderson Farms, 114
Apostle Island Dressing, **212**
Apostle Island Fish Company, **162**
apples, 12, 50, 90
    Apple Jelly, Savory and Sweet, **240**
    Applesauce and Apple Butter, Savory and Sweet, **51**
    Braised Red Cabbage, variation with apples, **86**
    Fresh Apple and Sage Sauce, 3
    Ginger Squash and Apple Soup, **11**
    Mom's Fall Fruit Crisp, **50**
    Pheasant with Hard Cider, Apples, and Chestnuts, **20**
    Rich Applesauce Cake, **53**
    Sausage with Apples and Onions, **73**
    Smoked Trout, Apple, and Fennel Salad in Cider Vinaigrette, **5**
    University of Minnesota Apples, 12
    Upsetting the Apple Cart, 52
applesauce:
    Rich Applesauce Cake, **53**
    Savory and Sweet Applesauce and Apple Butter, **51**
Arner, Audrey, 82
arugula:
    Melon, Feta, and Arugula Salad, **171**
    New Potato, Fiddlehead Ferns, and Arugula Salad, **125**
    Pizza with Arugula and Feta, **107**
Asian Chicken Noodle Soup, **10**
asparagus:
    Grilled Asparagus with Chive Vinaigrette, **128**
    Light and Lemony Asparagus Soup, **110**
    Simple Spring Sauté, **132**
    Spring Sauté, **105**
    Vegetable Frittata with Goat Cheese, **123**
Au Bon Canard, 17
Autumn Garden Slaw, **3**
Autumn Squash or Pumpkin Bars with Cranberry Glaze, **48**
Autumn's Bounty: Harvest Meals (menus), 55

b

Backyard Grape Jelly, **242**
bacon:
    Maple Bacon Bites, **59**
    Scandinavian Brown Beans with a Kick, **43**
    Watercress Salad with a French Twist, **106**
Barbecue Ribs with Honey Jalapeño BBQ Sauce, **166**
Barley Pilaf with Chickpeas and Autumn Vegetables, **29**
Basic Sage Stuffing, **40**
Basil Pesto, Traditional, **167**
beans, dried:
    Heartland Dried Beans and Native Harvest Hominy, 70
    Scandinavian Brown Beans with a Kick, **43**
    Spicy Bean and Hominy Stew, **70**
beans, fresh:
    Dilly Beans, **230**
    freezing, xvii
    Green Bean, Corn, and Fennel Sauté, **176**
beef:
    Classic Beef Stock, **66**
    free range, xi
    Hanger Steak with Fresh Horseradish Sauce, **16**
    Hungarian Steak and Mushroom Soup, **65**
    Marinated Beef Pot Roast, **82**
    Oxtails with Stout and Onions, **78**
beer:
    Beer-Braised Pork Chops with Pears, **14**
    Dave's Brewfarm, 165
    Seasonal Beers, 14
    Surly Brewing, 14, 219
Beer Can Chicken, **164**
beets:
    Spiced Beet Caviar, **146**
    Spiced Pickled Beets, **231**
berries:
    Wild Berry Love, 185
    Upside Down Summer Berry Crisp, **184**
    see also individual berries
Best Butter, 222
Bison Steaks with Blue Cheese Butter, **76**
blueberries, 185
    Fresh Blueberry Ice Cream, **186**
Blue Cheese Butter, **223**
blue cheeses, Heartland, 77
Braised Red or Green Cabbage, **86**
Braised Root Vegetables in Mustard Sauce, **89**
Braising—A Key Technique for Winter, 79
bread:
    Baking Real Bread with Brett, 201
    Daily Bread—Cress Spring Bakery, 198
    Daily Loaf, A, **199**
    Forgotten Bread, uses for, 202
    Old-Fashioned Bread and Butter Pudding, **99**
    Rich Brown Soda Bread, **198**
    Whole Wheat Bread, **201**
Bread and Butter Pudding, Old-Fashioned, **99**
Bresette, Keith, 162
broccoli:
    freezing, xvii
    Roast Broccoli or Cauliflower with Garlic and Hot Pepper, **36**
Brown Butter Vinaigrette, **213**

Brussels sprouts:
    Caramelized Brussels Sprouts, **35**
    freezing, xvii
    Oven-Blasted Brussels
        Sprouts, **87**
    Spiced Brussels Sprouts, **59**
buffalo:
    Bison Steaks with Blue Cheese
        Butter, **76**
    Wild Idea Buffalo, 76
Buffler, Rob, and Tom Dickson: *Fishing*
    for Buffalo: A Guide to the Pursuit
    and Cuisine of Carp, Suckers, Eelpout,
    Gar, and Other Rough Fish, 161
butter:
    Best Butter, 222
    Blue Cheese Butter, **223**
    Brown Butter Vinaigrette, **213**
    Flaky Butter Crust, **206**
    Honey Cinnamon Butter, **223**
    Lemon-Parsley Butter, **222**
    Maple Nut Butter, **223**
    Thyme Butter, **222**
buttermilk:
    Buttermilk Scones, Sweet or
        Savory, **196**
    Comfort Lodge Buttermilk
        Pancakes, **205**
    Real Buttermilk Ranch
        Dressing, **211**

C

cabbage:
    Braised Red or Green Cabbage, **86**
    Spicy Savoy Coleslaw, **31**
cakes and cupcakes:
    Favorite Carrot Cupcakes, **98**
    Ginger Stout Cake, **97**
    Pound Cake with Rhubarb
        Strawberry Sauce, **137**
    Rich Applesauce Cake, **53**
    Zucchini Spice Cakes, **189**
canning:
    Yes We Can, 227
    see also individual recipes
Capital Brewery, 188
Caplan, Leah, 220
Caramelized Brussels Sprouts, **35**
Caramelized Onion Soup, **64**
Carnitas, **72**
Carp-ing. Can't Beat Them? Eat
    Them!, 161

carrot(s):
    Carrot and Parsley Salad, **83**
    Carrot Cashew Bisque, **62**
    Favorite Carrot Cupcakes, **98**
    freezing, xvii
    Pickled Carrots, **229**
    Spiced Roast Carrots, **3**
    Sweetest Carrots, **62**
Cather, Willa, 2
cauliflower:
    freezing, xvii
    Grilled Cauliflower Steaks, **174**
    Roast Broccoli or Cauliflower with
        Garlic and Hot Pepper, **36**
Cedar Summit Farm, 187
Chanterelles, 8
Chard, Silky, 32
Charmoula (Moroccan Green Sauce), **67**
chestnuts:
    American Chestnuts, 7
    Cooking with Chestnuts, 7
    Fresh Chestnut Soup, **6**
    Parsnip and Chestnut Puree, **84**
    Pheasant with Hard Cider, Apples,
        and Chestnuts, **20**
cheeses:
    artisan, 101
    see also individual types and recipes
chèvre:
    Honeyed Chèvre, **105**
    Toasted Chèvre, **59**
chicken:
    Asian Chicken Noodle Soup, **10**
    Beer Can Chicken, **164**
    Chicken Braised with Mexican
        Spices, **74**
    Classic Tarragon Chicken
        Salad, **159**
    New Breed, The, 75
    Oven-Fried Chicken, **119**
    Quick Roast Herb Chicken, **22**
    Simple Chicken Stock, **10**
    Turkey or Chicken Pot Pie with
        Cheddar Chive Cobbler
        Crust, **25**
chocolate:
    Chocolate Mousse with Maple
        Cream, **134**
    Oatmeal Chocolate Chip and Dried
        Cranberry Cookies, **49**
    Spiked Chocolate Truffles, **100**
chokecherries, wild, 185

chutney:
    Fresh Mint-Cilantro Chutney, **115**
    Rhubarb Chutney, **237**
Cilantro, Mint, and Cashew Pesto, **168**
Classic Tarragon Chicken Salad, **159**
Come to the Table, xiii–xiv
Community Supported Agriculture,
    xv–xvii
compound butters, 222–23
Concord grapes:
    Backyard Grape Jelly, **242**
    Concord Grape Tart, **190**
Confit, Duck, **18**
Considering Eggplant, 175
cookies:
    Hazelnut and Dried Cherry
        Biscotti, **95**
    Linzer Cookies, **93**
    Maple Sugar Shortbread, **136**
    Oatmeal Chocolate Chip and Dried
        Cranberry Cookies, **49**
Cool Cucumber Yogurt and Mint Salad, **169**
Cool Fruit Soup, **145**
corn:
    CORN!, 155
    Farmstand Corn Chowder, **154**
    freezing, xvi
    Fresh Corn Relish, **234**
    Green Bean, Corn, and Fennel
        Sauté, **176**
    Grilled Sweet Corn with Thyme
        Butter, **173**
    Very Fresh Sweet Corn Salad, **145**
cornmeal:
    Cornmeal-Dusted Panfish, **71**
    Cranberry Tartlets in a Sweet
        Cornmeal Crust, **96**
    Heartland Polenta, 28
    Heartland Polenta with Mushroom
        Ragout, **27**
    Real Cornbread, **197**
    Sweet Cornmeal Crust, **208**
Cracked Wheat Tabouli with Herbs, **133**
cranberries:
    Autumn Squash or Pumpkin Bars
        with Cranberry Glaze, **48**
    Cranberry Cordial, **54**
    Cranberry Ginger Salsa, **239**
    Cranberry Sorbet, **44**
    Cranberry Tartlets in a Sweet
        Cornmeal Crust, **96**
    Ruby Fields: The Cranberry
        Harvest, 45

Savory Cranberry Compote, **41**
Wild Rice Cranberry Pilaf, **38**
Crème Fraiche, **181**
Cress Spring Bakery, 198
Crispy Fried Fish, **116**
cucumbers:
    Cool Cucumber Yogurt and Mint
      Salad, **169**
    Pickle This, **226**
currants, 185
Curried Eggplant, **175**
Curried Melon Salad, **145**
Curried Vegetable Soup, **9**

d

Daily Loaf, A, **199**
Dave's Brewfarm, 165
Death's Door Spirits, 188
Deviled Eggs, Speedy, **59**
Diffley, Atina and Martin, 26, 33, 109,
    144, 178
Dilly Beans, **230**
DIY, xiii
Dowling Community Garden, 180
dressings:
    Apostle Island Dressing, **212**
    Real Buttermilk Ranch
      Dressing, **211**
duck:
    Duck Confit, **18**
    Duck Confit Salad, **19**
    Duck Eggs, 123
    Rendered Duck Fat, **18–19**
    Sure Fire Roast Duck, **17**

e

Eckmeier, Mary, 196
eggplant:
    Considering Eggplant, 175
    Curried Eggplant, **175**
    freezing, xvii
    Tomato, Eggplant, Zucchini, and
      Potato Bake, **163**
eggs:
    Duck Eggs, 123
    Pickled Eggs with Horseradish and
      Beets, **232**
    Showy Spinach Soufflé, **122**
    Speedy Deviled Eggs, **59**
    Vegetable Frittata with Goat
      Cheese, **123**

Watercress Salad with a French
    Twist, **106**
elderberries, 185
Elixirs, Herbal, **141**
Entrepreneurs, x–xi
Extending the Seasons, 227

f

Farmers' Markets, x
farming, xv, 178, 75, 82
Farm-Raised Fish, 13
Farmstand Corn Chowder, **154**
Farrell, James, **209**
Favorite Carrot Cupcakes, **98**
Featherstone Farm, 62
fennel:
    Fennel Kohlrabi Slaw, **170**
    Green Bean, Corn, and Fennel
      Sauté, **176**
    Porketta with Oregano and
      Fennel, **81**
    Rabbit with Pancetta and Fennel, **21**
    Smoked Trout, Apple, and Fennel
      Salad in Cider Vinaigrette, **5**
fiddlehead ferns, 125
    New Potato, Fiddlehead Ferns, and
      Arugula Salad, **125**
Firelight Inn, 189
Fischer, Tim, 114
Fischer Family Farms, 114
fish and fishing:
    Cornmeal Dusted Panfish, **71**
    Crispy Fried Fish, **116**
    Farm-Raised Fish, 13
    Great Lakes Fishing, 162
    see also individual recipes and
      types of fish
Five Fall Dishes in Five Minutes or
    Less, 3
Five Spring Dishes in Five Minutes or
    Less, 105
Five Summer Dishes in Five Minutes or
    Less, 145
Five Winter Dishes in Five Minutes or
    Less, 59
Flaky Butter Crust, **206**
flour, fresh, 200
foie gras, 17
Fourth of July Brats, **157**
freezing guidelines, xvi
Fresh Blueberry Ice Cream, **186**
Fresh Chestnut Soup, **6**

Fresh Corn Relish, **234**
Fresh Tomato Sauce for Pasta, **156**
Fresh Tomato Soup with Basil Ice
    Cream, **153**
Fried Green Tomatoes, **180**
Frittata with Goat Cheese, Vegetable, **123**
frosting, cream cheese, **98**
fruit:
    Cool Fruit Soup, **145**
    Minted Yogurt Cream for Summer
      Fruit, **182**
    Mom's Fall Fruit Crisp, **50**
    see also individual recipes and
      types of fruit
Furious Mustard, **219**

g

game:
    see individual recipes and
      types of game
Gardens of Eagan, 178
garlic:
    Garlic—A Rose by Any Other
      Name, 179
    Lamb Shanks with Garlic and
      Rosemary, **80**
Gasset, Christian and Liz, 17
Gazpacho, Watermelon, **150**
Gedney Pickles, 226
gin:
    Juniper-Gin Marinade, **214**
    Venison Medallions with Juniper
      and Gin, **15**
ginger:
    Cranberry Ginger Salsa, **239**
    Ginger Squash and Apple Soup, **11**
    Ginger Stout Cake, **97**
    Honey Pumpkin Ginger Pie, **46**
Gingrich, Mike, 121
goat, 72
    Carnitas, **72**
Goat Cheese, Vegetable Fritatta with, **123**
Goeke, Virginia, 126
Good Tomatoes, Worth the Wait, 149
gooseberries, 185
grains:
    Muesli, **195**
    New Grain Exchange, 30
    Rolled Grains 101, 204
    Simply Granola, **204**
Grandmother's Strawberry Jam, **241**
Granola, Simply, **204**

Grant, Leslie, 226
grapes:
    Backyard Grape Jelly, **242**
    Concord Grape Tart, **190**
    Grape Juice, **242**
Grasp the Nettle, 109
Green Bean, Corn, and Fennel Sauté, **176**
green tomatoes:
    Fried Green Tomatoes, **180**
    Green Tomato Marmalade, **238**
grilling:
    Grilled Cauliflower Steaks, **174**
    Grilled Plums, **145**
    Grilled Radicchio, **3**
    Grilled Sweet Corn with Thyme
      Butter, **173**
    Grilled Tofu with Spirited
      Marinade, **158**
    Whole Grilled Whitefish or Trout
      with Warm Tomato
      Vinaigrette, **160**
Growing Power, 171
Guthrie, Bob, 182

h

Hanger Steak with Fresh Horseradish
    Sauce, **16**
Harvest Stuffed Squash, **26**
Haslett-Marroquin, Regi, 75
Hayden-Smith, Rose, 180
hazelnuts:
    Hazelnut and Dried Cherry
      Biscotti, **95**
    Hazelnuts and Hickories, 94
    Linzer Cookies, **93**
    Morels and Sunchokes with Toasted
      Hazelnuts, **129**
Heartland Blues, 77
Heartland Dried Beans and Native
    Harvest Hominy, 70
Heartland Peas, 108
Heartland Polenta, 28
Heartland Polenta with Mushroom
    Ragout, **27**
Hedin, Jack, 62
Hello, Goat!, 72
Herbal Elixirs, **141**
Herb Vinegar, 218
herbs, freezing, xvi
heritage foods, xi
Heynen, Jim, 58
hickory nuts, 35, 94

Hilgendorf, Doug, 200
Hillside Farmers Cooperative, 75
Hmong, 111
Hoch Orchard, 52
hominy, 70
    Spicy Bean and Hominy Stew, **70**
honey:
    Honey Cinnamon Butter, **223**
    Honey Jalapeño BBQ Sauce, **216**
    Honey Mustard Vinaigrette, **210**
    Honey, Oh Honey, 47
    Honey Pumpkin Ginger Pie, **46**
    Horseradish and Honey-Glazed
      Root Vegetables, **34**
Honeyed Chèvre, **105**
Hope Creamery, 221
horseradish:
    Hanger Steak with Fresh
      Horseradish Sauce, **16**
    Horseradish and Honey-Glazed
      Root Vegetables, **34**
Hot and Sour Vegetable Soup with
    Tofu, **111**
Hungarian Steak and Mushroom Soup, **65**

i

Ice cream:
    Fresh Blueberry Ice Cream, **186**
    Fresh Tomato Soup with Basil Ice
      Cream, **153**

j

Jam, Grandmother's Strawberry, **241**
Jaus, Loretta and Martin, 187
Jaus Farm, 187
jelly:
    Apple Jelly, Savory and Sweet, **240**
    Backyard Grape Jelly, **242**
Juniper-Gin Marinade, **214**

k

Kahleck, Khaiti, 123
Kale:
    Crispy Kale, **33**
    No Fail Kale, **33**
    Squash Lasagna with Walnuts
      and Kale, **68**
Ketchup, Real, **235**
Kiwifruit?, 182
Koch, Kishori, 135

l

Laidlaw, Brett, 201
Lake Superior Smoked Fish, 5
lamb:
    Pan-Roasted Lamb Chops with Fresh
      Mint-Cilantro Chutney, **115**
    Shanks with Garlic and
      Rosemary, **80**
La Quercia, 61
Leasman, Nancy and Ron, 210
Leatherwood Vinegary, 210
Lemon-Parsley Butter, **222**
Lemon Verbena Syrup, **141**
Leopold, Aldo, 104
Light and Lemony Asparagus
    Soup, **110**
Lindberg, Lisa, 65
Linder's Nursery, 182
Linzer Cookies, **93**
local food, x, xii–xiv
Local Kitchen, The, xiv
Luby, Jim, 182

m

Mandan Bride corn, 28
Many Muffins—One Recipe, **194**
maple:
    Chocolate Mousse with Maple
      Cream, **134**
    Maple Bacon Bites, **59**
    Maple Mustard Basting Sauce, **217**
    Maple Mustard Vinaigrette,
      variation, **210**
    Maple Nut Butter, **223**
    Maple Sugar Shortbread, **136**
    Maple Syrup: The Sweet Taste of
      Spring!, 135
marinades:
    Juniper-Gin Marinade, **214**
    Rosemary-Mint Marinade, **215**
    Spirited Marinade, **158**
Marinated Beef Pot Roast, **82**
Marrone, Theresa: *Abundantly Wild:*
    Collecting and Cooking Wild Edibles
    in the Upper Midwest, 124
Mashed Potatoes, Thanksgiving, **37**
mead, 100
Melon, Feta, and Arugula Salad, **171**
Melon Ice, **188**
menus, 55, 103, 142, 192
Meringue Tart, **183**
Meyers, Kent, 225

milk, organic, 187
Minar, Florence, 187
Mint-Cilantro Chutney, Pan-Roasted
    Lamb Chops with, **115**
Minted Pea Soup, **108**
Minted Yogurt Cram for Summer
    Fruit, **182**
Mint Syrup, **141**
Mom's Fall Fruit Crisp, **50**
Moonstone Farm, 82
morels:
    Morel Madness, 130
    Morels and Sunchokes with Toasted
        Hazelnuts, **129**
    Simple Spring Sauté, **132**
Morgan Creek Vineyards, 152
Moroccan Green Sauce (Charmoula), **67**
Mrotz, Victor, 221
Muesli, **195**
Muffins—One Recipe, Many, **194**
mulberries, 185
mushrooms:
    Chanterelles, 8
    Heartland Polenta with Mushroom
        Ragout, **27**
    Hungarian Steak and Mushroom
        Soup, **65**
    Morel Madness, 130
    Morels and Sunchokes with Toasted
        Hazelnuts, **129**
    Wild Rice and Wild Mushroom
        Soup, **8**
Mustard, Furious, **219**

n

Native Harvest, 70
nettles, 109
New Grain Exchange, 30
New Potato, Fiddlehead Ferns, and
    Arugula Salad, **125**
Nodinens, 135
No Fail Kale, **33**
Nuessmeier, Tom and Tim, 114
nuts:
    Hazelnuts and Hickories, 94
    Simply Granola, **204**

o

Oatmeal Chocolate Chip and Dried
    Cranberry Cookies, **49**
O'Brien, Dan, 76

Old-Fashioned Bread and Butter
    Pudding, **99**
Olsen, Erik, 193
Once a Year Rhubarb Pie, **138**
onions:
    Caramelized Onion Soup, **64**
    freezing, xvii
Organic Milk, 187
Organic Valley, 187
Oven-Blasted Brussels Sprouts, **87**
Oven-Dried Pears, **42**
Oven-Fried Chicken, **119**
Oxtails with Stout and Onions, **78**

p

Pancakes, Comfort Lodge
    Buttermilk, **205**
Panfish, Cornmeal-Dusted, **71**
Pan-Roasted Lamb Chops with Fresh
    Mint-Cilantro Chutney, **115**
Pan-Roasted Radishes, **127**
Panzanella Picnic Salad, **147**
Parsley and Walnut Pesto, **167**
Parsnip and Chestnut Puree, **84**
pears:
    Beer-Braised Pork Chops
        with Pears, **14**
    Oven-Dried Pears, **42**
    Roast, **3**
peas, 108
    freezing, xvii
    Minted Pea Soup, **108**
pesto:
    Cilantro, Mint, and Cashew
        Pesto, **168**
    Parsley and Walnut Pesto, **167**
    Traditional Basil Pesto, **167**
Peterson, Mike, 162
Pheasant with Hard Cider, Apples, and
    Chestnuts, **20**
pickles:
    Dilly Beans, **230**
    Pickled Carrots, **229**
    Pickled Cherry Peppers, **228**
    Pickled Eggs with Horseradish
        and Beets, **232**
    Pickle This (cucumbers), **226**
    Spiced Pickled Beets, **231**
    Watermelon Rind Pickles, **236**
pie:
    Cranberry Tartlets in a Sweet
        Cornmeal Crust, **96**

    Once a Year Rhubarb Pie, **138**
    Honey Pumpkin Ginger Pie, **46**
    Turkey or Chicken Pot Pie
        with Cheddar Chive Cobbler
        Crust, **25**
piecrusts:
    Flaky Butter Crust, **206**
    Pie Crust Primer, 206
    Rich Tart Crust, **207**
    Sweet Cornmeal Crust, **208**
Pig in a Patch, 114
Pigs at Play, 114
pin cherries, 185
pizza:
    Pizza Dough, **203**
    Pizza with Arugula and Feta, **107**
    Potato, Prosciutto, and Rosemary
        Pizza, **61**
    Roast Mushroom, Red Pepper, and
        Sage Pizza, **4**
Planked Whitefish, **162**
Pleasant Ridge Reserve, 121
Plums, Grilled, **145**
polenta:
    Heartland Polenta, 28
    Heartland Polenta with Mushroom
        Ragout, **27**
pork:
    Barbecue Ribs with Honey Jalapeño
        BBQ Sauce, **166**
    Beer-Braised Pork Chops with
        Pears, **14**
    Pork Ribs, 166
    Pork Tenderloin with Lemon and
        Herbs, **114**
Porketta with Oregano and Fennel, **81**
potatoes:
    freezing, xvii
    New Potato, Fiddlehead Ferns, and
        Arugula Salad, **125**
    Potato and Sorrel Gratin, **120**
    Potato, Prosciutto, and Rosemary
        Pizza, **61**
    Simple Potato Gratin, **91**
    Thanksgiving Mashed Potatoes, **37**
    Tomato, Eggplant, Zucchini and
        Potato Bake, **163**
    When Are Potatoes in Season?, 92
Pot Roast, Marinated Beef, **82**
Pound Cake with Rhubarb-Strawberry
    Sauce, **137**
Prairie Grass Farms, 215
Prosciutto Americano, 61

pumpkins:
    Autumn Squash or Pumpkin Bars
      with Cranberry Glaze, **48**
    Harvest Stuffed Squash, **26**
    Honey Pumpkin Ginger Pie, **46**
    Picking Pumpkins, 26

q

Quick Roast Herb Chicken, **22**

r

Rabbit with Pancetta and Fennel, **21**
Radicchio, Grilled, **3**
radishes:
    Pan-Roasted Radishes, **127**
    Radish Sandwiches, **105**
Ramps, 112
raspberries, 185
    Raspberry Cordial, **191**
    Raspberry Vinegar, **218**
Real Bread, 201
Real Cornbread, **197**
Real Ketchup, **235**
Red Lake Fisheries, 118
Relationship Commerce, xi
Relish, Fresh Corn, **234**
research, food, xi
Reynolds, Greg, 43, 149
rhubarb:
    Once a Year Rhubarb Pie, **18**
    Rhubarb Chutney, **237**
    Rhubarb Lemonade, **140**
    Rhubarb Vinaigrette, **124**
Rich Applesauce Cake, **53**
Rich Brown Soda Bread, **198**
Rich Tart Crust, **207**
Riddle, Jim, 227
Riesling Soup, Sour Cherry, **151**
Roast Broccoli or Cauliflower with Garlic
    and Hot Pepper, **36**
Roasted Root Salad with Honey Mustard
    Vinaigrette, **60**
Roasted Salsify, **88**
Roasted Tomato-Chipotle Salsa, **233**
Roasted Tomato Vodka Sauce, **220**
Roast Mushroom, Red Pepper, and
    Sage Pizza, **4**
Rolled Grains 101, 204
root vegetables:
    Braised Root Vegetables in Mustard
      Sauce, **89**

freezing, xvii
    Horseradish and Honey-Glazed
      Root Vegetables, **34**
    Roast Root Salad with Honey
      Mustard Vinaigrette, **60**
    see also individual vegetables
rosehips, 185
Rosemary-Mint Marinade, **215**
Rosemary Syrup, **141**

s

salads:
    Carrot and Parsley Salad, **83**
    Classic Tarragon Chicken Salad, **159**
    Cool Cucumber Yogurt and Mint
      Salad, **169**
    Curried Melon Salad, **145**
    Duck Confit Salad, **19**
    Melon, Feta, and Arugula Salad, **171**
    New Potato, Fiddlehead Ferns, and
      Arugula Salad, **125**
    Panzanella Picnic Salad, **147**
    Roasted Root Salad with Honey
      Mustard Vinaigrette, **60**
    Smoked Trout, Apple, and Fennel
      Salad in Cider Vinaigrette, **5**
    Spring Greens and Strawberry Salad
      with Rhubarb Vinaigrette, **124**
    Sweet Potato, Radish, and Walnut
      Salad, **85**
    Tomato, Watermelon, and Feta
      Salad, **145**
    Very Fresh Sweet Corn Salad, **145**
    Warm Spinach Salad, **105**
    Watercress Salad with a French
      Twist, **106**
    Zucchini, Summer Squash, and
      Lemon Salad, **172**
salsa:
    Cranberry Ginger Salsa, **239**
    Roasted Tomato-Chipotle
      Salsa, **233**
Salsify, Roasted, **88**
Sandhill Farm community, 97
sauces:
    Honey Jalapeño BBQ Sauce, **216**
    Maple Mustard Basting Sauce, **217**
    Minted Yogurt Cream for Summer
      Fruit, **182**
    Rhubarb-Strawberry Sauce, **137**
    Roasted Tomato Vodka Sauce, **220**
    Sweet Bell Pepper Sauce, **221**

Sausage with Apples and Onions, **73**
Savory Cranberry Compote, **41**
Scandinavian Brown Beans with a
    Kick, **43**
Schafer Fisheries, 161
Scones, Sweet or Savory Buttermilk, **196**
Seed Savers Exchange, 126
serviceberries, 185
Showy Spinach Soufflé, **122**
Silky Chard, **32**
Simple Chicken Stock, **10**
Simple Potato Gratin, **91**
Simple Spring Sauté, **132**
Slade, Andrew, 117
slaw:
    Fennel Kohlrabi Slaw, **170**
    Spicy Savoy Coleslaw, **31**
Slow-Roasted Tomatoes, **179**
Smelt Run on the North Shore, 117
Smoked Trout, Apple, and Fennel Salad
    in Cider Vinaigrette, **5**
Smoked Trout or Salmon Spread, **59**
Soda Bread, Rich Brown, **198**
Sorghum, 97
soup:
    Asian Chicken Noodle Soup, **10**
    Caramelized Onion Soup, **64**
    Chicken Stock, **10**
    Classic Beef Stock, **66**
    Curried Vegetable Soup, **9**
    Easiest Vegetable Stock Ever, **110**
    Farmstand Corn Chowder, **154**
    Fresh Tomato with Basil Ice
      Cream, **153**
    Ginger Squash and Apple Soup, **11**
    Hot and Sour Vegetable Soup with
      Tofu, **111**
    Hungarian Steak and Mushroom
      Soup, **65**
    Light and Lemony Asparagus
      Soup, **110**
    Minted Pea Soup, **108**
    Sour Cherry Riesling Soup, **151**
    Spring Spinach and Nettle
      Soup, **109**
    Squash Soup with Thai Spices, **63**
    Watermelon Gazpacho, **150**
    Wild Rice and Wild Mushroom
      Soup, **8**
Sorghum, 97
Speedy Deviled Eggs, **59**
Spiced Beet Caviar, **146**
Spiced Pickled Beets, **231**

Spicy Bean and Hominy Stew, **70**
Spicy Savoy Coleslaw, **31**
Spiked Chocolate Truffles, **100**
spinach:
  Showy Spinach Soufflé, **122**
  Spring Sauté, **105**
  Spring Spinach and Nettle
      Soup, **109**
  Warm Spinach Salad, **105**
Spring Greens and Strawberry Salad with
    Rhubarb Vinaigrette, **124**
Spring Things: Fresh Fare (menu), 142
Spring Vegetable Curry, **112**
squash:
  Autumn Squash or Pumpkin Bars
      with Cranberry Glaze, **48**
  freezing, xvii
  Ginger Squash and Apple Soup, **11**
  Harvest Stuffed Squash, **26**
  Soup with Thai Spices, **63**
  Squash Lasagna with Walnuts and
      Kale, **68**
Star Prairie Trout Farm, 13
stew:
  Oxtails with Stout and Onions, **78**
  Spicy Bean and Hominy Stew, **70**
strawberries:
  Grandmother's Strawberry Jam, **241**
  Rhubarb-Strawberry Sauce, **137**
  Rhubarb Vinaigrette, **124**
  Strawberry Sorbet, **139**
Stuffed Zucchini Blossoms, **177**
Stuffing, Basic Sage, **40**
sturgeon, 161
Summer's Splendors: Sunshine and
    Moonlight (menu), 192
Summer Wines, 152
sunchokes, 131
  Morels and Sunchokes with Toasted
      Hazelnuts, **129**
  Roast Sunchokes with Herbs, **105**
  Sunchoke Chips, **131**
Sunrise Flour Mill, 200
Sure Fire Roast Duck, **17**
Surly Brewing, 14
sustainable growers, x
Sweet Bell Pepper Sauce, **221**
Sweet Cornmeal Crust, **208**
sweet potatoes:
  Sweet Potato, Radish, and Walnut
      Salad, **85**
  Sweet Potatoes with a World of
      Topping, **90**

Sweet Spuds in the Heartland, 85
syrups:
  see Herbal Elixirs; Maple Syrup

t

Tabouli with Herbs, Cracked Wheat, **133**
Tagine, Winter Vegetable, **67**
tarts:
  Concord Grape tart, **190**
  Cranberry Tartlets in a Sweet
      Cornmeal Crust, **96**
  Meringue Tart, **183**
  Tomato, Tomato, and Tomato
      Tart, **148**
Ten Good Reasons to Eat Seasonal and
    Local, xii
Thanksgiving Bird—Fast!, **23**
Thanksgiving Mashed Potatoes, **37**
Thyme Butter, **222**
Tilapia with Sage, Prosciutto-
    Wrapped, **13**
tofu:
  Grilled Tofu with Spirited
      Marinade, **158**
  Heartland Tofu, 158
tomatoes:
  freezing, xvi
  Fresh Tomato Sauce for Pasta, **156**
  Fresh Tomato Soup with Basil
      Ice Cream, **153**
  Good Tomatoes, Worth the
      Wait, 149
  Roasted Tomato Vodka Sauce, **220**
  Slow-Roasted Tomatoes, **179**
  Tomato, Eggplant, Zucchini, and
      Potato Bake, **163**
  Tomato, Tomato, and Tomato
      Tart, **148**
  Tomato, Watermelon, and Feta
      Salad, **145**
  Warm Tomato Vinaigrette, **160**
  see also green tomatoes
trout:
  Smoked Trout or Salmon Spread, **59**
  Star Prairie Trout Farm, 13
  Whole Grilled Whitefish or Trout
      with Warm Tomato
      Vinaigrette, **160**
turkey:
  Turkey Cutlets with Spring
      Vegetables and Tangy Pan
      Sauces, **113**

Turkey Gravy, **23**
Turkey or Chicken Pot Pie with
    Cheddar Chive Cobbler
    Crust, **25**
Turkey Talk, 24

u

University of Minnesota, 12, 182
Uplands Cheese Pleasant Ridge Reserve
    (and Extra Aged Reserve), 121
Upside Down Summer Berry Crisp, **184**

v

Vander Puy, Nick, 39
Vegetable Frittata with Goat
    Cheese, **123**
Venison Medallions with Juniper and
    Gin, **15**
Victory Garden, 180
vinaigrettes:
  Brown Butter Vinaigrette, **213**
  Chive Vinaigrette, **128**
  Cider Vinaigrette, **5**
  Honey Mustard Vinaigrette, **60**
  Rhubarb Vinaigrette, **124**
  Warm Tomato Vinaigrette, **160**
vinegars:
  Herb Vinegar, 218
  Raspberry Vinegar, 218
Vinegary, 210

w

walleye, 118
  Walleye Meunière, **118**
Washington Island Hotel, 188
Watercress Salad with a French
    Twist, **106**
watermelon:
  Tomato, Watermelon, and Feta
      Salad, **145**
  Watermelon Gazpacho, **150**
  Watermelon Rind Pickles, **236**
We Don't Farm with Headlights, 82
Wendt, Nate, 13
What Do Local and Regional Really
    Mean?, xiii
Whipped Cream, Spirited, **46**
White Earth Land Recovery Project, 70
whitefish
  Planked Whitefish, **162**

Whole Grilled Whitefish or Trout with Warm Tomato Vinaigrette, **160**
White Winter Winery Mead, 100
Whole Grain Milling, 200
wild mushrooms, 8, 130
    Chanterelles, 8
    Morels and Sunchokes with Toasted Hazelnuts, **129**
    Wild Rice and Wild Mushroom Soup, **8**

Wild Rice, 39
    Harvest Stuffed Squash, **26**
    Wild Rice and Wild Mushroom Soup, **8**
    Wild Rice Cranberry Pilaf, **38**
wines, summer, 152
Winter's Pleasures: Warm and Cozy Suppers (menus), 102
Winter Vegetable Tagine, **67**
Wisconsin Sturgeon, 161

y
yogurt, 181
    Cool Cucumber Yogurt and Mint Salad, **169**
    Minted Yogurt Cream for Summer Fruit, **182**

z
zucchini:
    Stuffed Zucchini Blossoms, **177**
    Tomato, Eggplant, Zucchini, and Potato Bake, **163**
    Zucchini Spice Cakes, **189**
    Zucchini, Summer Squash, and Lemon Salad, **172**

BETH DOOLEY has covered the local food scene in the Northern Heartland for twenty-five years: she is the restaurant critic for *Mpls.St.Paul Magazine,* writes for the Taste section of the Minneapolis and St. Paul *Star Tribune,* and appears regularly on KARE 11 (NBC) television in the Twin Cities area. She is coauthor with Lucia Watson of *Savoring the Seasons of the Northern Heartland* (Minnesota, 2004) and teaches cooking classes at the University of Minnesota Landscape Arboretum. She lives in Minneapolis with her husband and three sons.

Jazzy Gumbo

4 oz. avacado oil
4 oz. white flour
2 fresh yellow onions, chopped
4 cloves garlic, minced
½ gal chicken stock
1 T. Dry Italian seasonings
1 lb. smoked turkey sausage
1 T. Cajun seasoning
1 tsp. Kitchen Bouquet
Diced chicken (1 lb.)
2 T. Worcestershire sauce
1 lb. frozen okra, thawed + drained
1 T. white vinegar

White rice.
Bunch parsley.

Popovers
Recipe from Brickyard Pottery

Beat together with whisk, just until smooth.
(Don't overbeat.)

> 1 cup flour
>
> 1 cup milk
>
> 1/2 tsp. salt
>
> 2 eggs

Pour into well-greased popover cups. Pam cooking spray works well. Bake at 425 degrees until golden brown—about 40-45 minutes. Serve immediately.

Makes 3 giant popovers.

Rhubarb Dream Bars

2 cups all-purpose flour
2/3 cup confectioners' sugar
1 cup butter, softened
3 cups white sugar
1 1/2 teaspoons salt
1/2 cup all-purpose flour
4 eggs, beaten
4 1/2 cups chopped fresh rhubarb

Preheat the oven to **350 degrees** F (175 degrees C). In a medium bowl, mix together 2 cups of flour, confectioners' sugar and butter until it forms a dough, or at least the butter is in small crumbs. Press into the bottom of a **9x13 inch baking dish**. Bake crust for **10 minute**s in the preheated oven. While this bakes, whisk together the white sugar, salt, flour and eggs in a large bowl. Stir in rhubarb to coat. Spread evenly over the baked crust when it comes out of the oven. Bake for another **35 minutes** in the preheated oven, or until rhubarb is tender. Cool and cut into squares to serve.